CHINA'S
CIVILIZATION

CHINA'S
CIVILIZATION

*A Survey of its History,
Arts, and Technology*

by Arthur Cotterell
and David Morgan

PRAEGER PUBLISHERS
New York

This book is dedicated to
Joseph Needham, F.R.S., F.B.A.
Master of Gonville and Caius College, Cambridge,
whose studies of China have done so much to foster
international understanding

Published in the United States of America in 1975
by Praeger Publishers, Inc.
111 Fourth Avenue, New York, N.Y. 10003

Library of Congress Cataloging in Publication Data

Cotterell, Arthur.
    China's civilization: a survey of its history, arts, and technology
    Bibliography: p. 314
    Includes indexes.
    1. China—Civilization. I. Morgan, David, 1947—joint author. II. Title.
    DS721.C83   915.1'03   74–17887
ISBN 0–275–33550–X
ISBN 0–275–85140–0 pbk.

Printed in the United States of America

Preface

This book attempts to provide a context for understanding China's current re-emergence as a leading world power. It aims to make accessible to the general reader and mature student the kind of information that will provide some answers to the questions often asked about the Chinese. We have adopted an integrated approach because China should be seen in the round, if any real insight into its nature and historical experience is to be gained.

For assistance with translations and invaluable advice on 'how it appears to a Chinese' we should like to thank Mrs Yong Yap Cotterell. Also, we are greatly indebted to Dr Needham for his encouragement when we were beginning the 'impossible' task of surveying Chinese civilization within a single volume.

A.B.C. and D.W.M. 1974

Acknowledgments

For permission to use copyright material, thanks are due to the following: Messrs George Allen and Unwin, Ltd, for an extract from *Monkey*, by Wu Chêng-ên, and for the verses 'To Tan-chiu', by Li Po, and 'On his Baldness', by Po Chü-i, all translated by Arthur Waley, the verses appearing in *More Translations from the Chinese*; Messrs Constable and Co., Ltd, for 'Fighting South of the Ramparts', by Li Po, and 'The Chancellor's Gravel Drive', by Po Chü-i, both from *One Hundred and Seventy Poems*, translated by Arthur Waley; the Hong Kong University Press, for 'The Spin-dance Girl', by Po Chü-i, translated by Shih Shun Liu, from *One Hundred and One Chinese Poems*; Grove Press, Inc., and Mrs. J. K. Rideout for permission to print an extract from 'Memorial on the Bone of Buddha', by Han Yu, translated by her late husband, appearing in *An Anthology of Chinese Literature*, also to Grove Press and to Mr A. C. Graham for translations of 'On Wine', by Li Po, and part of 'Autumn Meditation', by Tu Fu, both being by Mr Graham and appearing likewise in *An Anthology of Chinese Literature*; 'The Chancellor's Gravel Drive', 'To Tan-chiu', 'Fighting South of the Castle (Ramparts)' and 'On his Baldness' from *Translations from the Chinese*, by Arthur Waley. Copyright 1919, 1941 by Alfred A. Knopf, Inc. Copyright renewed 1947 by Arthur Waley, 1969 by Alfred A. Knopf, Inc. Reprinted by permission of the publisher.

Where efforts to trace the holders of copyright material have proved unavailing, apology is offered for any inadvertent infringement of rights.

The authors also wish to thank the following for their permission to reproduce copyright illustrations: *An Introduction to Chinese Art*, by Michael Sullivan (Faber and Faber), pp. 108, 286; Bodleian Library, pp. 215, 224; British Museum, pp. 67, 104, 162, 167, 235, 237; Camera Press, pp. 84, 163, 170, 223, 271, 293, 296, 298, 299, 300, 304; *China: a short cultural history*, by C. P. Fitzgerald (Cresset Press), pp. 37, 96, 240; Cultural Properties Commission, Tokyo, p. 112; Dominique Darbois, p. 107; *Everyday Life in Imperial China*, by Michael Loewe (B. T. Batsford, Ltd), p. 73; Field Museum of Natural History, Chicago, p. 137; *Happiness Pictorial Monthly*, pp. 17, 33, 165, 166, 171, 213; J. Allan Cash, p. 151; *Japan: a short cultural history*, by G. H. Samson (Cresset Press), p. 184; John Hillelson Agency, pp. 88, 89, 174, 175, 223, 273, 274, 278, 285; Mansell Collection, pp. 210, 222, 243, 249; National Maritime Museum, p. 239; National Palace Museum, Peking, pp. 119, 130, 134; National Palace Museum, Taipeh, Taiwan, pp. 23, 132, 133, 135; Dr Joseph Needham and Allen and Unwin, pp. 27, 35, 39, 53, 57, 65, 74 (top), 81, 86, 126, 173; Dr Joseph Needham and Cambridge University Press, pp. 74 (bottom), 76, 80, 138, 139, 141, 145, 154, 155, 156, 159, 164, 169, 261; New York Public Library, pp. 143, 144; Nicholas Bouvier, p. 157; Paul Popper, Ltd, pp. 50, 51, 69, 172, 174, 175, 195, 221, 280, 294; Radio Times Hulton Picture Library, pp. 218, 238, 263, 267, 270; Royal Geographical Society, p. 217; St Louis Art Museum, p. 168; Victoria and Albert Museum, pp. 69, 227.

Contents

INTRODUCTION

Prehistory

In 1971 the People's Republic became a member of the United Nations. Her population approaches 800 million and when her leaders have something to say, then the world listens. The Chinese form a large part, about one quarter, of mankind, but outside China little is known generally about the way these people think and get on with the business of living together. What does the Chinese citizen expect from life? How does he see the place of his own country among the present-day community of nations? Where would his hopes for the future lead us? What contribution can China make to the last third of the twentieth century?

For these urgent questions some answers will be found in our study of China. In order that they do not seem strange and incomprehensible we have tried to provide a background for the Chinese viewpoint, as far as possible keeping a balance between Chinese and non-Chinese sources. This book attempts to discover what it has been like to be born and brought up within the Great Wall. The tense change, from present to past, is deliberate, because no understanding of China would be complete unless the historical experience of the Chinese people has been taken into full account. This is the case for several reasons. Firstly, the Chinese see themselves as the direct descendants of an ancient civilization. It is a fact that China is the oldest continuous civilization surviving today. Secondly, this great tradition was isolated from the rest of the world for centuries at a time so that many of its developments are unique and require our special attention. Thirdly, the influence of even remote times is evident in the happenings of the 1970s; old ways die hard in China. What we hope this book will offer is a 'context' for the current re-emergence of China as a world power. The emphasis is on the historical development of Chinese civilization because this is not the first occasion that its greatness has been acknowledged by the rest of mankind.

WHO ARE THE CHINESE?

Although we think of the Chinese as people who live in, or come from China, the present political boundary of the People's Republic encloses a much larger area than the first Chinese Empire. It embraces many diverse races, each having its own history and culture. So where did China proper originate? When can it be said to have begun? And, most important, why has it become such a powerful country?

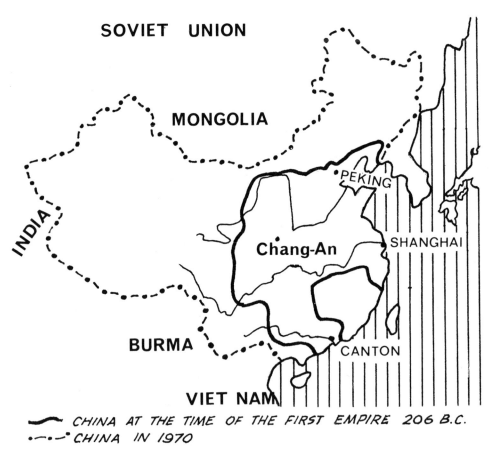

CHINA AT THE TIME OF THE FIRST EMPIRE 206 B.C.
CHINA IN 1970

THE HEARTLAND OF CHINA

The original centre of China lies along the middle course of the great Yellow River. The river is so called because of the large

10

amount of yellow silt it carries from the high plateau lands of Inner Mongolia. From the Desert of Ordos to the North China Plain, squeezed between the Lu Liang and Chin Ling Highlands, lies an area known as 'The Land within the Passes.' The earliest Chinese settlements developed here over 5000 years ago. By 1000 B.C. the Chinese had spread eastwards along the Yellow River valley and southwards to the valley of the Yangtze. Many different races were absorbed, while others were repelled to the highlands and wastelands of Yüeh and Yunnan.

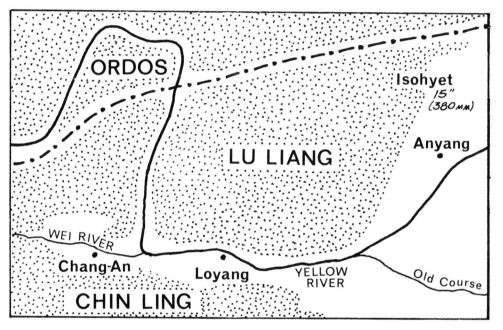

The Land within the Passes showing ancient capitals

The Land within the Passes
The physical environment of this area had a great formative effect on Chinese culture. Early man was totally dependent on the natural elements, the seasons, rainfall, the régime and flow rate of the river. As a result his whole way of life, his beliefs, superstitions, fables, his work and leisure, were all dominated by them. The physical environment not only determined the basic nature of Chinese culture but ensured its preservation by the formidable barriers it imposed between the unique civilization of

11

the Yellow River valley and the other great civilizations of the ancient world.

Ancient Cultural Centres
a—Egypt   b—Babylon   c—Indus Valley   d—China

Major Physical Barriers
1 Gobi Desert and Mongolian Plateau
2 Himalayas, Pamirs and Tibetan Plateau
3 Yunnan Plateau

The Isolation of China

THE MAJOR PHYSICAL INFLUENCES

- The continental (inland) situation
- The highly seasonal and erratic nature of rainfall
- The loess covering of the region
- River flooding
- Earthquakes

The inland nature of the Land within the Passes affects life in two main ways. Monsoon rains starting over the Indian Ocean have been largely deposited by the time they reach North China. The resulting decrease in cloud cover makes for great ranges in both daily and seasonal temperatures, since insolation is lost. If winter comes early, or is prolonged, the whole cycle of agriculture is affected. The winters are bitterly cold with the dominant winds coming from Mongolia. The second result is of course *the problem of light and erratic summer rainfall* which scarcely exceeds 762 millimetres, which leads to drought and crop failure. In effect, the limit of settled agriculture is roughly the line of 15 inch (380 mm) isohyet. Beyond this live the nomadic stock rearers. But it should not be forgotten that excessive rainfall can be equally disastrous to the easily eroded soil.

The region is covered by *thick deposits of windblown yellow earth called loess.* This soil originated on the Mongolian Plateau at a time when it was well watered and fertile. Changes in climate, brought about by a glacial period and the uplift of the Tibetan plateau which cut off monsoon rains from the Indian Ocean, reduced the soil to a fine dust which was carried southwards by

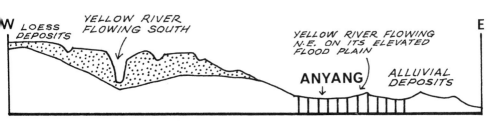

W–E Sketch—section through site of Anyang.

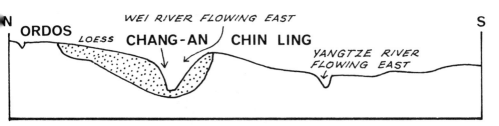

N–S Sketch—section through site of Ch'angan.

the cold winds. It was deposited over a large area of North China in depths over 75 metres in some valleys. Not only was the soil fertile but it was laid down on successive growths of grass, creating a capillary effect. Agriculture could be supported by the utilization of underground moisture even where rainfall was limited. High population densities were maintained but unfortunately the loess suffered from wind and rain erosion. Sheet and gully erosion have carved steep-sided gorges and denuded whole hillsides.

13

MISFORTUNE   This is the character for calamity or misfortune. The original meaning is dramatically clear since the strokes show a large river with some form of obstruction across it, thus causing the calamity of floods. The character has two distinct elements, a river 川 and a bar — : it is pronounced *tsai*. It is shown in its ancient form, the general practice adopted for Chinese characters in this book.

The loess is carried by the Yellow River and its tributaries in exceptional amounts. This has been gradually deposited on the flood plains of the river, raising its level above the surrounding land. This has led to *periodic flooding and complete changes in river courses.* The last major flooding of the Yellow River in 1931 caused nearly 4 000 000 deaths. The factors mentioned so far have been aggravated by *earthquakes.* Cave houses built in the loess cliffs were cool in the hot dry summers and warm in the cold windy winters. But they rapidly disintegrated during earth tremórs. As late as 1920 a quarter of a million deaths resulted from earthquakes in this region.

The effect of these physical influences on the way of life of the Chinese is particularly reflected in the Yin-Yang philosophy. Rituals and ceremonies to avert disaster recognized the delicate balance of the extreme forces of nature.

Yin-Yang

This design illustrates the interaction of the Yin and the Yang. The harmony of the universe was thought to depend on the balance of these two natural forces—Yin, negative, female and dark; Yang, positive, male and light. They were not fighting each other, but rather existing together in precarious balance, which if disturbed would bring disasters to mankind.

Heaven, the sky, was Yang, while Earth, the land on which man dwelt, was Yin. Heaven, the origin of weather, was looked upon as a chief god whose goodwill had to be ensured with sacrifices made by the chief man, the ruler, the Son of Heaven.

This perception of the natural forces stems from the everyday experience of the early farmer of the Yellow River valley. The loess soil is fertile with adequate rainfall, but in time of drought little more than dust. A sudden deluge, or flooding from rivers, can alter the landscape itself. The ancient kings preserved the people by maintaining a proper relationship with the heavenly powers and undertaking practical works in the countryside. They were priests as well as kings.

Yin-Yang has remained a basic concept of the Chinese mind. The natural world is seen as a single intricately balanced organism in which mankind must find the way to play its own correct part. Harmony, attunement, is vital. This very old idea has had a tremendous influence on Chinese thinking—in politics, science and the arts.

THE MOVEMENT SOUTH

As population pressure built up in the middle valleys of the Yellow River there was a movement eastwards to the flat alluvial plains. Here the problems of river control were greatest, but more reliable rainfall and the fertility of the soils encouraged a more diverse agriculture, and the population continued to expand. As the Chinese moved south into the Huai and Yangtze valleys they encountered a different climate and different cultures. Subtropical rain forest was the natural vegetation cover. Rice replaced millet as the staple food. The problems of erosion and flooding were not as destructive in the south, since rice growing involved water control through the use of ditches, canals and basins. The point is that despite a movement into another climatic region the basic elements of traditional Chinese culture remained unchanged. Moreover, the South like the North was cut off from other centres of civilization by the Tibetan and Yunnan Plateaux. Between 221 and 206 B.C. both North and South China adopted a standardized form of writing, coinage and weights.

PREHISTORIC CHINA

Our knowledge of 'Prehistoric China' is dependent upon archaeological excavations. As yet there are many gaps in our knowledge. Evidence of human habitation can be divided into three main groups:
- Palaeolithic, or early Stone Age finds;
- Neolithic or late Stone Age finds;
- Bronze Age finds.

Early Sites

The earliest evidence of human-type culture was found in the 1920s at Chou Kou Tien. Peking Man as he is called lived between 300 000 to 500 000 years ago, and was a hunter with a knowledge of fire. Similar evidence of such encampments has been discovered in the Desert of Ordos, the Upper Yangtze Valley, and Kwangsi in South China.

Late Stone Age Settlements

There is a great gap between such finds and later ones. During such time the climate factors changed considerably and many sites are probably buried beneath loess and alluvial deposits. Certainly northern China has had a far more benevolent climate in the past, with lush pasture supporting a wide variety of wild animal life. A Stone Age settlement buried under loess at Chou Tong Kou has been dated at 50 000 B.C. Evidence of later cultures shows them to be largely located in the river valleys of North China. These are of much more recent origin, being around 5 000 years old. There were two main cultural groups—the Yang Shao and the Lung Shan, named after important sites illustrating their ways of life. They were sedentary agriculturalists as well as hunters, fishers and collectors of wild vegetation. Yang Shao on the loess plateau is the older of the two. This culture spread throughout the middle course of the Yellow River and its tributary the Wei.

At Pan Pei, near ancient Chang-an, further information on the form of these settlements has been revealed. At its height Pan Pei had over two hundred houses with a population of between five and six hundred people. Such a population could only be supported by the cultivation of cereal crops, such as millet, and domesticated swine. Their cultivation often accelerated the process of erosion by the removal of tree and grass cover. One of the major features of the Yang Shao people was their painted pottery, none of which was turned on a potter's wheel. Remains of three-legged cooking vessels called *li* have established a link with later Chinese cultures. The Lung Shan were more advanced and lived on the eastern coastal and river plains. Their settlements were surrounded by defensive walls not ditches and their agriculture was more diverse including cattle, sheep and goats and wheat and rice where conditions were favourable. The best known artifact of the Lung Shan was a highly polished, very hard, wheel-made black pottery.

16

Reconstructions of the types of houses discovered at Pan Pei, near ancient Chang-an.

Cookery and medicine. The *li,* three pots joined as a tripod, dates from the neolithic period and is peculiar to China. It represents an immense advance in terms of using heat, as the hollow legs both provide support and present a greater surface to the fire, while the internal division allows the preparation of several things at once. Chinese skill in cooking would seem very old. Today the Chinese housewife knows a great deal about medicine. In meals she makes for the family she uses herbs and special ingredients intended to ensure the health of all members. Should this connection between cooking and medicine be an ancient tradition, as the discovery of the *li* suggests, then we may have found one of the reasons for the large size of the Chinese population from early times. A proverb runs: 'The beggar is an Emperor when he eats.'

17

The Bronze Age

The Lung Shan take us to the Dawn of Civilization, from the Stone Age to the Bronze Age. Our knowledge of the descendants of the Lung Shan is supplemented by legend. The first dynasty, the Hsia, was supposedly founded by Yü, the great tamer of the Yellow River, but little evidence as yet exists to back up its historical authenticity. The following dynasty, the Shang, were regarded as mythological until 1928 when the last of their six capitals was uncovered at Anyang. Shortly after another at Cheng Chou was discovered. Important elements of these finds include:

- their large scale organization, and architecture;
- the sophisticated use of bronze;
- the highly complex record of pictogram writing on oracle bones and turtle shells.

Anyang was founded in 1300 B.C. It had a carefully planned, almost extravagant royal palace and carefully segregated semi-subterranean dwellings for the lower orders. The consecration of new important buildings required ritual sacrifices of both animals and humans.

Ancient symbol for sacrifice to ancestral spirits. The ancestor is standing above a hand offering food.

Language. A factor which may have contributed to the age-long unity of China despite marked geographical differences between regions is the unique nature of the Chinese language. An ideographic script, the individual characters have value as ideas rather than sounds, so that the meaning is accessible to speakers of different dialects. For example, the character for king, 王 , is pronounced *wang* in Mandarin, *ong* in Hokien dialect and *w'ong* in Cantonese dialect. No difficulty of understanding can exist once the character has been written down, since the character is exactly the same for each dialect. All pronunciation given in this book is Mandarin, now the national speech.

18

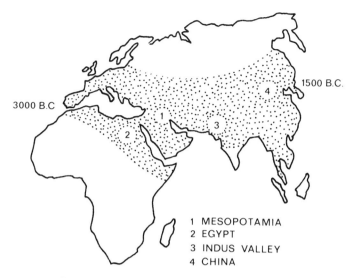

3000 B.C

1500 B.C.

4

1
3
2

1 MESOPOTAMIA
2 EGYPT
3 INDUS VALLEY
4 CHINA

Bronze Cultures of the Prehistoric World.

We have learned much from the complex and sophisticated writing found on the oracle bones which were used to foretell the future. Animal bones or turtle shells were heated with a live coal or a red-hot bronze poker, the resulting cracks being interpreted as the reply of the gods and carved on the bone. The beginning of the pictogram writing came later than that of Mesopotamia and Egypt but as the basis of the Chinese language it has outlived them to the present day. Over 2000 different characters have been noted for the Shang period. Similarly, the use of bronze spread to China much later than to the West, from its Middle Eastern origins. Yet the Chinese became technically more advanced than other bronze users. Alongside the diffusion of bronze by about 1500 B.C. came wheat cultivation; the spread of the two was closely linked.

China, then, had links with the West but was sufficiently isolated to develop a very original form of civilization and science. Anyang proved myth to be reality.

CHINA—AN ECOSYSTEM

China has a unique culture which has been maintained despite changes in boundaries. It is not that China has lacked communication with the outside world, despite the formidable mountain barriers. The Chinese had overland trading links with the Middle East and Europe before the birth of Christ. They were exploring

19

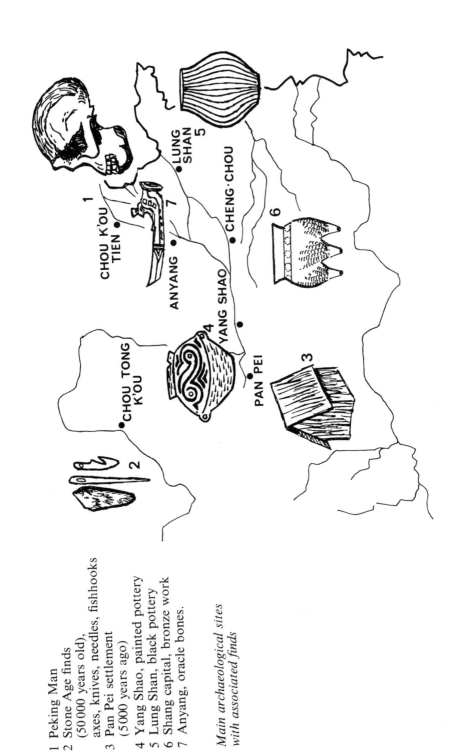

1 Peking Man
2 Stone Age finds
  (50 000 years old),
  axes, knives, needles, fishhooks
3 Pan Pei settlement
  (5000 years ago)

4 Yang Shao, painted pottery
5 Lung Shan, black pottery
6 Shang capital, bronze work
7 Anyang, oracle bones.

*Main archaeological sites
with associated finds*

the East coast of Africa long before the Europeans rounded the Cape of Good Hope. They were not static, their territorial boundary ebbed and flowed, generally at the expense of immediate neighbours. The mobile nomadic peoples from the Mongolian steppe swept through the valleys and plains on several occasions in spite of the natural physical barriers and man-made walls. But such movements seem incidental when compared with the unbroken traditions of China, the language, philosophy, architecture, cooking, and the status of teachers and peasants as twin pillars of society. Because of the basic stability of Chinese culture in the face of continual inflows and outflows of ideas and people, we can call China an ecosystem. An ecosystem is a state of equilibrium between nature in all its forms and man in all his works. Man has learned to survive by working with nature just as Yü the Great Engineer succeeded in controlling the floods, not by building dams, but by deepening the river beds. China has always been self-sufficient and remains so today. At times the ecosystem has been disturbed, even severely shaken, but always it has succeeded in absorbing what was useful and rejecting the unhelpful or irrelevant. More than most countries China has pursued its own distinct way.

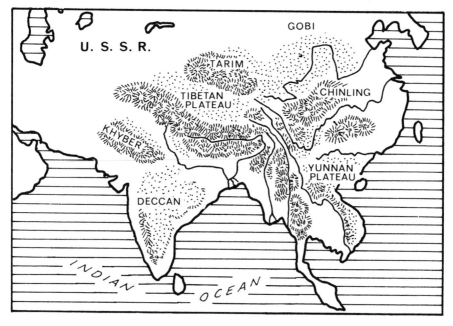

MYTHOLOGY AND LEGENDARY FIGURES

Since ancient China was isolated from the other early centres of civilization, Egypt, Mesopotamia and the Indus valley, the first thoughts of the Chinese, their legends, are worth our attention. They belong to China alone. From them we may be able to identify what are the original and distinct elements in the Chinese consciousness.

A legend of the creation of the universe concerns Pan Ku, primeval man. At the beginning the universe was an egg. One day the egg split open. The top half became the sky and the bottom half the earth. Pan Ku, who emerged from the broken egg, grew three metres taller every day, just as the sky became three metres higher and the earth three metres thicker. After eighteen thousand years Pan Ku died. Then, like the original egg, he split into a number of parts. His head formed the sun and moon, his blood the rivers and seas, his hair the forests, his sweat the rain, his breath the wind, his voice thunder and, last of all, his fleas became the ancestors of mankind.

What stands out most in this story for a Westerner is the lowly position the Chinese have ascribed to man. Not the centre of creation, not a colossus in the landscape, but rather a small figure in the great sweep of natural things. This view of the world is expressed in Chinese painting where men are set down amid the magnificence of Nature, mountains and valleys, clouds and waterfalls, trees and flowers. The first inhabitants of the Yellow River communities must have regarded themselves as members of a vast order of living things, with whose processes they had to seek a harmonious relationship. Life was a matter of reciprocity, mutual interchange between its many parts.

After Pan Ku came a series of emperors, largely divine, since Huang Ti, the Yellow Emperor, is considered by Chinese historians to be the earliest human ruler. Under the Yellow Emperor and his four successors, Chuan Hsiu, K'u, Yao and Shun, the people learnt the ways of civilized life. Arts and crafts flourished; government and moral conduct were established; the gods received regular sacrifices. The throne was not passed on to the next emperor according to birth, but each successor was chosen by merit. Yü the Great Engineer, selected for power by Shun, was the founder of the first dynasty, the Hsia.

Around Yü many stories have collected. They all praise his devotion to duty. Thirteen years Yü spent 'mastering the waters' without once returning home to see his wife and children. By his

A Mountain View *by Hsia Kuei (A.D. 1190–1230) shows Man in a Chinese landscape: it is a small section of a large scroll.*

large scale conservancy schemes he made the country safe from floods and well irrigated for agriculture. The legend of Yü reveals that from very early times the Chinese began to develop a technology capable of transforming their homeland into a region suited to a settled pattern of life. The Hsia dynasty ended with the defeat of its last king, Chieh, a cruel tyrant, by a people and nobility driven to rebellion. The new dynasty, the Shang, had a similar fate in store for it, though Chou Hsin, the last Shang king, is reputed to have outdone Chieh with his viciousness. Much later the philosopher Mencius was to construct a theory of the Right of Rebellion from this event. But records of Hsia and Shang times are scarce; the historical period in China does not start till the Chou dynasty.

WORLD CHRONOLOGY 3000–1000 B.C.

3000 B.C. 2900	2800	2700	2600	2500	2400	2300	2200

EUROPE

WEST ASIA and NORTH AFRICA

EGYPT
● 2900 Unification of
the country under Narmer
    ● 2700 Cheops'
    pyramid at Giza 
      ● 2626 Death of Imhotep
      the Great Builder

MESOPOTAMIA   ASIA MINO▮
  ● 2600 Cities with   ● 2225 Troy
ziggurats for their
gods   ● 2370 Sumer unde▮
    Sargon becomes pow▮
    state controlling vall▮

SOUTH ASIA

INDUS VALLEY
  ● 2500 Great cities   ● 210▮
Mohenjo-Daro and Harappa Seals s▮
flourish – each a masterpiece contac▮
of town planning   with S▮

EAST ASIA

CHINA
  ● 2200
Yü the Great Engin▮
founds
the Hsia dynasty

ENGLAND
- 1850 Stonehenge, a Neolithic monument

GREECE
- 1700 Mycenae and Tiryns

- 1500 The coming of the Dorian Greeks

CRETE
- 1900 The great palace at Knossos

- 1400 The destruction of Knossos

- 1700 Hyksos invade Egypt

- 1570 Hyksos expelled

- 1480 Pharaoh Tuthmosis III conquers Palestine and Syria

- 1250 Moses leads Israelites from Egypt

- 1750 King Hammurabi of Babylon introduces his code of laws, first known in history

- 1400 Hittites develop iron

- 1123 Death of King Nebuchadnezzar I

- 1500 Aryan invasion of India – a new people and a new civilization; the *Rig Veda*, ancient book of Hindu religion, dates from this time

- 1500 Shang period in China. Notable achievements in bronze working

1027 ● Chou dynasty founded

1 Classical China

From early times to 221 B.C.

HISTORICAL OUTLINE

One of the first events which can be said to be certain was the overthrow of the Shang kingdom by Chou, a vassal state on the western frontier. About 1027 B.C. Anyang, the capital, fell to the rebel armies and the last Shang king was slain. The new dynasty, the Chou, was destined to have the longest rule in China's history, and even though the last centuries were filled with civil wars, this was the 'Classical Age'. Chinese society found its pattern during this period. Great thinkers appeared, leaving their mark on the minds of all future generations. Science and technology developed; cities and towns multiplied.

The second ruler of the new dynasty was too young to take charge of the government on his father's death so Chou Kung, or the Duke of Chou, acted as regent. This man firmly established the new kingdom and seems to have found a way of saving the best things from Shang times. There was no abrupt break, but continuation and improvement. Two of his actions illustrate the smoothness of the change-over. The descendants of Shang were awarded the tiny state of Sung so that they would have sufficient revenue to keep up the sacrifices such a princely family had to make to its ancestral spirits. And the officials of the defeated kingdom were added to the Chou civil service. Looking back on these early years from the confusion at the end of the Chou dynasty many people, the philosopher Confucius among them, came to look upon this period as a lost ideal. The Duke of Chou had shown proper respect for the Shang family and his treatment of the scholar officials was a sign of the value he attached to peace. Order, balance, respect for elders and learning—these were the virtues they thought they saw. How correct these wistful glances into the past were it is not possible to know. Though the Chinese were one of the first people to write history as we know it today, accurate records do not survive before the last four

26

Here the Duke of Chou is seen making an announcement to the officials of the defeated Shang kingdom. The drawing comes from a nineteenth-century edition of the Shu Ching (Historical Classic), *a work dating from 850 B.C. and a main source for details of the Chou dynasty.*

hundred years of the Chou kingdom. What the rise of Chou most probably represents is a major expansion of Chinese civilization, for there is mention of the Yangtze valley, not then considered to be part of Chou, or the Middle Kingdom, a name still used to denote China.

27

The Period of the Warring States (481–221 B.C.)
This last part of the Classical period, known as the Warring States, marks the breakdown of the feudal system and ends in the unification of all China, the foundation of the first Chinese Empire. The royal house of Chou gradually lost control of its vassal states. In 771 B.C. the ninth ruler was expelled from his capital by a mounted army from the Mongolian steppe. This barbarian invasion was an unexpected setback for the Chou dynasty and, though they rebuilt their capital on a new site at Loyang, the old authority over the other feudal powers was permanently weakened. Ch'u and Ch'in, large semi-barbarous states on the fringes of the Middle Kingdom, steadily became more developed and acquired greater military strength. There was an overall tendency for the smaller and weaker states to be absorbed by the stronger ones, particularly after 500 B.C.

THREE These three strokes stand for the number of heaven, earth and humanity. Therefore, the king is the one **|** , the man who connects together heaven, earth and humanity. The title for king, pronounced *wang,* was restricted to the supreme monarch during the Classical Age. It was borne only by the king of Chou, the leading feudal power. From 221 B.C., the accession of the king of Ch'in as first emperor, the term *huang* was introduced for the idea of the sole ruler of an empire. On top

KING

of the character for king the sign for antiquity was added ѣ .
Although the 'Tiger of Ch'in' overthrew the feudal states and dispossessed the noble classes, he claimed to be an emperor, a ruler like the famous figures of ancient times, Huang-ti, Chuan Hsui, K'u, Yao and Shun.

EMPEROR These renowned ancestors were looked upon as 'the five sages', ideals for following ages to respect and emulate. The Chinese consciousness of being part of a long civilization existed even before the birth of Christ.

Soon the Chou kings were rulers of little more than their own city, powerless to prevent Ch'in in the west and Ch'u in the south from gaining territory through the quarrels of their Chinese neighbours. Although Sung was annexed by Ch'i in 286 B.C., the King of Ch'u had gained the greater share of the spoils with Wu, Yüeh and Lu.

But a real shock went through Chinese society when the ambitions of Ch'in were translated into action on the battlefield. In 259 B.C. the army of Chao was starved into surrender and the Ch'in commanders ordered the slaughter of all prisoners. It is said that 400 000 heads were cut off. Then, three years later,

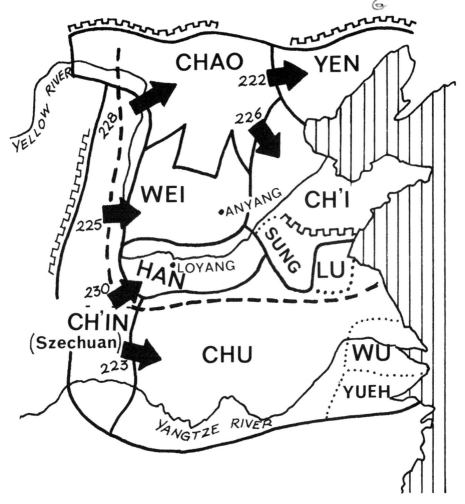

LINES OF FORTIFICATIONS

BOUNDARIES OF RECENTLY
ABSORBED STATES

LIMIT OF CHINESE STATES, ORIGINAL
MEMBERS OF THE MIDDLE KINGDOM

223 CH'IN CONQUESTS WITH DATES

Map showing the growth of Ch'in power 230–221 B.C.

Ch'in attacked the remaining possessions of the royal house of Chou and the Son of Heaven was dethroned. The Chou dynasty passed into history, its ancestral spirits into neglect. From this point onwards all eyes apprehensively watched as Ch'in reduced one state after another, like 'a silkworm devours a mulberry leaf.' There seemed to be an exceptional force behind the advance of Ch'in. Several factors that contributed to the ultimate Ch'in victory can be noted:

● Unlike Ch'u, its chief rival for supreme power, Ch'in occupied the loess areas and had need of vast irrigation schemes. Organizing such public works greatly strengthened the authority of the king at the expense of the nobles. A more streamlined state emerged, a predecessor of the bureaucratic system to be developed in the Chinese Empire.

● There is evidence to suggest that Ch'in was well advanced in terms of industry and may have been the first state to use iron.

● The School of the Law, the official philosophy of Ch'in, was a severe military code that made the people virtually slaves. Society had only two purposes—agriculture and war. Nothing else should be tolerated by the monarch. Cruel and merciless punishments were reserved for anyone foolish enough to disagree. Ch'in has been called a 'fascist state.'

● In 246 B.C. the future First Emperor, Shih Huang Ti, became King of Ch'in. He was a very determined man. Besides defeating all the other feudal states and unifying China for the first time, he was responsible during his reign as emperor for another event of lasting significance, namely the building of the Great Wall.

● The early conquest of modern Szechuan provided Ch'in with additional manpower resources and turned the flank of Ch'u.

● The Chinese kingdoms were always divided and involved in wars with each other. Moreover, the general decay of feudalism had encouraged internal conflicts as the old loyalties were forgotten. Confucius himself had resigned his office in his native state of Lu on account of the goings-on at court.

The 'Tiger of Ch'in' took just a quarter of a century to make himself the First Emperor in 221 B.C. After a decade of preparation the Ch'in armies were ready to devour the other states. Han went down in 230 B.C., but the decisive encounter did not occur till 223 B.C., when the great rival state of Ch'u was completely overrun. Another year saw remote Yen fall and the end of all serious resistance to the will of the Ch'in monarch.

SOCIETY

At the apex of Chinese society was the feudal hierarchy, before the First Emperor swept away this highly privileged class. The titles held by its members are usually translated duke, marquis, count, viscount and baron. After the foundation of the Empire this aristocracy was to be confined to the relatives of the reigning imperial house, and its members, carefully watched and kept out of the civil service, were never a powerful force in public affairs. Below this feudal group the rest of the population was divided in the famous four estates:

- *shih*, lesser nobility, that is the gentry and scholars;
- *nung*, the peasant farmers;
- *kung*, the artisans;
- *shang*, the merchants, the last of all.

The low social position given to the merchants was the natural outcome of economic development in the Classical Age, for the feudal kings had assumed most of the responsibility for industry and public works. Irrigation schemes have already been mentioned. Metal working had come under royal control too. In the Han Empire, the Chinese dynasty that was to oust the Ch'in in 207 B.C., there were further extensions of nationalization, placing under imperial care the making of wine and beer. Another emphasis unusual to people brought up in the West was the Chinese attitude to the military. 'Good iron is not made into nails, nor good men into soldiers,' a proverb that indicates soldiers were also put at the bottom of the social scale. Experience of the harshness of Ch'in rule confirmed this view, though the philosopher Mo Tze had earlier taught the folly of war and insisted upon the brotherhood of all men. Yet the importance attached to learning, the respect for one's teacher, ensured that the pattern of Chinese society was based on a civil ethic. Good behaviour meant knowing how a citizen should behave. The poor status of merchant and soldier has remained down the centuries. Most important, perhaps, there was no enormous slave class. The institution of large-scale slavery as understood in the Ancient World—Egypt, Mesopotamia, Greece and Rome—was unknown in Classical China. Society rested on the peasant farmers, whose comparative freedom was confirmed after the Ch'in dynasty by the early Han emperors. The absence of slavery seems to have had an influence on the social outlook of the philosophers, except the School of Law. But the barbarous actions of Ch'in were greeted with universal disapproval.

31

The Family
Large families were preferred. Confucius stressed the duties of children to parents, seeing loyalty as the cornerstone of the whole social structure. 'The hundred families' had long been a name for the Chinese people. Primitive ancestor worship was gradually transformed into a ritual observance ensuring the continuation of the family. 'Five generations in one hall' became the great aim. Custom and tradition were enshrined in the Chinese family.

GOOD This is the ancient way of writing the character which means 'what is good'. It tells us a lot about the way Chinese people think too. On the left side of the character the strokes represent a woman, a wife, and on the right they show children. So important in China is the continuation of the family that the word for good is a drawing of a mother with her children. The character is pronounced like the English word 'how' and today it is written 好.

What might be called an off-shoot of large families, or clans, were the numerous secret societies. These associations may have grown in response to the general decay of society during the Warring States period. They offered protection in uncertain times, such as the decline of a dynasty, and were often directly connected with popular rebellions.

'BUYING A DEAD HORSE'

BUYING A DEAD HORSE A fable of the Warring States period tells how one of the kings desperately wanted a fast steed. For three years he sought after such a horse but without success. One day an official asked to be entrusted with the task and the king agreed. This official searched for three months before he heard about a place where a very fast horse was kept. But when he got there he found the horse had died. He considered the situation for a while and then purchased the dead horse for 500 pieces of gold. Returning to court with a dead horse made the king very angry, but nonchalantly the official said: 'I have spent five hundred pieces of gold and bought this dead horse on your behalf so that all the people under heaven will learn of your love for fast horses. This news will bring horses to court.' And so it˙ happened that before a year had elapsed the king possessed three fast steeds.

IDEAS

The centuries of ever-increasing political confusion down to the triumph of Ch'in were accompanied by great intellectual ferment. Men cast about for explanations of contemporary failure. This was the time of the 'Hundred Schools,' when roving philosophers offered advice to any ruler who chose to listen to them. The kingdom of Ch'i welcomed philosophers of every school but Confucius was ill-used in Lu. Of the many different schools there were two that became the main currents in Chinese thought:

- Taoism, the philosophy of Lao-tzu (? born 604 B.C.) and Chuang-tzu (350–275 B.C.);
- Confucian philosophy, the ideas of Confucius (551–479 B.C.) and Mencius (374–289 B.C.).

Taoism

Lao-tzu, the Old Philosopher as he is known in China, may have been keeper of the royal archives at Loyang, the Chou capital, but few details are known of his life. He was 'a hidden wise man,' reluctant to found a school and gather a following. 'When he foresaw the decay of Chou,' the Han historian Ssu-ma Ch'ien tells us in the oldest biography, 'Lao-tzu departed and came to the frontier. The customs official, Yin-Hi, asked the sage to write a book before he retired from the world. So Lao-tzu wrote a book consisting of five thousand words, in which the proper way to live was set forth. Then he went on. No one knows where he died.'

The book mentioned here is *Tao Teh Ching*, or *The Way of Virtue*, a collection of profound sayings, many of which date from the earliest times. It is significant that in the legend about Lao-tzu's departure he was only persuaded to leave a record of his wisdom at the very last moment. Saddened by the short-sightedness of his fellow men, their tragic perversity, their inability to follow natural goodness, Lao-tzu decided to leave so-called civilization behind him. Making statements, trying to explain his ideas, would only add to the current confusion, since words have an unpleasant way of limiting what should really be said. Unlike the philosophers of the Confucian school, the Taoists held written words in mean respect.

Though the figure of Lao-tzu is wreathed uncertainly in the mists of legend, the characters in his book stand out with pristine strength. 'Conduct your triumph as a funeral': this saying has lost nothing since it was first applied to the senseless rivalry of

34

Lao-tzu meeting Yin-Hi on the frontier.

the Warring States. 'He who feels punctured must have been a bubble.' What concerned Lao-tzu most was man's rootedness in Nature, the inner power that made all men wiser than they knew. 'Knowledge studies others; wisdom is self-known.' The artificial demands of society had disturbed the natural abilities of men. Instead of following the Way, the *Tao*, codes of love and honesty were introduced. Learning and charity became necessary. Men have to return to the natural way of behaviour:

> As the soft yield of water cleaves obstinate stone,
> So to yield with life solves the insoluble:
> To yield, I have learned, is to come back again.
> But this unworded lesson,
> This easy example,
> Is lost upon men.

This verse may partly explain China's age-long survival. To yield and then come back again. The conquest of Ch'in was neither the last nor the worst invasion that the country was to suffer. When Marco Polo reached Cathay over a thousand years later the government was in the hands of the Mongols, fierce descendants of Genghiz Khan. Yet Chinese civilization endured the Mongols as well as other warlike peoples from the steppes. Water's being a strong element is an interesting thought, so

35

different from firmness of rock praised in the West. The formidable rivers of China were there for everyone with eyes to see, but the humility of water, ever seeking the lowest level, was an appropriate route for the descendants of Pan Ku's fleas to tread.

Taoist philosophy received its classical form in the works of Chuang-tzu. By then it was a tradition for Taoist hermits to shun human society in order to contemplate Nature. A story about him illustrates the point. Because of intrigue and dishonesty at court a certain Prince determined to send two high officials to ask Chuang-tzu to take charge of the government and become Prime Minister. A long and weary journey brought them to the remote valley in which the sage's hut was situated, but they did not mind the hardship since they were sure that the new leader would reward them once in office. They found Chuang-tzu fishing. Intent on what he was doing he listened without turning his head. At last he said: 'I have been told there is in the capital a holy tortoise which has been dead for over a thousand years. And that the Prince keeps this tortoise carefully in a temple there. Now would this creature rather be dead but considered holy, or alive and wagging its tail in the mud?' The two officials answered that it would prefer to be alive and wagging its tail in the mud. 'Clear off from my valley then—you and your offer!' shouted Chuang-tzu. 'Like the tortoise I will wag my tail in the mud here.'

Chuang-tzu had turned down the highest office of state, something a member of the Confucian school would never have done. 'A thief steals a purse and he is hanged,' Chuang-tzu wrote, 'another man steals a kingdom and becomes a Prince.' From the Taoists came the conviction the government was a necessary evil. China needed some form of organization, they admitted, but it should be reduced to the minimum, lest restrictions hinder the natural way of doing things. Another legacy could well be Chinese science, which was far in advance of the West till the Renaissance. It has been suggested that Taoist experiments in alchemy were the beginnings of science.

Confucian Philosophy

Historically younger than Taoism, the school of philosophy that derived from Confucius' ideas became the dominant one from the Han Empire onwards. Confucius himself was a descendant of the Shang kings. His family were related to the rulers of Sung, whose Shang ancestors had been awarded this small state by Chou Kung, near the beginning of the Chou dynasty. He felt himself to be an active member of the feudal system but the

An engraving of Confucius. Contrast the formality and correctness of his clothes with the attire of Lao-tzu riding on the ox.

abuses prevalent during his lifetime set his mind on a course of reform. Finding his own state of Lu uninterested in what he had to say, he became the first of the 'wandering scholars,' moving from one capital to another seeking a monarch who would listen to his instructions and put his philosophy into practice. Often the reception at court was cordial enough. Yet there was always hesitation over taking virtuous advice. By Mencius' time the prolonged struggle between the Warring States had closed royal ears altogether. Mencius found that the sole concern of the King of Wei was any scheme likely to harm his rivals.

Still, Confucius collected numerous followers and his philosophy took shape in words. It was a feudal ethic, an attempt to shore up the breaches in the society of his own day, but, above all, it was essentially social-minded. The monarch must rule with benevolence and sincerity, avoiding the use of force at all costs. He should manage affairs so that justice was enjoyed by every subject. Soldiers were a sign of bad government. The virtue of the king would call forth the virtue concealed in all men. For the breakdown of society had caused men to be corrupted from their natural goodness. The duty of the subject was loyal service to the king.

The *shih*, the scholars and gentry, were responsible for the maintenance of morality too. They must display an independence of mind in the service of their king. When Confucius was asked how a Prince should be served, he answered: 'If it becomes necessary to oppose him, withstand him to his face, and don't try roundabout methods.' This firmness of principle was destined to be the cardinal rule of the imperial civil service; officials were to perish at the hands of impatient emperors, only to be admired for generations afterwards. Mencius went further in propounding the theory of justified rebellion against wicked rulers. The Mandate of Heaven was withdrawn from a corrupt dynasty whenever a successful rebel arose. This theory has been called the Chinese Constitution.

Although Confucius agreed with the Taoists over the natural goodness of men, his remedy for the times was quite different. He placed the emphasis on nurture, not Nature. Men had to learn how to conduct themselves properly. Education was given a central place in society. Young people were to be nurtured in the ways of virtue—loyalty, respect for elders, attention to ceremonies and rites, decorum. Referring to the Taoists Confucius said: 'They dislike me because I want to reform society, but if we

Mencius' mother. This popular story explains how wise the mother of the philosopher was in knowing how to bring him up. It is the classic account of the importance of nurture.

At first they lived in a cottage near some tombs. Finding young Mencius interested in funerals and tomb construction, she moved to a house by a market. But the activity in the market attracted the boy and she moved house again. Next to a college she was pleased to see Mencius watching the comings and goings of scholars. She said: 'This is the right place for my son'.

Returning from school one day Mencius found his mother weaving on her loom. 'Have you learnt everything now?' she asked. 'Yes', he replied, 'I know enough.' Immediately she picked up her scissors and ripped across the cloth. Mencius was shocked and worried. 'Your stupidity about learning is like my cutting through this unfinished piece of work. Men only attain fame for their knowledge after hard work and great effort. Wise men possess a breadth of learning, live in peaceful places, and shun bad things. Realize this and you will come to no harm. . . .'

are not to live with our fellow men with whom can we live? We cannot live with animals. If society was as it ought to be, I should not be wanting to change it.'

Finally, the Confucian school of philosophy introduced a sense of balance in the supernatural world as well as on the earthly level. 'I stand in awe of spirits,' Confucius said, 'but keep them at a distance.' This rational attitude ensured that a certain amount of scepticism was always available during religious crises. The T'ang scholar, Han Yu (A.D. 768–824), drew on this tradition when he composed his famous *Memorial on the Bone of Buddha*, a stinging attack on the excesses of the court. Han Yu was exiled, not executed. Taoism tended to shade too easily into magic. In the Chinese mind, however, there was room for elements from both of these main schools of thought. This capacity to retain diverse viewpoints at the same time is a notable feature of Chinese thought.

TECHNOLOGY

Major developments in technology helped to transform China into a centralized, well-organized state by 221 B.C. Furthermore, they ensured that China could maintain its independence, thus preserving the cultural pattern they had helped create. The improvements can be divided into five groups which are inter-related:

- building;
- agriculture;
- communications;
- hydraulics;
- metal working.

Improvements in these fields must be seen against changes occurring in the Chinese economy. An increasing number of people were non-food producers. Because administrators, scholars, craftsmen and soldiers depended on others to provide their food, the traditional subsistence agriculture had to be made more productive in order to guarantee a regular surplus. Increased state taxation, levied in grain, was a further stimulus to agricultural improvement. The specialists congregated in the growing number of cities which acted as administrative and military centres as well as market and service centres. In exchange for loyalty and the payment of taxes the cities were built for the benefit of the country peasants, providing winter shelter for them and giving protection from marauders. To speed the flow of food between producers and consumers, and to maintain state security and protection, improved transportation by land and water was introduced. Metallic money became acceptable instead of cowrie shells and barter for transactions and a merchant class developed. But the foundation of the whole system remained the peasant food producer.

Building

Wall building was particularly important to the early Chou since it was the foundation of both house construction and city defences. Subterranean wattle and daub cave dwellings remained in use but 'earth' walls became increasingly important in the construction of dwellings. A wall could be built of layers eight to ten centimetres thick. Each layer would be added with the use of a wooden frame into which earth was rammed until solid. This wooden shuttering would then be removed and the process repeated at the next level. Bamboo might be placed between each layer to absorb moisture, and rubble stone was often used as a foundation.

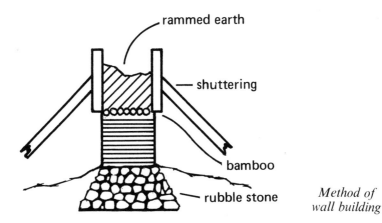

rammed earth

shuttering

bamboo

rubble stone

Method of wall building

These walls were particularly useful where little weight had to be carried or where protection from erosion could be obtained from overhanging eaves. In the later Chou period adobe, or sun-dried bricks, were used to construct or 'face' walls and in the Warring States period fire-baked bricks were introduced. These were often skilfully inscribed for ornamental and burial purposes.

Rival powers in the Warring States period constructed large defensive walls along their boundaries to halt invasions. The First Emperor, Ch'in Shih Huang Ti, linked and extended a number of these in order to thwart potential cavalry attacks by the nomadic peoples of the North. This was a prototype for the later Great Wall of China, which marked the border between the steppe and the sown lands. City walls date back to 1500 B.C. Prior to this the nomads and primitive hunters had used ditches or earth mounds for protection. By the Shang period city walls were up to twenty metres thick at the base and later Chou capitals had similar dimension. Hantan founded in 386 B.C. had walls over 1350 metres long, 15 metres high and 20 metres wide at the base. Some of the city walls built before the First Empire were still in use at the beginning of this century.

Agriculture
The basic foodstuff of the early Chinese farmers of the Yellow River valley was millet. By the time of the Chou dynasty this was supplemented by the other indigenous crops, kaoliang and buck wheat. The ancient method of clearing land was 'slash and burn' which accelerated erosion. The only fertilizers were ash and silt. The peasantry were obliged to work on the lord's land and spent the winters in the shelter of the cities. Along the flood plain of the Yellow River the field system was geometric with an equal re-distribution of land each year to each family. The final amount they received depended on the relative fertility and nature of the land. Livestock such as pigs, dogs, cattle, sheep, goats, water buffaloes and elephants probably originated in the forests of the South.

TWO OLD CHARACTERS
CONNECTED WITH FARMING

Chiang, meaning bounds. The two fields ⊕ were separated by barriers.

Tzu The uncultivated areas; a field exposed to floods.

The population of China may have grown fivefold to around fifty million in the Chou period. This was supported partly by an extension in farming land along the coastal lowlands but also by improvements in technique. Irrigation was first recorded around 560 B.C. and manuring seems to have become common-place by the late Chou period. New forms of livestock and crops were assimilated from the South whenever climatic conditions allowed. The northern limits of China became increasingly identified with the marginal agricultural lands on the edge of the Mongolian Plateau. This was an area of continual friction between the settled farmers who eked out a living from the dry and easily eroded soil, and the nomadic herdsmen of the steppes, the Hsiung Nu, who encroached southwards. At the same time the Chinese themselves were moving southwards into different climates. Rice had penetrated from India by about 3000 B.C. but until the Chinese had moved south of the Chin Ling mountains they did not encounter it. Rice was initially considered as having medicinal value. It was a very productive cereal which could support high population densities. As a result the southern states of China became increasingly influential. Rice could not easily be adopted north of a line drawn east from the Chin Ling for climatic reasons, but there was a definite two-way movement of agricultural knowledge between these differing economies. A great amount of organization was required for the efficient growing of rice; there must be careful control of stored water at vital times in the growing cycle. After the land had been divided into small rectangular basins, it was ploughed and harrowed before being flooded. The seeds were then sown and when the plants were thirteen to fifteen centimetres high they were planted out. The water was drained off before flowering and seeding, and flooded again afterwards. Thus co-operation was essential to the success of the rice farmers.

Communications
Good communications were necessary for strong, centralized government. The ancient *Book of Odes* records:

> The roads of Chou are smooth as whetstone,
> Straight as an arrow

and this probably helped account for the long reign of this feudal dynasty. As the stability broke down so each individual state took charge of its own road system, and it was not surprising that the eventual dominance of the Ch'in was related in part to its engineering skills.

In the early Chou period the main routeways ran east–west along the Yellow River valley and then south to the Huai and Yangtze valleys. Chinese road-building techniques were quite different from those used by the Romans. While the latter favoured enormous foundations and heavy surfacing, the Chinese relied on the use of thin, convex, watertight 'shells' over ordinary subsoil as the base. (This technique was to be adopted by McAdam in Britain over 2 000 years later.)

'The radiation of virtue,' Confucius is reported to have said, 'is faster than the transmission of imperial orders by stages and couriers.' The Posting System was used for the speedy relay of royal orders and to obtain systematic intelligence reports from frontier regions. Ch'in became skilled in building roads as they forged southwards over the Chin Ling barriers towards the important area of modern Szechuan. The 'five-foot [1·5 metres] way' was a remarkable feat, which included many kilometres of 'hanging galleries,' suspended along the sides of precipitous slopes.

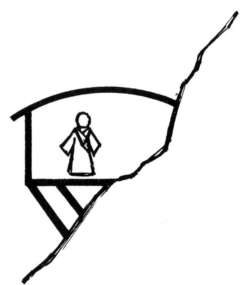

Hanging galleries.

Great importance was attached to bridge building and several forms were developed. The simplest was the wooden-beam bridge which was seldom more than 6 metres long. This could be extended into a trestle bridge resting on partly submerged piers. Records exist of bridges over 600 metres long with 68 spans and a deck 17 metres wide. Since these lay close to the water they were often submerged in floods. Stone-arch bridges were also constructed.

Hydraulics

In the Yellow River basin eighty per cent of the rainfall falls in the three summer months when the cold dry continental winds are replaced by the warm moist monsoons. However, the quantity and timing of rainfall was so irregular that drought or flooding were equally likely. The Yellow River was the most difficult to master, followed by the Huai and Yangtze rivers. It carries up to 1 000 million tons of silt every year and deposits much of this on its flood plain, elevating it above the surrounding lowlands, and making it very vulnerable to changes in course and flooding when the banks burst.

Yü the Great Engineer initially controlled the waters by deepening the existing channels rather than building dams. Before 600 B.C. Duke Huan of Ch'i built levels or dykes along the nine branches of the flood plain. Usually the policy of containing the river has failed because it proved impossible to control nature.

One scheme carried out in the Ch'in State stands out as being highly successful. In 246 B.C. the Cheng Kuo Canal was built parallel to the Wei river. It was the organization of this scheme which consolidated the power of Ch'in. The scheme still operates today.

The importance of controlling floods and drought was not seen purely in agricultural terms. Political considerations were present too. An official might have reasoned along these lines: If floods should break the dykes along the rivers, this would cause drowning and distress among the people. Distress leads to a disregard for morality and increases the problem of maintaining order. Hence, it is in the interests of political stability to encourage hydraulic engineering developments. The way out of the problem is for men to act in disciplined unity. Reaching such a conclusion, the official would see to it that the labour was organized through the *corvée* (obligatory unpaid labour for the state) and engineers appointed.

Metal Working

Though bronze reached China as late as 1500 B.C., the Chinese reached a far higher level of technique than other bronze users. Iron arrived in China about 700 B.C. and the earliest examples of work include cauldrons inscribed with the code of law. We know that the King of Wu had weapons of iron by 500 B.C., but the use of iron probably permeated eastwards via the passes of the Tarim Basin. This could account for the development of iron in Ch'in, a factor in its military superiority.

Iron was used for tools, such as hoes and ploughshares, besides weapons. What is important about iron production in China is the fact that it was smelted and cast almost as soon as it was known. In the West iron working was to be limited to the forge until A.D. 1350. Possible reasons for this great advance were:

● high phosphorus content of Chinese iron which lowered the melting point of the ore;

● good refractory clays for making crucibles for steel production and moulds for casting;

● the development of double acting piston bellows which maintained high and constant draughts into the furnaces, thus keeping temperatures high;

● the extremely advanced traditions of copper and clay working.

In China this knowledge did not fundamentally alter the nature of society as it did in the West.

2 One Empire Under Heaven
The unification of China under the Ch'in and Han dynasties, 221 B.C.–A.D. 220

HISTORICAL OUTLINE

By 221 B.C. the Ch'in armies had crushed all remaining pockets of resistance and the King of Ch'in was able to proclaim himself Shih Huang Ti, 'the First Emperor.' In place of the old feudal system of government belonging to the Classical Age a centralized monarchy was established. For the future development of China the significance of the revolutionary change that Shih Huang Ti began and Liu Pang, the founder of the following purely Chinese dynasty, the Han, completed cannot be underestimated. Under the Han Emperors the political structure assumed a pattern that was to serve China right down till 1912, when the Empire was overthrown and the Republic founded.

The Triumph of Shih Huang Ti
The ruthless determination that had directed the 'Tiger of Ch'in' in his defeat of the ancient feudal kingdoms soon became evident in the organization of the new Empire. Indeed, Shih Huang Ti was one of the great destroyers of history. He was conscious of the insecurity of his Empire, which lacked any degree of economic integration. Strict military control he decided was the quickest and most efficient way of bringing stability. Insecurity came from two sources:

● In the east there was an internal political threat from the aristocracy of old feudal states.

● In the north the Hsiung Nu nomads, probably the Huns who invaded the Roman Empire in the fourth century A.D., were a continual danger.

To break the power of the nobility Shih Huang Ti abolished all the feudal states and divided the Empire into new administrative areas, under military governors. Great landowners lost their estates and all the nobles were forced to reside at the Ch'in capital, where isolated from their supporters they remained without influence. The *nung*, the peasant farmers, were given greater rights over their land, but were liable for taxes.

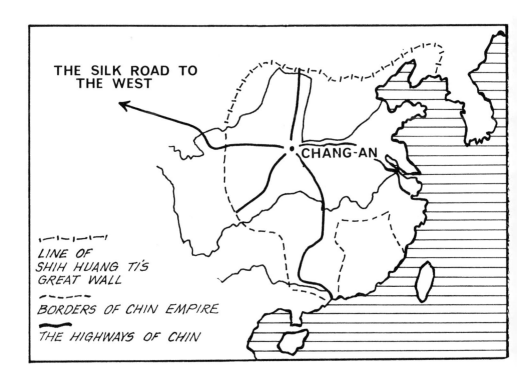

China 206 B.C.

Unification and centralization were synonymous for Shih Huang Ti. Since the capital could hardly be considered central to the Empire, a good communication system was essential both for dispatch of messages and for transport of armies and taxes. To ease communication between previously independent provinces it was not sufficient merely to extend the superior roads and canals of the Ch'in State. The written language was standardized as were currency, weights and measures. These eased the collection of the all-important grain taxes on which prosperity depended. It was impossible to have a large administrative capital without a constant supply of foodstuffs to feed it. The Emperor made it his policy to visit all points of the Empire in order to check on the work of his administrators, though his movements were always kept secret. The first Emperor was a harsh ruler, but his policy of centralization helped foster a feeling of national identity among the Chinese.

The location of the imperial capital itself, near Chang-an, in the heart of Ch'in, caused deep resentment. The Ch'in, inhabiting the Wei Valley, were disliked by the lowland Chinese because of their contact with the nomad peoples, which had led to some intermarriage, and because they were essentially a war-orientated society with distinct military advantages. They had adopted cavalry and obtained iron weapons in the preceding centuries. From their favoured geographical position, protected on three sides by mountain or desert, the Ch'in could sweep down into the lowlands and retire into an almost impregnable stronghold whenever the forces of the Great Plain were organized. Thus in choosing Chang-an, Shih Huang Ti increased his chances of holding the capital and, by extending the highly efficient radial road system to link the extreme points of the Empire, he could ensure his orders were transmitted rapidly to the farthest outposts.

Perhaps most important the First Emperor refused to grant fiefs, feudal holdings of land, to his sons or relatives, since he felt they might revive the local divisions which had caused rivalry in the period of the Warring States. When the *shih*, the scholars, argued for the maintenance of the boundaries of the feudal kingdoms, Li Ssu, Shih Huang Ti's tough minister, made it clear that the Empire was going to last for 'ten thousand years' because the throne had reduced everything 'in a uniform manner.'

Although Confucius had not condemned empire, he had been unaware of such a possibility, so that his followers at this moment in time were opposed to the end of feudalism. Finding this alliance between the dispossessed nobles and the scholars dangerous for the régime, Li Ssu made his infamous proposal to Shih Huang Ti. Throughout the Empire, on pain of death, teaching should be banned and all books except those dealing with technical subjects like agriculture burnt. Only the history of Ch'in was to be read. In this way, Li Ssu hoped, the people would have to adopt the philosophy of the School of Law.

The Burning of the Books was the death-blow for feudal ideals: it caused a definite break in consciousness. When, in Han times, the ancient texts were painfully reconstructed, from memory and the badly tattered copies that had been hidden at great personal risk, the feudal world seemed remote. Education, not birth, appeared the important social qualification. Li Ssu had dealt a decisive blow at the aristocracy, but he had weakened the Ch'in dynasty too. The *shih* were united in hatred against the imperial house. Only the official class of Ch'in remained loyal.

49

The Great Wall of China

It was *the measure introduced to deal with the Hsiung Nu,* namely the Building of the Great Wall, that unified the ordinary people against the Ch'in dynasty. Along the northern boundaries of the feudal states walls had been constructed as a means of defence against raids from nomadic tribes. Such an invasion had shaken the power of the Chou kingdom in 771 B.C. To give the Empire permanent protection, to divide the steppe from the sown, Shih Huang Ti ordered that the old walls be joined together as a continuous 'Great Wall.' The completed line of the wall ran from the western frontier of Ch'in to the sea in the east, a distance of 2 250 kilometres. It has close proximity to the 15 inch (380 mm) isohyet which effectively marks the limits of settled agriculture and may have moved further south since the second century B.C. through desiccation of the region.

'A wall between is a mountain' runs an ancient Chinese proverb. The Great Wall of Shih Huang Ti did act as an immense barrier between the steppe and the sown. The construction was rubble filled walls faced with stone, topped by a brick roadway edged with a parapet and battlements. Towers were sited at strategic points and gateways had additional defensive walls.

Hundreds of thousands toiled on the immense task of construction, prisoners of war and conscripted labourers, working and dying in the cold mountains of the north. The terrible lot of these people has remained a constant subject for Chinese folksong ever since. Forced labour on the Great Wall and the road network became an everyday fact of life for the people under the harsh rule of the School of Law. Ch'in governors, backed with large garrisons, enforced one severe decree after another. But not all the reforms of Shih Huang Ti were pitiless. He standardized weights and measures, transport, currency and the written script. As an administrator he worked hard, handling 'fifty-four kilos of reports' daily, and he travelled widely.

The Fall of Ch'in
No rebellion occurred during the eleven stern years that Shih Huang Ti ruled, but his less able successor was soon engulfed with risings in every province. Heavy taxes, forced labour, unjust laws, cruel tortures, widespread crime—all the ingredients for popular rebellion were there awaiting an opportunity: it came with an intrigue over the succession. Li Ssu concealed the fact of the First Emperor's death in 210 B.C. long enough to force the Crown Prince to commit suicide by a forged imperial command. The Crown Prince had objected to the treatment of the scholars and had been banished to the northern frontier. Fearing for his own safety now his old master was dead, the minister had the second son declared Er Shih Huang Ti, or the Second Emperor. He proved too young and incompetent to deal with the rebels.

As soon as the Ch'in generals put down one rising another broke out. Soldiers mutinied, peasants took up arms, and rebel armies gathered strength. The civil war was a long contest between several leaders, who at first pretended to restore the old feudal kingdoms, till Liu Pang gained overall control in 207 B.C. A man of obscure origins, possibly the son of a village headman and certainly illiterate, he was forced into active rebellion by the excessive rigour of Ch'in law. Having lost a group of convicts and being doomed to execution for this failure of responsibility, Liu Pang deserted and became the leader of a band of such fugitives.

The Foundation of the Han Empire
That a part of the inspiration for the popular rebellions against the Ch'in dynasty was a desire to put the clock back to feudal

Here the legendary Emperor Shun is shown going carefully through piles of reports and other documents brought to a terrace by his secretaries. The drawing comes from a Ch'ing edition of the Shu Ch'ing. *Shih Huang Ti was an efficient ruler too.*

times cannot be doubted. 'The Avenging Army of Ch'u' was the name of one rebel force. But so thorough had been Shih Huang Ti's measures against the old order that in the hour of Ch'in's collapse all attempts to re-establish feudal authority were unsuccessful.

However, Liu Pang, as the Emperor Han Kao Tsu, or 'High Ancestor,' sought a compromise. He saw that though Ch'in policy was correct in reducing everything 'in a uniform manner,' it was necessary to go about it more tactfully. He was prepared to move slowly and undermine feudal institutions over a number of decades. Fiefs were permitted and a few of the old royal houses received small territories, but future Emperors could only come from his own family. Besides, the principal areas came directly under the Emperor's control through the appointment of imperial officers in the Ch'in manner. To make completely sure of his position the Emperor Kao Tsu steadily eliminated possible rivals, loyal generals included, so that his successors inherited undisputed sway over 'the Empire of all beneath Heaven.'

Two things hastened the decline of what was left of feudal influence:

● In 144 B.C. it was decreed that all the sons of a feudal lord were co-heirs of their father, and his estates must be divided among them. This measure accelerated the breakdown of large feudal holdings into little more than substantial country estates.

● Then it was decided that many of the aristocrats should live on their rents in the capital, Chang-an. This measure combined with the threat of dispossession for misconduct caused ties between feudal families and their traditional localities to wither away.

By 100 B.C. the Court was the undisputed centre of power and authority.

The Court

As the Liu family enjoyed great prestige and produced a succession of excellent rulers, the Han Empire was not much troubled by rebellions. Where political difficulties arose was in the palace, with plots and intrigues centred on the Consort Family, the relations of the Empress. With the passing of the feudal kingdoms a China isolated from the rest of the world could not provide royal brides for each new Emperor. The advantage of a foreign Empress or Queen, as European states have found, is that she has no relatives in the country and cannot readily become the centre of a faction. Since in China marriage within the same family was strictly forbidden by immemorial custom the choice of a new Empress became a matter of immense importance. As relatives of the imperial house her kinsfolk automatically became 'the Second Family.' They expected high offices and rewards. Each new Empress would wish to see her people enjoying the status they deserved and the Emperor could be expected to grant her requests. The conflict became intense when two Consort Families were struggling for position. This situation occurred when the new Consort Family, the relatives of the Emperor's young bride, were opposed by the old Consort Family, the relatives of the Emperor's mother.

Such court intrigue remained a permanent feature of the Chinese Empire. Only the sixth Han ruler, Emperor Wu, 'the Warlike,' who reigned from 140 to 86 B.C., ever solved the problem. He took a desperate course; he executed all the members of the Empress' family. Though this left his court free from family strife, later Emperors did not follow his example. As a result the Wang family succeeded in temporarily taking over the Empire for fourteen years (from 9 to A.D. 23). But the usurping uncle, Wang Mang, found the provinces solidly against his rule so that at last another branch of the Liu family was able to reinstate the Han dynasty in a new capital at Loyang.

Away from the imperial city itself these intrigues, short of civil war, were hardly noticed. Governors might change but the system of government went on unaffected. Liu Pang had founded the Empire well. The Han dynasty (207 B.C.–A.D. 220) made united China a reality for centuries and an ideal for which in times of later division men would always strive. 'Men of Han,' in fact, became one of the names for the Chinese thereafter.

The End of the Han Empire
Not surprisingly the Han dynasty lost the Empire through a struggle with an all-too-important Consort Family, the Liang. In A.D. 159 the Emperor Han Huang Ti used the palace eunuchs to oust the Liang from office. Yet this dependence on the eunuchs eventually proved more disastrous than the old trouble with the Consort Families. Unable to found families of their own and recruited from the lowest levels of society, the eunuchs took advantage of their new power to gather personal wealth. Weak Emperors failed to check their activities and corruption became rife. When a loyal general, the brother of a dowager Empress, was assassinated by the eunuchs in A.D. 186, his infuriated soldiers stormed the palace and massacred them. The ensuing

civil war destroyed the Han Empire and split China into the Three Kingdoms.

THE CIVIL SERVICE AND THE REVIVAL OF LEARNING

Despite his lack of education the first Han Emperor did not persecute the *shih*. He allowed the scholars to reconstruct the ancient texts and reopen their schools. Employment for large numbers of them was provided in the body of government officials that became necessary for the smooth running of the Empire. In 206 B.C. the harsh Ch'in laws were repealed, and gentler ones introduced. The growing influence of Confucian philosophy can be observed from this event onwards. An episode concerning the Emperor and his chamberlain, Lu Chia, reveals the civilizing efforts of Confucian scholars.

Lu Chia constantly quoted from the ancient books to the Emperor, who ended by becoming exasperated. 'I conquered the empire on horseback,' he cried, 'what is the good of these sayings?' Lu Chia replied: 'That is true, but it is not on horseback that you will be able to govern it. War and peace are two aspects of an eternal art. If the Ch'in, having become masters of the empire, had governed it in humanity and righteousness, if they had imitated the ancient sages, you would not have got it.' The Emperor changed colour and said: 'Show me then what it is that lost the empire for Ch'in, and how it was I got it, and what it was that won and lost kingdoms of old.' So Lu Chia wrote a book about the causes of the rise and fall of states. There were twelve chapters in all. He read them one after the other to the Emperor, who never failed to praise them.

The School of Law was identified with the worst excesses of Ch'in rule. Those who believed in the values of this stern code soon disappeared from imperial service. During the long reign of the Emperor Wu not only did a regular civil service become the accepted basis of organization for the Empire, but the means of selection for entry into its ranks included the examination of a candidate's understanding of the teachings of Confucius. The ideal candidate was distinguished by 'abundant talents,' respect for family, moral rectitude and learning. In 124 B.C. the Poh Shih Kuan, or the Imperial University, was set up, with a department for each of the ancient books. Many of its students were recruited as government officials. Provincial centres of learning were founded at this period too.

A photograph taken in 1925 of the old examination cells at Nanking.

Under the system of imperial examinations candidates who had won their bachelor's degrees locally used to assemble at the provincial capital for the examinations for the master's degree. Each candidate spent his days in one of a vast range of cells like riverside changing-cabins, guarded by invigilators and supplied with frugal meals brought in from the outside. In the Ming and Ch'ing Empires, the subjects were confined to orthodox literature and philosophy; but during the T'ang and Sung Empires the examinations were more concerned with concrete administrative, governmental and economic problems, while technical subjects such as astronomy, engineering and medicine could be taken too.

The ruling *shih* were recruited through this examination system, whose origins date from the Han Empire. In the nineteenth century European countries adopted the idea of competitive entry to their own civil services. Today, the People's Republic has moved away from such a system—it is considered élitist and undemocratic.

Inevitably the socially well-placed families were able to take the most advantage of this system. They could afford for their sons the many years of education necessary to obtain literary success. At first there were built-in advantages for these people, special exemptions and other rights, but gradually the examination system gained authority and served as 'an open door' for the gifted son of humbler parents. The members of the civil service became a learned élite; families rose into this estate and sank out of it. It was not hereditary. These cultivated officials and lesser gentry, the *shih*, and the peasant farmers, the *nung*, formed the two great pillars on which the structure of the Empire rested till its final overthrow in 1911. The *nung* supported the system, while the *shih* made it work.

The assimilation of the *shih* into the very heart of the Han Empire was possible through the disappearance of feudalism. The followers of Confucius, with their strong sense of duty and their desire to have an orderly society, were naturally drawn into government service. Confucian philosophy was applied to Empire and founded the 'most glorious of the hundred schools.' The Han Emperors encouraged the process for good reasons, not least connected with their own humble origins and lack of noble blood. A system of promotion based on education, not blood, was not inappropriate for a family that had raised, by its own efforts, a member to the exalted position of Son of Heaven.

A revival of learning sprang directly from the tolerance of the Han Emperors. The ancient texts were reconstructed, from memory and surviving fragments. New commentaries were written. Historical writing became a major interest. Ssu-ma Tan, the father, and Ssu-ma Ch'ien, the son, wrote their *Shih Chi* (*Historical Memoirs*). As officials at the court of Emperor Wu they had access to the imperial library and archives. Ssu-ma Ch'ien also travelled the length and breadth of the Empire. The invention of the brush pen began to make a notable change in the style of the characters when used on silk. The beginnings of later achievements in calligraphy, the writing of Chinese characters, and painting date from the Han Empire.

ECONOMY AND SOCIETY

> The law honours farmers, yet farmers have become poorer and poorer; the law degrades merchants, yet merchants have become richer and richer.
>
> *The view of a* shih *in the second century B.C.*

Feudalism had not been destroyed for the benefit of the fifty million peasants but to create absolute power for the First Emperor and his descendants. Political changes were immaterial to the *nung* until they actually prevented them from earning a living. This could occur through greedy administrators, high taxes or an abuse of the *corvée*; or through inconsiderate or non-existent government action to ease periodic famine. But since Confucian philosophy interpreted natural disasters as a sign that a régime had lost the Mandate of Heaven, only a foolish ruler did not consider the feelings of the *nung*. They were the vast majority of his subjects and they provided the food for the maintenance of cities and armies.

The King Emperor and the Peasant Emperor
Shih Huang Ti did a creditable job in uniting the Warring States during his eleven years as Emperor. He did reduce a great deal 'in a uniform manner.' The standardization of cart axles is a good example of Shih Huang Ti's attention to detail. Previously the cart-wheels of one state would not fit the ruts made by the cart-wheels of another state. Loads had to be transferred at borders, where reweighing slowed down transport considerably. Common weights and measures, coupled with a reduction of local corruption and inefficiency, encouraged the growth of trade throughout the Ch'in Empire. The freer interchange of people and goods gave impetus to the Chinese nationalist movement, which came to maturity in the Han Empire.

Although Liu Pang followed this policy, there was a fundamental difference in his attitude towards the four estates of society. The first Han Emperor avoided the harshness of the School of Law. It should not be forgotten that each great feat of Ch'in civil engineering from the Great Wall to the reconstruction of the capital at Hsien Yang (near to Chang-an) required hundreds of thousands of labourers who were conscripted in an outright abuse of the *corvée*. Such large-scale projects completely disrupted the agricultural cycle of entire regions. Up to 700 000 coolies had been involved in the construction of Shih Huang Ti's palace, which towered above the two hundred and seventy other palaces built at Hsien Yang to house the exiled nobles from the Warring States.

Liu Pang was a man of the people; he ruled by obtaining their support. He is remembered also as a lover of women and wine. When he had to leave his homeland of Chou in order to take residence at the new capital Chang-an, he left with tears after throwing a farewell party for his poorer friends. Such stories reflect the human image of a man who was called the Great Ancestor, 'Kao Tsu.'

Commerce in Chaos

Liu Pang was disturbed to see merchants filling the power gaps left in the provinces after the collapse of feudalism, but he found this process hard to check. Because the merchant had a local monopoly he could buy grain at very low prices at harvest time, then hoard it until scarcity forced the price up. In periods of famine the monopolists could become extremely wealthy. A policy of discrimination and taxation against these speculators failed to alter this situation and it was repealed soon after the death of Emperor Han Kao Tsu.

The economy had come under stresses that are quite familiar to us, today.

● Government reserves were drained by maintaining forces in the North. As a result taxes had to be increased.

● The minting of money by private individuals led to a continual rise in the price of grain and also threatened to make such people financially stronger than the Emperor.

● In salt and iron production too the manufacturers became increasingly richer, through virtual monopolies.

● Because a few were wealthy there was only a veneer of prosperity, concealing underlying chaos.

● The *nung* were suffering at the hands of the grain speculators and their incomes were always falling behind the level of prices.

Nationalization

In 140 B.C. Emperor Wu came to power and in his incisive manner attempted to wrestle the wealth from the merchants and industrialists in order to finance his military expeditions. At first he courted them, taking the most able into the civil service, a course of action that upset the *shih*. Always short of money, Wu subjected China to heavy taxation and increasing production of worthless coinage. He nationalized the iron and salt industries, employing their former owners to run them. By 100 B.C. all iron was supposedly produced in forty-nine government factories. Later in the Han Empire beer and wine production were nationalized too. None of these measures had the desired effect of reducing rampant inflation. Barter began to replace cash transactions and eventually the sheer low value of each unit of currency led to a cessation of the illegal minting of coins, which had become something of a business for many families.

A Notable Success
To prevent fluctuation in food prices provincial officials were ordered to establish public granaries, to buy grain when prices were low, and to sell in times of shortage. This was the *p'ing chun* or 'levelling system,' specifically designed to break the monopoly of local merchants. Of all Emperor Wu's measures the 'ever normal' granary was admitted to be most effective, even by the traditional *shih*. The merchants remained wealthy enough to be able to buy titles and positions with grain or livestock, but the *nung* were safeguarded against heavy speculation.

After Wu's death the Empire tottered on the verge of economic and military ruin. From the signs of famine and war it could be interpreted that the days of the Han Empire were numbered, and Wang Mang, a highly esteemed member of the Empress's family, considered that he had received the call from Heaven to save China. Establishing himself as the founder of the brief Hsin dynasty (A.D. 9–23), he was popular and unpopular by turns. A great rebellion ended his reign of fourteen years and named him posthumously 'the Usurper.' But his controversial efforts deserve our attention.

The Revolutionary Reformer
Increasingly, great landlords were dominating agriculture, buying out smaller farmers, who could not compete. The Ch'in and Han dynasties had not prevented this trend for two reasons. First, it permitted an increase in productivity, which a growing population needed. Secondly, the landowners were influential and some account had to be taken of their interests.

A small farmer in debt through a bad harvest might mortgage his land, eventually being forced to give it up when debts could not be repaid. A tenant farmer had to pay half his produce in rent and the rest was split between his family, the government and seed for the following year.

Wang Mang decided on the following reforms:
● no buying and selling of land was allowed, as it belonged to the nation;
● each farmer was to be allocated land in proportion to his needs;
● idle land should be triply taxed;
● there should be a reintroduction of the 'levelling system,' which had been allowed to lapse;
● government banks were to give small loans to farmers at low interest;

61

- administrative expenses were to be met out of the existing monopolies of liquor, salt, iron and coinage;
- no buying and selling of slaves should be allowed.

Thrust upon an ill-prepared country the administration of these schemes created chaos and bitterness on all sides. Eventually the *nung*, who were suffering as much as anyone from the measures intended to help them, joined with the landowners and the outraged *shih* to overthrow the Hsin dynasty.

CHINESE EXPANSION AND THE DISCOVERY OF THE WORLD

The area occupied solely by Chinese within the Empire was limited to the flood plains of the Yellow River. From 'The Land within the Passes' the Chinese had continually moved southwards, particularly from 400 to 200 B.C. when the population expanded rapidly with improved agriculture. This movement was always accelerated by famine, whether caused by drought, flood or war.

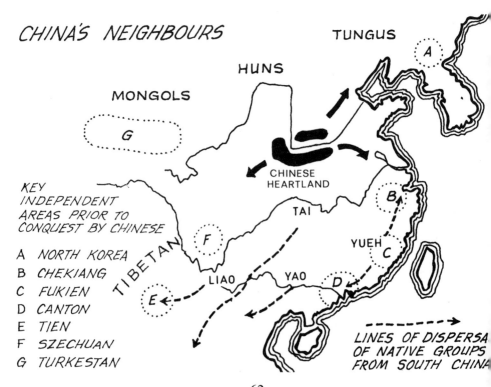

CHINA'S NEIGHBOURS

TUNGUS

HUNS

MONGOLS

G

CHINESE
HEARTLAND

TAI

YUEH

KEY
INDEPENDENT
AREAS PRIOR TO
CONQUEST BY CHINESE

A NORTH KOREA
B CHEKIANG
C FUKIEN
D CANTON
E TIEN
F SZECHUAN
G TURKESTAN

LIAO   YAO

LINES OF DISPERSA
OF NATIVE GROUPS
FROM SOUTH CHINA

Often conflict with the indigenous peoples of the South was limited, for the most primitive were hill-forest dwellers, while the Chinese farmed the plains. Shih Huang Ti encouraged such movements southwards but discouraged any movement to the North fearing that the farmers of the northern outposts might abandon their often marginal farms to take up stock raising and join the nomadic herders.

China's Neighbours in the South
The main groups of non-Chinese peoples in contact with the Empire were as follows:

● *The Liao* These were a very primitive tribe originating in the forested hills of Hupei and Hunan to the south of the Yangtze River. The Chinese tended to avoid them because of their backwardness.

● *The Yao* These too originated in Hunan but spread throughout the hill country of South China. They practised primitive agriculture unlike the Liao, who were entirely hunters and collectors.

● *The Tai* They came from the flatter lands of the Yangtze valley and later spread throughout South-East Asia, particularly in Thailand and Burma. They had a sophisticated agricultural system based on rice and it was through contact with these people that the Chinese improved their own agriculture, adopting many new crops and animals like the water buffalo.

● *The Yüeh* The greatest resistance to Chinese encroachment was displayed by the Yüeh. They were a well-organized people who may have been related to those previously mentioned. As the inhabitants of the south-east coastlands they were masters of maritime enterprise. Their supremacy in coastal waters, coupled with the mountainous terrain encircling their coastal states, gave them greater protection from Chinese dominance.

China's Neighbours in the North
To the north and west of the Empire dwelt tribes of nomadic herdsmen. They were all regarded by the Chinese as 'barbarians,' but formed basically four geographically distinct groups. These were:

● *The Tibetans*, whose economy depended on sheep. Although not highly organized as a military and political force, they came into conflict with the Chinese during the Han dynasty. They usually fought on foot as their horses were inferior to the cavalry chargers of more organized armies. However, in their fastness of high mountains they remained largely undisturbed. Altitude sickness always hampered later imperial forces sent from China.

● *The Mongols* They inhabited the steppes and plateaux which rolled down from the Tarim Basin to North China. Their economy was based on cattle, though like the Turkish group they also had sheep, camels and goats. Since they lived across the overland trade routes to Central Asia, the Chinese had contact with them over a long period.

● *The Turks* These were the Hsiung Nu, or Huns, that were a constant threat to the northern frontier of China. Horses comprised the basis of all wealth in their economy, though other animals were kept. They were highly mobile and well-organized. Their reputation as fierce fighters was fully deserved. After 200 B.C. they abandoned what little farming they had done and became involved in barter trade as well as pillage of neighbouring agriculturalists, such as the Chinese.

● *The Tungus* of Manchuria and Hopeh. These differed in many respects from the other northern peoples. As forest dwellers with an economy based on pigs they had little occasion for fighting the Chinese.

The Great Wall and the Huns
The success of Shih Huang Ti's wall was noticeable between about 200 and 140 B.C. when the Hsiung Nu were persuaded to adopt a policy of peaceful coexistence and trade with the Empire. They accepted gifts of silk and other luxuries, and even copied some Chinese customs. But in 141 B.C. the Han Emperor, Wu (the Warlike), tried to ambush the Chief of the Hsiung Nu at a frontier post on the Great Wall. The Chief escaped and a very long war broke out in which the Chinese had greater success than in earlier encounters due to their increasing competence as horsemen. Two pieces of technology gave the Han Empire security in the north—the fortifications of the Great Wall and the longer range of the crossbow, invented at the end of the Chou dynasty but developed by the Han—yet for Emperor Wu this was insufficient. He wanted to dominate the steppelands too.

The struggle came to a temporary halt in 51 B.C. following civil conflict within the nomad nation. It resumed in A.D. 73 as nomad raiders took advantage of discord in the Empire. But the significance of the feud with the Hsiung Nu lay rather in China's attempts to obtain allies and outflank them. An era of exploration and conquest was stimulated by these goals and was to expand China's political boundaries far beyond the valleys of the Yellow

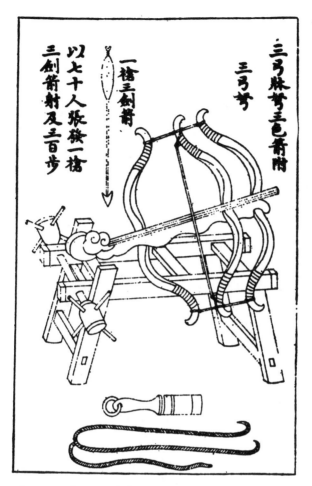

Large-scale use of the crossbow, from a handbook
(A.D. 1044).

and Yangtze Rivers. The Han Empire extended its authority over large areas of Central Asia, a relationship that persists even today, and by annexing Lak Lang province, now North Korea, Chinese culture came to flow down the peninsula and, eventually, across the sea to influence Japan. Incidentally, China discovered the West.

The Discovery of the West
Searching for allies against the Hsiung Nu in 138 B.C., Emperor Wu dispatched Chang Ch'ien to find the Ta Yueh Chi, nomads living to the west. In spite of being held prisoner by the Hsiung Nu for a decade Chang Ch'ien eventually located the Ta Yueh

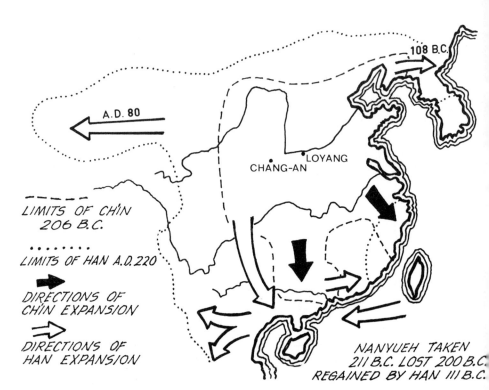

Imperial expansion 220 B.C.–220 A.D.

Chi, far removed from China and uninterested in returning. They had settled in Ta Hsia, now part of Russian Turkestan and Afghanistan, but what had been a few years before the Chinese envoy's arrival the Greek kingdom of Bactria.

Chang Ch'ien was amazed to discover a settled population: his report of the journey speaks of 'cities, mansions and houses as in China.' Here was another civilization, beyond the nomad lands. The description excited the Court in Chang-an, as did his news of India and Persia. But what interested Emperor Wu were the fine horses Chang Ch'ien had seen on his journey through Ta Yuan. These large animals could carry heavily armed men against the Hsiung Nu who rode the smaller Mongolian pony. Embassies and military expeditions were sent to Ta Yuan, the incredible distance of two thousand miles, until by 102 B.C. the forceful Emperor had obtained enough horses for breeding purposes.

Contact with states in Bactria and northern India was interrupted by troubles at the Han Court, the usurpation of Wang Mang (A.D. 9–23), and the Kushan invasion of India. When the second phase of Han discovery of the West took place at the end of the first century A.D., the chance of cultural exchange between European and Chinese civilization had gone. The Greek element in that region, with the exception of the arts, was submerged in Buddhist India and the ruling Kushans, a nomadic tribe recently converted to Buddhism, had adopted Indian culture. Between A.D. 73 and A.D. 102 General Pan Chao established Chinese overlordship of Central Asia, even reaching the shores of the Caspian Sea with an army of seventy thousand men, but his envoys did not open up relations with the Roman Empire. The other civilization that was to touch China, now that the 'Empire of all under Heaven' had learnt of other advanced worlds, was not Europe, but India. The transplanting of the Buddhist faith to China confirmed the oriental frame of Chinese society and continued it along its separate course, so remote from the historical experience of Western Europe.

Coin of King Menander. This silver coin was struck by Menander, King of North India; it has a bilingual inscription in Greek and an Indian language. After the death of Alexander in 323 B.C. the eastern provinces of his empire were ruled by the Seleucid dynasty from Antioch in Syria. But about 250 B.C. they broke off as an independent Greek kingdom. Under Demetrius I Bactrians, Greeks and Indians merged as a single people in the Buddhist kingdom of Bactria. His general Menander invaded the north of India around 190 B.C. and was made a separate king. A famous Indian book, the ancient *Milinda Panha*, records Menander's own conversion to Buddhism. Other Greek kings appeared in north-west India but they were swept away by the great invasion of the Kushan tribes during the first century B.C. Bactria and Ferghana, to the north, had many magnificent cities and towns at this time. Large-scale irrigation schemes permitted agriculture while international trade brought in commodities and wealth. The present-day desolation is largely due to the fury of the Mongols. Early in the thirteenth century A.D. Genghiz Khan devastated the entire area.

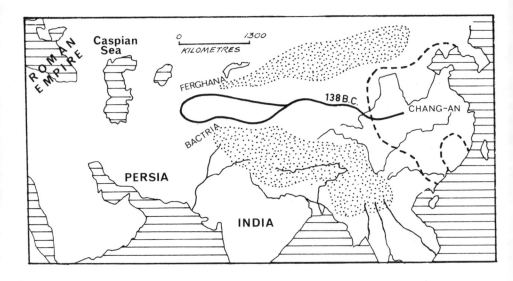

Probable route of Chang Ch'ien (138–126 B.C.) during his mission to the Ta Yueh Chi.

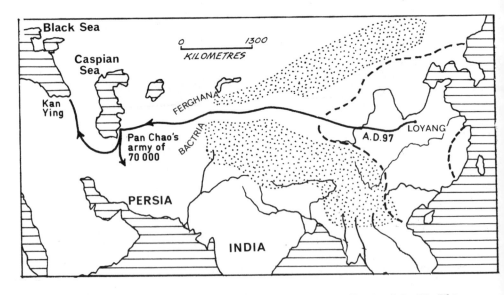

General Pan Chao reached the shores of the Caspian Sea in A.D. 97. This is the closest point that a Chinese force has ever approached Europe. But the majority of Pan Chao's troops were raised in the kingdoms of Central Asia which had accepted Han overlordship on the march westwards. An ambassador, Kan Ying, was sent towards the Roman Empire but he returned to Pan Chao's camp without making contact.

68

A tea caravan on a pass near Tachienlu on the borders of Tibet.

*A clay model
of a horse
(A.D. 220–589).
It is one of the
heavier breeds
that the
Han Emperors
sought for their
cavalry regiments.*

The Coming of Buddhism
The only significant foreign influence on the Chinese people
has been the teachings of the Buddha. Nothing else, till the nineteenth century, has ever modified the way of life followed by the
'Men of Han' to the extent achieved by this religion. The Han
Empire officially noticed Buddhism in A.D. 65, though it is
likely that some of Buddha's teaching had earlier travelled back
along the path trodden by Chang Ch'ien. An embassy was sent
to India to collect copies of the *sutras*, or holy books, and Indian
scholars to help translate them. Centuries of labour and many
pilgrimages to India were necessary before the Buddhist scriptures
became generally available in China. It was in the fifth and sixth
centuries A.D. that Buddhism developed into a great popular
religion.

The legend of Bodhidharma, the monk who is reputed to have
introduced the Ch'an school of Buddhism from India around
A.D. 520, retains something of the initial shock that many
Chinese must have felt from the impact of this Indian religion.
Arriving at the southern court, where the Chinese Emperor
Liang Wu Ti not only strongly supported the new faith but had
retired from the world himself on more than one occasion, to
the dismay of his subjects, Bodhidharma, a fierce-looking fellow
with a bushy beard and wide-open, penetrating eyes, baffled
nearly everyone. His interview with Emperor Wu was brief and
abrupt. For the Emperor described all that he had done to
promote the practice of Buddhism, and asked what merit he had
gained thereby—taking the popular view that Buddhism is a
gradual accumulation of merit through good deeds, leading to
better and better circumstances in future incarnations, or lives,
and finally release in *nirvana*, or eternal bliss. But Bodhidharma
replied, 'No merit whatever!' This so undermined the Emperor's
idea of Buddhism that he asked, 'What, then, is the sacred
doctrine's first principle?' Bodhidharma replied, 'It's just empty;
there's nothing sacred.' 'Who, then, are you,' said the Emperor,
'to stand before us?' 'I don't know,' was the final reply.

After this interview, so unsatisfactory from the Emperor's
point of view, Bodhidharma retired to a monastery in Wei,
where he is said to have spent nine years in a cave, 'gazing at
the wall.' The replies of Bodhidharma must have seemed very
strange to the *shih*, the scholar officials, in the court, but their
emphasis on inner values and the limits of what can be expressed
in words about eternal truth is not very far removed from Taoism.
Confucian philosophy consistently opposed the rising tide of the

Buddhist faith, while Taoism paralleled and competed with it in the hearts and minds of the *nung*, the peasant farmers. Ch'an Buddhism, a fruitful interaction, even amalgam, of the teachings of Lao-tzu and Gautama, was to reach its climax in Japan as Zen.

An Agricultural Calendar from one by Tsui Shih (A.D. 100–170) for Loyang.

71

SCIENCE AND TECHNOLOGY

Because of the fundamental role of Nature in Chinese culture, specialists such as astronomers, engineers and magicians were absorbed into the civil service. Science and sorcery could exist side by side because natural phenomena, like flooding or eclipses, were related to supernatural powers. It would have been silly to confine efforts for their control to practical measures.

By the end of the Han Empire, China had acquired much experience in science, accumulated a mass of information, formulated some fundamental principles, and anticipated many discoveries associated with the West. In the past it has been fashionable to criticize Chinese advances as being unscientific in their methodology and for being practical rather than theoretical. We are now reassessing this view. Science and technology were inevitably linked. Without engineering precision scientific instruments could not be used to record accurate data; by the first century B.C. Chinese craftsmen were using sliding callipers graduated in decimals.

Chang Heng (A.D. 78–139)

An example of a government official well versed in science was the mathematician and astronomer from Hupeh, Chang Heng. Among his notable achievements were:

- the most accurate calculation of the value of π at that time;
- the improvement of the armillary sphere and other precision instruments used in the plotting and understanding of heavenly bodies;
- the modification and clarification of existing astronomical theory in the light of his findings;
- the introduction of the grid system of co-ordinates in cartography;
- the construction of a seismograph to record the direction of earthquakes.

Magnetism

The very first dial and pointer readings, the magnetic compass, was developed in Han China. It evolved from a piece of lodestone embedded in a wooden fish floating in water. A needle projecting from it indicated South. The 'South controlling spoon' was used by diviners, being carved from lodestone which rotated on highly polished plate used to foretell the future.

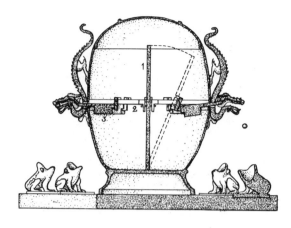

A cross section of Chang Heng's seismograph. A tremor would disturb the pendulum (1) causing the arm (2) to open the dragon's mouth (3) and releasing a ball which fell into the mouth of the frog below, thus indicating the direction of the tremor.

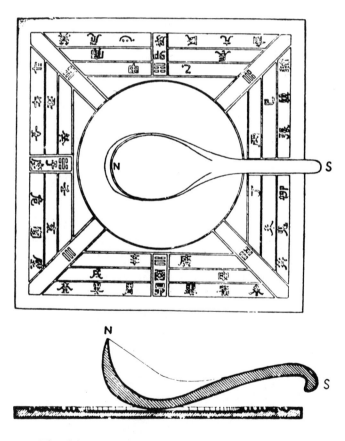

The diviner's board and south-pointing spoon.

The Iron and Salt Industries. From the fourth century B.C. cast iron hoes, ploughshares, axes, swords and picks are recorded. Cast iron was produced at a very early stage aided by man- and water-powered double-acting piston bellows, as illustrated. The picture also shows production of wrought iron by 'puddling,' a technique not developed in Britain until the eighteenth century. Steel making was undertaken as early as the sixth century A.D. by the forerunner of the later Siemens-Martin method, known as co-fusion—both wrought and cast iron were heated together, thus 'averaging' out carbon content.

Salt production utilized steel drilling bits to extract brine from underground sources up to 600 metres. Extracted through bamboo tubes it was evaporated in large iron pans. In Szechuan natural gas was used for this as early as the second century B.C. The illustration below shows a deep drilling operation for brine and natural gas.

74

An invention often confused with magnetism was the 'South pointing carriage.' Invented by Ma Chun around A.D. 260, the carriage carried an indicator which always pointed South on journeys. This was not magnetic. It rotated by means of a simple differential gear and therefore utilized toothed wheels or cogs.

Chinese Inventions of Daily Significance

● *The harness.* Down to A.D. 1000 in Europe a 'throat-and-girth' harness was used, giving inefficient haulage. Only China had developed the 'breast strap' harness as early as 200 B.C. This forerunner of modern collar harness increased the haulage capacity of horses. Chinese chariots were larger and carried more passengers than either Greek or Roman chariots.

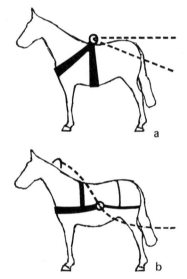

a. Western 'throat-and-girth' harness.
b. The more efficient 'breast-strap' harness of ancient China.

● *The wheelbarrow.* No evidence exists of this labour-saving device in the West until the thirteenth century. In China it was used for supplying the armies of Chu Ko Liang, a Shu general, in the third century A.D.

● *Stirrups.* Probably stimulated by the Indian toe stirrup, the foot stirrup appeared in China in the second century B.C., a thousand years before it reached Europe. It made Chinese cavalry a rival force to the Huns for the first time, fusing horse and rider into one immovable force.

● *The rudder*. The stern-post rudder is found in model boats dating from the first century B.C. in the Canton area, though Chinese boats did not have a stern post as such—it was rather box shaped. The rudder reached Europe in the twelfth century (about the same time as the magnetic compass).

A pottery model of a ship from a Cantonese Han tomb, showing stern-post rudder.

● *Paper*. First announced by the eunuch Tsai Lun, the Director of Imperial Workshops in A.D. 105, the use of paper may have led to the loss of many important Chinese records that might have survived if written on cruder parchment or bark. Printing probably developed by the sixth century A.D. under Buddhist influence.

Technical Education
Medical examinations date from the Han period. State education in general originated in Szechuan under Governor Wen Ong. In 145 B.C. he founded a teacher's training college in Cheng Tu in order to spread civilization among the uncultured masses of the Red Basin. Scholars received special privileges and they obtained key government posts. In 124 B.C. the Po Shih Kuan or Imperial University was founded with a chair for each of the classical books. When Wang Mang was Chief Minister, he inaugurated the first assembly of scientific experts. More than a thousand attended the conference at Chang-an. Scientific bibliographies, dictionaries

and encyclopaedias were all drawn up by the end of the Han dynasty.

The Development of Medicine

Although the functions of priest and doctor were separated early on, the basis of medicine remained the balancing of the forces of yin and yang within the body's main organs. The Yellow Emperor is traditionally accredited with a systematic study of medicine, including the invention of acupuncture, but the Han period witnessed most of the earliest writings and personalities.

Diagnosis was developed in 255 B.C. by Pien Chiao. His work was furthered in the *Pulse Classic* of Wang Shu Ho in 280 A.D. On each wrist six pulses could be examined indicating the condition of each of the twelve internal organs. Pulse types could be superficial, deep, slow or fast. Altogether, over fifty-two chief varieties were recorded, including seven which signified impending death.

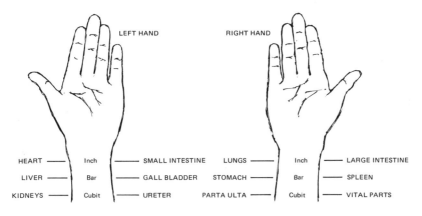

The twelve pulses of the body.

Acupuncture was the use of hot or cold needles of silver, brass and other metals which could be long or short, coarse or fine, to puncture the twelve invisible channels of the body. This was to release the yin and yang. Three-hundred-and-sixty-five points of puncture were recognized.

Three great medical men emerge in the Han period:
● Tsang Kung (around 180 B.C.) who was known as Father Tsang, developed the use of drugs rather than palpation or acupuncture.

● Chang Chung-ching, who was called the Hippocrates of China, graduated in medicine in A.D. 168. He was exceptional in his belief in clinical treatments, having no time for supernatural or magic cures. His most famous work was on typhoid and related diseases.

● Hua To, who was born in A.D. 190, became a famous surgeon with great knowledge of anaesthetics, despite the pressures of the orthodox *shih* who were against dissection of bodies. It is said that with his death surgery came to an end.

THE AGRICULTURAL BASIS OF THE FIRST EMPIRE

In A.D. 2 the first reliable census revealed that three-quarters of the total population of around fifty-eight million lived in the Wei and Yellow River valleys. The only other densely populated area was the Red Basin of Szechuan, while the Lower Yangtze valley was still a sparsely populated pioneer-frontier.

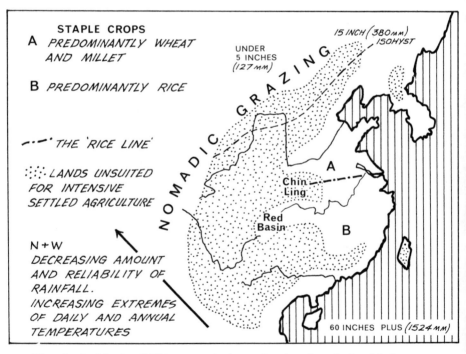

The physical basis of Chinese agriculture showing the relationship between climate, relief and subsistence types.

The Northern Farmer
By abandoning wasteful and destructive shifting cultivation the peasants of the Wei valley were able to increase output from the fragile loess soils of the hills and the easily-breached alluvial soils of the valleys.

A complex system arose based on:
- co-operative use of labour for irrigation and dyke building;
- high and continuous inputs of labour in the care of land;
- intensive use of fertilizers;
- adoption and development of new crops and techniques.

Irrigation and Flood Control
While many indigenous northern crops were drought resistant, yields could also be increased by the provision of summer water. This was initially supplied as a by-product of strategic military and transport canals. Experience gained in their construction proved valuable when rice was introduced from the sub-tropical South, for this needed complicated irrigation when taken from its natural environment.

The strength of Chang-an depended entirely on the canal systems of the Wei valley. Emperor Wu was criticized for developing them to the benefit of one corner of the realm only, as he neglected to repair the breached dykes of the lower Yellow River valley after disastrous floods.

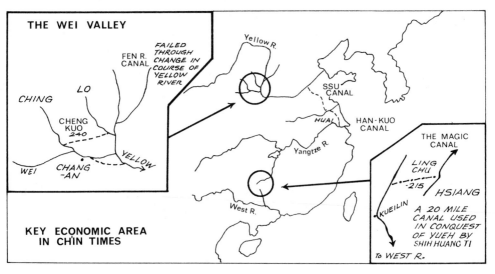

Some major canal schemes of the Han dynasty.

Some important schemes were the *Cheng Kuo Canal*, constructed in 246 B.C., which increased the power of the Ch'in State by watering over 182000 hectares and increasing productivity in the Wei valley fivefold. The *Chang-an Canal* of 129 B.C. reduced the distance from the Yellow River to the capital by half and irrigated a further 182000 hectares on land formerly fit only for sheep. An improvement of the Cheng Kuo Canal was made in the *Po Canal* (95 B.C.). A significant achievement outside the Wei valley was the *'Magic Canal,'* linking the Yangtze and West Rivers in 215 B.C. This allowed Shih Huang Ti to send troops into Yüeh and was a spearhead for the agricultural colonization of the South.

Tenure and Technology
Traditionally the Chinese were accredited with the 'well-field' system of farm-holding. Farms would be grouped in nines. Eight would be operated as family units and the ninth exploited jointly for the benefit of landlord or ruler. But this ideal may never have been attained, because the small farmer was frequently

A Han tomb model of a rotary mill (foreground), a pedal tilt-hammer, and a rotary winnowing fan with a crank handle (the oldest known illustration of a crank).

under pressure to sell his land and surrender his independence as a tenant of a great estate. Laws were introduced to prevent the handing-over of intact estates from father to son but this did not

Agriculture around the city wall. Fertilizer from the city helps explain why such fields had the highest yields.

prevent wealthy merchants from accumulating land at the expense of the farmer. Technically their estates were more advanced. Ox-drawn ploughs were fitted with iron ploughshares and moulding boards. Water and animal power were harnessed for the milling of grain by tilt hammers and circular stone grinding wheels. Prototype seed drills are mentioned. Water-buffalo, introduced from the south, worked in the increasing number of paddy fields, the small square basins used for rice growing. These contrasted with the long narrow strips winding around the loess hillsides on which dry crops would be grown. The 'endless chain' was devised for raising water by footpower from canal and well. The estate could boast all these and an impressive array of fruits and ornamental shrubs from far afield. The *nung* however were forced to retain the ancient methods and crops, depending on millets and beans, wooden hand hoes, and manually-operated grain mills, and carrying their water by yoke and bucket.

Fertilizers
River silt and canal mud were an initial source of fertility readily available to the Chinese. Up to twenty-eight tonnes per hectare were applied as it was recognized as essential to put back into the soil what had been taken out. All waste material was saved, including ashes, manure, silkworm debris and human excrement. The daily collection of city 'night soil', rich in phosphorus, potassium and nitrogen, was a major commercial enterprise. It could be stored as a liquid in stone jars for feeding to plants, or reduced to a fine powder for manuring soil prior to planting. Fertilizers were generally processed by composting and mixing with soil before application as it was thought the growth of the plant foods from it would compete with plant growth itself. This prior processing was an important time-saver. Plants such as clover and beans may have been ploughed into the earth as 'green fertilizer' and it is likely that crop rotation was developed to prevent soil exhaustion.

> In 1905 a peasant farmer in Shantung was keeping his family of ten, plus one pig and one donkey on two-thirds of a hectare. This is equivalent to 240 people, 24 donkeys and 24 pigs on 16 hectares, which at that time was considered too small an area to support the average American farming family.

The Oriental farmer has been called a 'time economizer beyond any other.' By careful use of the calendar and his spare time he should not need to rush or panic in any season. In the essential task of ploughing he was exhorted to attend to it during a drizzle or after rain thereby conserving moisture which would be invaluable in the summer. As early as the first century B.C. Chao Kuo, an agricultural minister, evolved the system of ploughing called 'tai-tien.' The traditional field was about 240 paces long by 1 pace wide, a pace being equivalent to about 1·5 metres. Each farmer would own several of these unenclosed strips. Chao Kuo advocated the digging of 3 shallow trenches or furrows separated by 3 raised ridges along each field. Improvements were immediate:

- seed previously sown broadcast was now efficiently channelled into the furrows;
- the position of ridge and furrow was alternated each year;
- the ridges would slowly be flattened during the growing season as weeding took place, giving extra support to the crop;
- the system could be adapted for growing two complementary crops at the same time, one on the ridge, the other in the furrow.

Another system of the period was the 'ou-t'ien' or shallow-pit system by which good land could be obtained from bad. Barren slopes or wastes could be made fertile by removing the earth, taking it to the village, composting it with organic refuse, and then replacing it. The method was also used to grow crops in very shallow soils.

Crops and Stock

The Chinese remained primarily crop growers even when imperial expansion gave control of the grasslands and new livestock, such as camels, were introduced. Shih Huang Ti was aware that the poor peasants of these semi-desert lands would become nomads, if given half a chance. Fearing the infiltration of the Huns southwards he created many settlements to act as focal points for agriculture. Discouragement of large-scale livestock raising had sound economic as well as political motives. Overgrazing was highly likely in an area of little and infrequent rain and this could hasten the whole cycle of erosion which so affected agriculture in the Wei valley. Further, livestock were poor 'converters' of vegetable products. In other words the end products in foodstuff terms did not justify the high vegetable inputs.

The Chinese regarded cows' milk as the drink of barbarians, and cattle were raised mainly as draught animals. Smaller, more economical livestock such as dogs, chickens, geese and pigs supplemented the largely vegetarian diet. The indigenous cereals of the north such as millets and wheat were supplemented by beans and root crops. Cereals, such as kaoliang, provided not only bread and porridge but also thatch, fuel and fertilizer. Soya beans were another versatile crop, having a high protein content,

Terraced and flooded paddy fields.

and being capable of having flour and paste made from them. (Today synthetic plastics and non-meat steaks are made from soya beans.)

Rice
This had been introduced successfully in the North by the first century B.C. North of the Yangtze River it could only be grown in the summer and with careful irrigation. As a result it was mainly a luxury crop accredited with medicinal value. But with improved techniques its productivity exceeded all other crops, and above all others it depended on co-operation and joint action by the farmers.

The rice would be planted by experienced sowers in seed beds covered with carefully smoothed liquid manure. A seed bed of one hectare would supply enough shoots to fill ten hectares after thirty to fifty days. Before transplanting, the paddy fields would be prepared by ploughing in clover or composted refuse and mud. Paddy fields and terracing are first recorded in the North, where farmers were exhorted to build small rice fields to allow greater control of standing water. Terracing was essentially designed to minimize erosion in hilly areas and probably preceded the introduction of rice. As the rice plants grew the water level of the fields went down until the final harvesting took place in dry fields.

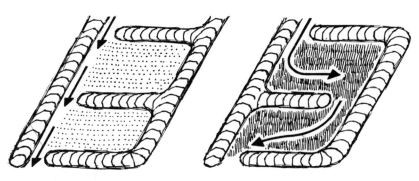

A Movement of water
in rice paddies in
early growing season

B Movement of water
at hottest part of
growing season

Water circulation in paddy fields. To keep water temperature up at the beginning of the summer growing season, water circulation was minimized. At the summer peak, temperatures were kept down by increasing the circulation.

85

Silk

Linen made from hemp was the commonest and cheapest form of clothing. Wool was used mainly as a protective padding between two layers of linen to combat the bitter northern winters. Other materials included rice straw for rain-resistant capes and sun shade hats. Cotton was introduced via the South much later.

Silk had been known from 1000 B.C. and the Chinese had a monopoly of its production until silkworm eggs were smuggled to Korea in the second century A.D. Cocoons spun by wild silkworms could be unravelled into a single thread of fibre of long staple and high tensile strength. These silkworms were domesticated and reared wherever mulberry trees could be grown for food. Each single thread could stretch for several hundred metres. The cocoons had first to be soaked in hot water before the silk was wound on to reels by means of a quilling wheel.

Spinning wheel possibly used for making thread from broken cocoons. Machinery for cloth production was far ahead of Europe by the first century A.D.

It has been recorded that, at hatching, seven hundred thousand silk-worms weigh just under half a kilogram. They shed their skin four times in thirty-six days before reaching maturity. By this time they weigh over four kilograms. In that time they have eaten nearly twelve tonnes of mulberry leaves. The cocoons they spin weigh up to nine hundred kilograms. About one-twelfth of this, i.e., seventy-five kilos becomes raw silk.

Silk was an extremely valuable luxury commodity. Ceremonial robes and 'best suits' would be made from it. The Romans valued it highly and the Chinese used it to 'buy off' potential enemies. It became an important element of taxation and was regarded as worth its weight in gold. Weaving and dyeing were developed to a high level at a very early stage. It was of course trade in silk which encouraged East–West contact and kept open the major trade routes via the Jade Gate and the Tarim Basin.

NEW TERRITORIES AND THE MOVEMENT SOUTH

During the Han dynasty military colonies were established in two directions:
- the northern arm of Kansu leading through Sinkiang to the Tarim Basin, and
- the lowland river valleys of the South.

The northern oasis settlements maintained garrisons to protect and extend Chinese influence along the Silk Roads. The southern settlements were intended to 'civilize' the native populations by spreading Chinese culture. As agricultural settlements both areas had limited initial success for climatic reasons. However, a two-way flow of crops and techniques was facilitated.

The South—'the land of rice and fish'—was peopled by two main groups of agriculturalists, the shifting cultivators of the hills and the settled farmers of the coast and valleys. The Chinese had most contact with the latter who were said to be lazy but never hungry thanks to the warm climate and abundant rainfall throughout the year. They could grow two crops of rice, and in the extreme South East a third crop of cabbages, beans, or other vegetables was possible. Tea growing was referred to by A.D. 273 and sugar-cane had already been established for four hundred years by then. Sea products and domesticated fish also figured commonly in the diet. By A.D. 150 there had been a major population shift away from the overpopulated Wei valley. The

Fragmented holdings, kitchen gardens, and fish ponds in a southern village.

overall population had remained at around fifty million after disastrous floods, famine and civil wars, but the heartland of the empire had lost eighteen million people while the South gained nine million. The rest were found in the Shantung peninsula and the Red Basin. As a result the lower Yangtze valley became the new key economic area of China, as a major supplier of grain to the imperial capitals.

Paddy fields and peasant farmers in the South.

The middle Yangtze valley. The watery landscape helped to make it a new key economic area of the later Han dynasty.

CHINA	'The Three Kingdoms' succeeded the Han Empire: the long struggle between these contending powers ended with the victory of Wei over Shu (264) and Wu (280). The older 'core area', the northern region in which the Middle Kingdom originated, had reasserted its control over the west and south, two newly developing economic regions. The advanced agricultural and communication systems of Wei were the decisive factor. But the new dynasty, the Tsin, proved unable to unify China in the face of pressure from the steppes. The Hsiung Nu, and other nomad tribes brought in as allies during civil wars proved impossible to expel or control. By 316 everything north of the Yangtze watershed was lost to Tsin. • In the North, the most populous region and the stronghold of Chinese culture, the Tartar tribes set up a series of dynasties, but they were not able to alter the pattern of life. The sown quickly began to absorb the steppe. Chinese agriculture and administration continued. Intermarriage was general. Confucian and Taoist thought was too rooted in the mass of the people to be lost even though the presence of non-Chinese rulers did facilitate the growth of Buddhism. In 500 a decree was actually issued banning Tartar speech, dress and customs. • In the South, Chinese dynasties were secure after the invading Tartar army was defeated in the battle of Fei Shui (387). The Yangtze Valley, in fact, proved entirely unsuited to the Tartar cavalry. The Court of Emperor Wu, of the Liang dynasty, was an impressive cultural centre when Bodhidharma visited it in 520. Reunification came from a movement starting yet again in the north region of China. Seizing the throne, Yang Chien, a Chinese general with Tartar blood, invaded and easily conquered the South. The new Sui dynasty (589–618) was welcomed by the southern population since it offered the return of the ideal, lost at the end of the Han dynasty, of a united China, 'One Empire of All under Heaven'. Over three hundred years of division had ended.
INDIA and WEST ASIA	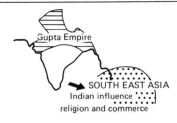
EUROPE	• The Roman Septimius Severus died in York after campaigning in Scotland against the fierce tribes there and rebuilding Hadrian's Wall, the northernmost frontier of the Empire. • 410 Rome sacked by the Goths. The British cities were told that they must fend for themselves: the legions were needed closer to the capital. By 450, the Anglo-Saxons had overrun the province. • 476 The last Roman Emperor in the West abdicated. Unlike the Tartar invaders in China (316–590), the 'barbarians' who overran the Roman Empire could neither maintain their own cultural traditions nor fully adopt those of the Empire. Roman culture had been spread thin in the Western Empire; the Eastern Empire was more compact and urban. Also the large slave element meant that there was no cultural reservoir equal to the Chinese peasant farmers. The Church was a unique survival.

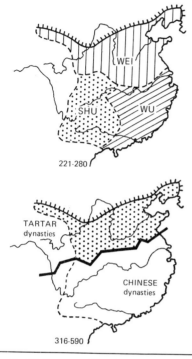

221-280

TARTAR dynasties

CHINESE dynasties

316-590

But the Sui dynasty, not unlike the Ch'in at the end of the Warring States period, overstretched itself and caused a popular uprising that ended in the establishment of the great T'ang dynasty (618). The second Sui emperor, Yang Ti, undertook vast projects. Communications between North and South were improved by canals linking the Yellow and Yangtze rivers; later this became the basis of the Grand Canal and effectively united the two key economic regions of China. Forced labour on this scheme and military failure in Korea precipitated rebellion.

• 455 Emperor Skanda Gupta repelled White Huns but the Empire was seriously weakened. By 550 it had disintegrated. Lacking a defence system, like China's Great Wall, the great plains of northern India were open to invaders from Central Asia.

• 399 Fa Hsien, a Chinese monk, set out for India and returned via Ceylon and Java. Pilgrimage to Holy India became a familiar event in China.

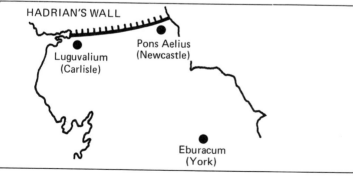

HADRIAN'S WALL

Luguvalium (Carlisle)

Pons Aelius (Newcastle)

Eburacum (York)

continued

CHINA	Major canal development in China 1 Cheng Kuo Canal, opened in 246 B.C. It irrigated a vast area of land and prov excellent water-transport facilities: Ch'in gained a decisive advantage over the Warring States by this project, unusual for its time. 2 Chang-an Canal, completed 129 B.C., was used for navigation and the moveme silt-laden water, a rich fertilizer, downstream to the lower middle course of the Y River. 3 Suen Fang Canal, and others in this area, formed part of a strategic network du Wei during the Three Kingdoms period and later Tartar dynasties. 4 The Old Pien Canal was dug partially by the King of Wu, one of the Warring (486 B.C.). It was intended to facilitate the northern expansion of this state. 5 The New Pien Canal, built A.D. 616–18, effectively joined the North with the S This involved the re-opening of older sections of existing but derelict water cours well as the cutting of extensive lengths of new canal. It was the product of Sui aut tarianism. 6 Cheng-tu Canal System was begun by Li Ping, a Ch'in governor of Shu, and Pa, tured from Ch'u in 316 B.C. Although it was originally constructed for water-tran purposes, the numerous canals were extensively used for irrigation. Soon the Che plain was called 'sea-on-land' and the agricultural prosperity of the area was f established. The Red Basin took advantage of this economic base to assert its ind dence whenever the central authority declined: it was known as Shu in the Kingdoms period too. 7 Yuan Grand Canal was dug by the Mongol conquerors as a means of connecting capital at what is now Peking with the Yangtze Valley, the stronghold and econ base of the defeated Sung dynasty. Its route was followed by the larger Ming Canal, which is still in use today.
INDIA and WEST ASIA	● Persia under the native Sassanid dynasty grew powerful. King Shapur attacked India and Rome in the West. Ctesiphon PERSI (500
EUROPE	● Emperor Justinian (died 565) found it impossible to reunite permanently the M ranean provinces of the former Roman Empire. The old language cleavage, West sp Latin and East Greek, was decisive. A single language, as prevailed in China, was la There was internal conflict within the eastern provinces too. Islam (after 636) v release the region from the last vestiges of Roman rule.

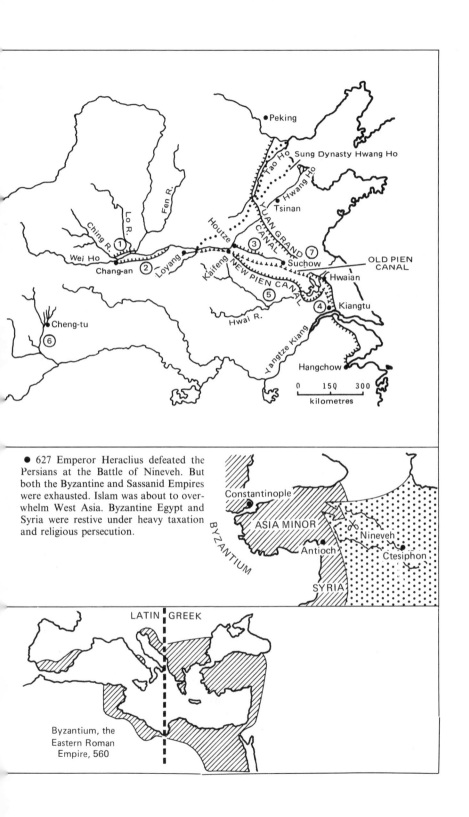

Peking

Tao Ho Sung Dynasty Hwang Ho

Hwang Ho

Tsinan

Fen R.

Lo R.

Ching R.

Houtze

YUAN GRAND CANAL

① Wei Ho

③

⑦ Suchow

OLD PIEN CANAL

Chang-an ② Loyang

Kaifeng NEW PIEN CANAL

Hwaian

⑤

④ Kiangtu

Hwai R.

Cheng-tu

⑥

Yangtze Kiang

Hangchow

0   150   300
kilometres

● 627 Emperor Heraclius defeated the
Persians at the Battle of Nineveh. But
both the Byzantine and Sassanid Empires
were exhausted. Islam was about to over-
whelm West Asia. Byzantine Egypt and
Syria were restive under heavy taxation
and religious persecution.

Constantinople

BYZANTIUM

ASIA MINOR

Nineveh

Antioch

Ctesiphon

SYRIA

LATIN ┊ GREEK

Byzantium, the
Eastern Roman
Empire, 560

3 A Golden Age

The restoration of unity under the T'ang Dynasty, A.D. 618–907

HISTORICAL OUTLINE

The successful way in which the T'ang dynasty built on the foundations laid by the short-lived Sui not only restored the Empire but ensured that the Chinese would always prefer unification during future generations. Henceforth, the country was united for far longer than it was divided either by internal conflict or external conquest. In the Chinese mind it is the T'ang Empire that has become the Golden Age.

Yet the restored Empire was not the same as the Han Empire. It was a more open society. Internally, the re-establishment of the examination system for entrance to the civil service on a more regular basis than the largely oral tests used since the Han period led to an enormous expansion in education. The invention of block printing some time in the eighth century A.D. met the demand for textbooks as well as encouraging the spread of literacy. Recommendation continued as a slight advantage for the relatives of the *shih*, but it became a familiar event for a group of *nung* to club together and pay for the education of a promising village boy. Literary achievement was the hallmark of the T'ang Empire, with its Confucian prose writers like Han Yu and its Taoist poets like Li Po. The Empire evolved a bureaucratic system in place of the lesser aristocratic one that had replaced feudalism.

Externally, too, a more flexible attitude appeared in the ready acceptance of foreign peoples and their ideas. The streets of the capital, Chang-an, were thronged with priests from India and South-East Asia, merchants from Central Asia and Arabia, and travellers from Persia, Korea and Japan. The second T'ang Emperor, T'ai Tsung or 'Supreme Ancestor,' came out to meet personally the famous Buddhist monk Hsuan Tsang when he returned from India with scriptures in A.D. 645. Although the

A block-printed scroll found at Tun-huang. It shows Buddha addressing his disciples. This copy of the 'Diamond Sutra' was made in 868; the earliest known example of block printing is a Buddhist charm (770). The demand for copies of the Scriptures as well as Confucian Classics led to this invention. For centuries the Chinese had used ink and paper besides being expert in stone engraving: put together they made block-printing, which may have been brought to Europe by the invading Mongols in the thirteenth century A.D.

Emperor was a Taoist, he supported the Confucians for the sake of the civil service, besides welcoming Buddhism and other foreign faiths. This distinction between the Han and T'ang Empires is expressed today in two common forms of address for the Chinese people. 'Men of Han' embodies a sense of exclusiveness, Chinese as opposed to Hsiung Nu or barbarians, while 'Men of T'ang' incorporates the diversity of a China stretching from the steppes to the tropics on one hand and from land-locked mountains to the sea on the other.

The Imperial Administration

A strong civil service, recruited by examination, was the foundation of the hundred-and-fifty years of peace and prosperity that the reign of Emperor T'ai Tsung (627–49) inaugurated. It shifted the power centre from the military to the civil. During the Three Kingdoms and the Tartar partition a military aristocracy had developed at the expense of the old alliance between the ruling

An engraving of the Emperor T'ai Tsung.

house and the *shih*. The Li, T'ai Tsung's own family, belonged to this class so that as Emperor he was well aware of dangers from this quarter.

Until the rebellion of An Lu-shan in 755 had severely shaken the Empire, the central administration effectively controlled every province. Regular censuses informed the Emperor of the exact population and resources available. The T'ang Empire was certainly the largest and most populous state in the world. In 754 there were nearly 53 000 000 persons living in over 300 prefectures.

Empress Wu

To the horror of traditional Chinese historians, members of the *shih* class, the continued success of the T'ang dynasty was largely due to an ex-concubine who finally usurped the throne itself. That Wu Chao, concubine to T'ai Tsung, could escape the Buddhist convent where the concubines of a dead Emperor were required to live, win the favour of the new Emperor Kao Tsung, and then dominate the government for fifty years, tells us a lot about the power structure of the T'ang Empire. It reveals that the Court, supported by an improved civil service, was supreme.

Emperor Kao Tsung was an indifferent ruler but he had the sense to let his consort, now Empress Wu, deal with affairs of state during his long reign (649–83). After his death she dethroned two of her sons, both ineffectual: her official reign began in 690 and lasted for fifteen years; at the age of eighty, her health failing, Empress Wu, 'Holy and Divine,' was forced to abdicate (705). This was the first and last occasion on which a woman occupied the Throne of the Emperors.

Although Empress Wu was ruthless towards her political enemies, the period of her ascendancy was a good one for the Empire. Government was sound; no serious revolts occurred; the army was reorganized; and Korea was conquered, a task that no previous Chinese had ever managed. One of the few favourable comments on her reign by Chinese historians pinpoints her desire to find new blood for the Empire. We read:

> The Empress was not sparing in the bestowal of titles and ranks, because she wished to cage the bold and enterprising spirits of all regions. Even a wild reckless fellow who said something which she thought apt would be made an official without regard to the normal order of the degrees of rank; but those who proved unfit for their responsibilities were forthwith, in large numbers, cashiered or executed. Her broad aim was to select men of real talent and true virtue.

The T'ang Empire avoided civil disturbances over the succession through the emergence of the third great ruler of the dynasty, Emperor Hsuan Tsung, known as Ming Huang, 'the Brilliant Emperor,' the grandson of Empress Wu, whose court became a splendid cultural centre admired by later times. However, there was to be a terrible revolt near the end of his reign.

The Rebellion of An Lu-shan

Poets and playwrights have made the tragic events of An Lu-shan's rebellion famous. Every Chinese knows how the aging Emperor fell in love with a beautiful concubine, Yang Kuei Fei, who clouded his judgment and persuaded him to foolish policies. Through her urging Ming Huang bestowed undeserved honours on An Lu-shan, a barbarian general serving on the northern frontier. An Lu-shan was appointed commander-in-chief of the army, and this ambitious soldier took advantage of the idleness of the Court to make a bid for power. Almost unopposed, he captured Chang-an in 755; the Emperor had fled westwards. When the disheartened troops of the imperial bodyguard demanded that Yang Kuei Fei should be executed as a traitor, and backed their demand with a threatened mutiny, Ming Huang was obliged to consent.

Beneath these human episodes of the rebellion, the very stuff of character drama, there was an economic conflict. For An Lu-shan, though a Turk of the Kitan tribe, had the support of the eastern provinces. The burden of supplying grain to the upland capital may have been a root cause of the strife. In the reign of Emperor T'ai Tsung the annual shipment was around 10 000 tonnes, but by this time it had topped 160 000 tonnes. The cost and waste of transporting such amounts up-river for the benefit of an indolent Court may well have been too much for the *nung* to stomach.

The civil war was long (755–66) and bitterly fought. The North was devasted: the T'ang Empire lost most of its dynamic force. A Tibetan army was able to break through the weakened frontier defences and sack Chang-an, just recovered from the rebels.

The Last Years of the T'ang Dynasty
Though the Empire experienced general peace for another century, its organization was less efficient and less satisfactory. The central administration declined as military leaders became more independent of the throne; at Court the eunuchs became a political force again; the Tibetans in the East and the Turkish tribes to the North pressed hard; heavier taxation and levies were required to meet the various crises. Perhaps a crucial neglect was that of the hydraulic works, the traditional unifying factor in Chinese history. After the rebellion of An Lu-shan few projects were undertaken and many old schemes fell into decay. When the last T'ang Emperor was deposed in 907, the country fragmented into more than a dozen separate states. New methods of warfare might have accounted for the unusual extent of the disunity too. The first reference to the use of gunpowder is in 919.

EXPANSION AND ABSORPTION

Imperial expansion reached farther under the T'ang dynasty than under the Han. Most of the gains were made before the rebellion of An Lu-shan, whose victory at the battle of Ling Pao (755) opened the pass to the Wei Valley and placed Chang-an at the mercy of his rebel forces. The ensuing civil disturbances and contraction of the Empire may give the impression of decay, but these related events were really a function of two factors: internal economic changes and over-expansion.

● Internal conflicts were largely a result of the movement of the key economic area of China from the North to the Yangtze Valley. By 742 Chang-an and its satellites had a population approaching 2 000 000. The strain on the easily exhausted loess soils in supporting such an urban concentration could only be offset by imports from the South. At first this was feasible with the construction of the Grand Canal network, built by the Sui dynasty, but eventually the operation proved unworkable. Grain transport increased from 10 000 tonnes to 160 000 tonnes between 627 and 742. Consequently the capital was very insecure in event of civil war and every decade made it increasingly distant from the chief economic regions.

● The Empire had tended to overreach itself. The major gains before 755 were:
—pushing the Turkish tribes back to Inner Mongolia, where they accepted Chinese overlordship (648);
—obtaining control over Turkestan, where Sinkiang ('the new dominion') was established;
—the repenetration of Vietnam;
—the annexation of Korea and Manchuria;
—the alliance with Tibet through royal marriage of a Chinese princess, which did not ensure perpetual peace but caused an inflow of Chinese cultural influence;
—the acceptance of 'protection' from China by many states in Central Asia.

Only the hill-tribesmen of Yunnan remained obstinately independent of the Empire. But such a far-flung border was not easy to defend. It was impossible to maintain security on every frontier once civil wars broke out, and other imperial powers were eager to expand at China's expense. The Arabs, having crushed the Sassanid Empire in Persia (642), initially formed an alliance with the Chinese, but then began to take over the weaker states in Western Turkestan. A confrontation came just before the rebellion of An Lu-shan. In 751 the Chinese armies in the West were decisively beaten at the battle of Talas River, and Central Asia ceased to be Buddhist and became a part of the Moslem world. Slightly later Mongolia broke free, while in Korea the semi-independent state of Silla absorbed the Chinese territories there.

The Tibetans actually sacked Chang-an during An Lu-shan's revolt. After 750, in effect, the T'ang Empire contracted.

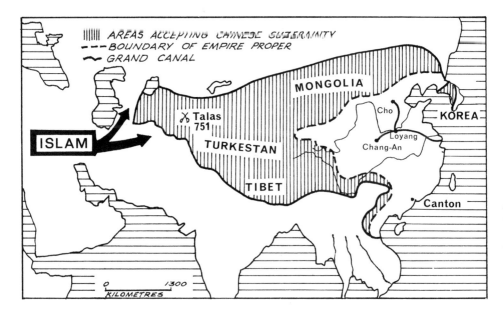

The T'ang Empire at its peak—A.D. 700.

Cross-cultural Assimilation

Besides the large numbers of scholars and diplomats welcomed in Chang-an there were many alien groups who were absorbed by Chinese society. With the fall of the Sassanid Empire, a colony of Persian refugees was established. Muslim soldiers, recruited against An Lu-shan, settled as permanent residents at the end of the fighting. In the South the city of Canton became a centre of international trade after the northern 'silk roads' came under pressure (751 onwards). There were colonies of Arabs, Jews, Persians and Christians. A similar openness existed with respect to foreign religions, though national crises towards the end of the T'ang dynasty were marked with the temporary restriction of alien creeds and occasional riots.

The Ecosystem Maintained

The T'ang Empire can be seen as the reassertion of China's natural unity. In the Introduction, the continuity of Chinese civilization was stressed because it remains a remarkable fact that China has a history of four thousand years. Our description of this unusual historical phenomenon as an ecosystem was put to the test following the fall of the Han Empire. The T'ang restoration at the end of three hundred years of division was a part of the self-adjustment of the ecosystem. The basic stability was evident in several ways:

- the balanced relationship between man and the natural world as a function of dependence on agriculture;
- cultural continuity from the ability to absorb and modify new ideas or innovations, such as the imperial control of early capitalist iron technology, or the introduction of Buddhism;
- geographical integrity despite changes in inputs and outputs, such as imperial expansion and contraction, alterations in key economic regions, and the growth of the Chinese 'core area' through large scale hydraulic works.

For the *shih* and the *nung* the pattern of production and the system of philosophy which had evolved slowly from ancient times still held good. A change of dynasty or a civil war did not change the necessity of providing food for the next day. Military exploits did not outlast the words of the sages. Moreover, early state influence over the capitalist activities of merchants and industrialists maintained the equilibrium of the ecosystem, ensuring that China was not fundamentally changed by the development of technology. Printing did not encourage a Reformation, the spur failed to elevate the knight, gunpowder was about to cause little more than an extra fragmentation between the T'ang and the Sung Empires, and the magnetic compass would not lead to overseas colonies. In short, China has always pursued its own distinct way.

RELIGIONS

Confucian philosophy had become a strictly moral code of conduct during the Han Empire. In the hands of the official class of scholars it was transformed into the yardstick for measuring correctness of behaviour in the 'Empire of all under Heaven.' But its appeal was confined largely to the *shih*, the gentry and the scholar officials themselves. Though the mass of the people agreed with Confucius about the importance of the family and respect for ancestors, they wanted something less austere and

101

clung to Taoism, at this time absorbing the magical rites and practices of the countryside. The local gods of ancient tradition found room under the spreading umbrella of Taoism; the followers of Confucius respected Heaven, but showered the cold water of ridicule over spirits and lesser deities. What completed the transformation of Taoist Ideas into a popular religion was competition with the new faith from India, Buddhism.

Later Taoism
Both Taoism and Buddhism had little patience with the world that Confucian philosophy admired. Inner space, the mystical elements in man's nature—these became their main concern. Lao-tzu had tired of life in the Chou capital and gone into the west. Chapter nineteen of his book, the *Tao Teh Ching*, runs:

> Rid of formalized wisdom and learning
> People would be a hundredfold happier,
> Rid of conventionalized duty and honour
> People would find their families dear,
> Rid of legalized profiteering
> People would have no thieves to fear.
> These methods of life have failed, all three,
> Here is the way, it seems to me:
> Set the people free,
> As deep in their hearts they would like to be,
> From private greeds
> And wanton needs.

Since Chuang-tzu's time there was a strong tradition for Taoist sages to live in retirement from the world.

> Who will prefer the jingle of jade pendants if
> He once heard stone growing in a cliff!

'The jingle of jade pendants' stands for the Court, its beautiful women and splendid life, which is a hollow-world for a person who has experienced the *Tao*. This was the highest form of Taoism, the holy man quietly living at one with Nature on a remote mountainside, but another aspect, alchemy, caught the imagination of many Chinese. Chang Tao-ling, the first T'ien Shih, or Heavenly Teacher of Taoist religion, spent most of his long life (A.D. 34–156, according to legend) in retirement studying alchemy. His purpose was to obtain the elixir of life, a drug capable of bestowing immortality. Gradually the Taoist adept became in the popular mind the magician. Wang Pi (A.D. 226–49) wrote an excellent commentary on the *Tao Teh Ching*, entirely in tune with its original spirit, and numerous *shih* embraced Taoist ideas as an alternative to Confucius, but the popular response was the decisive factor.

During the Tartar partition one royal house, the Wei in Shansi, sought a new book of charms on the accession of each ruler. Astrology only added strength to the Confucian opposition to Taoism. Yet it now seems likely that major scientific inventions and discoveries originated from Taoist experiments: new medical knowledge, the magnetic compass which was used to determine favourable positions for graves, and gunpowder which was used in ghost-scaring firecrackers. While Taoism was becoming more concerned with magic and identified with popular superstition, Buddhism did make a serious and sustained challenge to Confucian philosophy in the Court itself.

Buddhism

At every level in Chinese society the teachings of the Buddha have had a profound effect. Until the modern period only India, 'the Holy Land of the East,' has influenced China. Yet that singular Chinese ability to absorb and transform foreign peoples, whether Tartar, Mongol or Manchu conquerors, was active in the development of Buddhism too. In the end the Buddhist faith was adapted to suit Chinese society, rather than China being altered by the new religion.

Gautama (died 479 or 477 B.C.), the prince from North India who became the Buddha, 'the Enlightened One,' required his followers to be fully conscious of the nature of the universe and to exercise full self-control. The saffron robe worn by Buddhist monks represents the death of themselves to a worldly life: the colour was chosen because condemned men used to be dressed in such material on the day of execution. What was demanded from the individual believer was nothing less than the death of self, freedom from all desires and fears. A hard and lonely path to tread, for Buddha said, 'no man can help another.' To prevent himself becoming a god in the eyes of later followers after he had died and gone into *Nirvana*, or 'eternal bliss,' the Buddha prohibited pictures or sculptures of his life or deeds. An empty seat or a footprint was to be the only sign of the way he had discovered and taught. Enlightenment, like the *Tao* of Lao-tzu, could not be explained in words or represented visually. It was ineffable, something 'no man can help another' to experience. It was an individual quest.

Head of Buddha, a fine example of Gandharan sculpture, the Greek tradition in India (second century A.D.). The lips are folded into the cheek with the Enlightened One's consciousness of the heavy weight of the Flesh; skin sags laden with experience; and inner freedom lies deep down the channels of the sightless eyes, far below the weary drooping of the lids. India is the inwardness of the Vision as well as the acceptance of universal misfortune. The West, carved in the Greco-Roman modelling of the face, is the outer presentation of world-weariness. It is as if the descendants of Alexander's great army, the generations settled and reinforced on the shadowy edge of his vast imperial dream, had reached the same fundamental insight into life as prevailed in the country they inhabited.

The Buddha's consciousness of suffering is basic. As an infant prince it was prophesied that he would not be a great king, but a great holy man, if he became aware of the sufferings of the world. The king his father did his utmost to prevent him from having any contact with the outside world; a special palace was constructed in which all possible pleasures were offered to beguile the young prince's mind. However, one day Gautama saw a sick person, on another a tottering old man; these experiences troubled him considerably, but it was an encounter with a corpse that jolted him into active discontent with 'soft' living. The serene calm of a hermit suggested a course for him and, leaving throne, family and offspring, he became a wandering ascetic, bent on discovering Truth. Having tried the way of self-mortification for a number of years without success, Gautama resolved to sit in meditation till he finished his quest. His Enlightenment followed, whereby he became the Buddha.

104

But as Buddha foresaw his teachings became another religion over the centuries. The great tradition of Greek and Roman sculpture may have been an untimely influence, for marvellous statues of Buddha were carved in Bactria and the other regions where the Greeks had settled. The immense rock carvings to be found in China are an offspring of Greco-Indian tradition. A late Buddhist proverb explains what had happened: 'To mistake a finger for the moon.' When a man was asked by another to show him the moon, he pointed it out in the sky. But the questioner mistook the man's finger for the moon. The monasteries, the places of pilgrimage, the stories of Buddha and the saints had become accepted as the essence of Enlightenment.

By the time, then, that China received Buddhism it was a highly developed faith. The older Hindu beliefs of the Indian people had added much. Two distinct branches were evolved, Hinayana and Mahayana. And it was the more complicated and less other-worldly Mahayana version that had been introduced into Han China in A.D. 65. For Mahayana Buddhists Gautama was a single incarnation in an almost infinite series of Buddhas. Saints and gods had appeared capable of securing the believer a place in the 'Western Heaven.' Merit from good deeds in the world accumulated in better reincarnations till complete bliss was obtained in an after-world. Against this manageable system of belief, quite properly held by Emperor Liang Wu Ti in his capital at Nanking, the uncompromising doctrines of Bodhidharma came as a terrific shock.

The Ch'an school held contemplation to be the way to achieve Buddhahood. Everyone had this potential in him but most people failed to realize it. Although Bodhidharma is supposed to have brought this true version of the Buddha's teachings direct from India, the parallels with early Taoism are quite obvious. The Buddhist monk and poet Han-shan, living in the eighth century A.D., was very like a Taoist hermit. In a preface to his poems Yin Lu-ch'iu wrote:

No-one knows just what sort of man Han-shan was. There are old people who knew him: they say he was a poor man, a crazy character. He lived alone . . . at a place called Cold Mountain [Han-shan]. . . . He often went down to the Kuo-ch'in Temple. At the temple lived Shih-te, who ran the dining hall. He sometimes saved leftovers for Han-shan, hiding them in a bamboo tube. Han-shan would come and carry it away; walking the long veranda, calling and shouting happily, talking and laughing to himself. Once the monks followed him, caught him, and made fun of him. He stopped, clapped his hands, and laughed greatly—Ha Ha!—for a spell, then left.

He looked like a tramp. His body and face were old and beat. Yet in every word he breathed was a meaning in line with the subtle principles of things, if only you thought of it deeply. Everything he said had a feeling of the Tao in it, profound and arcane secrets. His hat was made of birch bark, his clothes were ragged and worn out, and his shoes were wood. Thus men who have made it hide their tracks: unifying categories and interpenetrating things. On that long veranda calling and singing, in his words of reply Ha Ha!—the three worlds revolve. Sometimes at the villages and farms he laughed and sang with cowherds. Sometimes intractable, sometimes agreeable, his nature was happy of itself. But how could a person without wisdom recognize him?

Cold Mountain was more than the name of a place or a man; it was a state of mind. Han-shan's verse tells us that he read 'Huang and Lao,' the ancient Taoist book of the Yellow Emperor and the *Tao Teh Ching*. These lines communicate what the hermit monk felt:

> Cold Mountain is a house
> Without beams or walls.
> The six doors left and right are open
> The hall is blue sky.
> The rooms all vacant and vague
> The east wall beats on the west wall
> At the centre, nothing.
> Borrowers don't bother me
> In the cold I built a little fire
> When I'm hungry I boil up some greens.
> I've got no use for the kuluk
> With his big barn and pasture—
> He just sets up a prison for himself.
> Once in he can't get out.
> Think it over—
> You know it might happen to you.

Tun-huang, the great Buddhist cave complex at the western end of the Great Wall, was started in A.D. 366. Although it has not always been within the Chinese Empire, the remoteness of the site and the dry conditions in that area have saved its marvellous frescoes and sculpture from destruction. It was a religious centre, with monasteries and schools.

A Buddhist Paradise, copy of the central section of a wall-painting at Tun-huang, painted during the T'ang dynasty.

A Golden Age

The Confucian Reaction

The growing strength of Buddhism in China alarmed the *shih*, who considered the ideas and practices it was introducing to be entirely 'un-Chinese.' The rational, sceptical outlook of the Confucian philosophy reacted strongly to the mass excitement which the new faith generated. Opposition became explicit in Han Yu's (768–824) famous defence of traditional values and behaviour, the *Memorial on the Bone of Buddha*. Addressing the credulous Emperor Hsien Tsung, the scholar official wrote:

> I humbly submit that Buddhism is but one of the religious systems obtaining among the barbarian tribes, that only during the later Han dynasty did it filter into the Middle Kingdom, and that it never existed in the golden age of the past . . .
> It was not until the reign of Ming-ti of Han that Buddhism first appeared. Ming-ti's reign lasted no longer than eighteen years, and after him disturbance followed upon disturbance, and reigns were all short . . .
> When Kao-tsu succeeded the fallen house of Sui, he determined to eradicate Buddhism. But the ministers of the time were lacking in foresight and ability, they had no real understanding of the way of the ancient kings, nor of the things that are right both for then and now. Thus they were unable to assist the wise resolution of their ruler and save their country from this plague. To my constant regret the attempt stopped short. But you, your majesty, are possessed of a skill in the arts of peace and war, of wisdom and courage the like of which has not been seen for several thousand years. When you first ascended the throne you prohibited recruitment of Buddhist monks and Taoist priests and the foundation of new temples and monasteries; and I firmly believed that the intentions of Kao-tsu would be carried out by your hand, or if this were still impossible, that at least their religions would not be allowed to spread and flourish.
> And now, your majesty, I hear that you have ordered all Buddhist monks to escort a bone of the Buddha from Feng-hsiang and that a pavilion be erected from which you will in person watch its entrance into the Imperial Palace. You have further ordered every Buddhist temple to receive this object with due homage. Stupid as I am, I feel convinced that it is not out of regard for Buddha that you, your majesty, are praying for blessings by doing him this honour; but that you are organizing this absurd pantomime for the benefit of the people of the capital and for their gratification in this year of plenty and happiness. For a mind so enlightened as your majesty's could never believe such nonsense. The minds of the common people, however, are as easy to becloud as they are difficult to enlighten. If they see your majesty acting in this way, they will think that you are wholeheartedly worshipping the Buddha, and will say: 'His majesty is a great sage, and even he worships the Buddha with all his heart. Who are we that we should any of us

109

grudge our lives in his service?' They will cauterize the crowns of their heads, burn off their fingers, and in bands of tens or hundreds cast off their clothing and scatter their money and from daylight to darkness follow one another in the cold fear of being too late. Young and old in one mad rush will forsake their trades and callings and, unless you issue some prohibition, will flock round the temples, hacking their arms and mutilating their bodies to do him homage. And the laughter that such unseemly and degenerate behaviour will everywhere provoke will be no light matter.

The Buddha was born a barbarian; he was unacquainted with the language of the Middle Kingdom, and his dress was of a different cut. His tongue did not speak nor was his body clothed in the manner prescribed by the kings of old; he knew nothing of the duty of minister to prince or the relationship of son to father. Were he still alive today, were he to come to court at the bidding of his country, your majesty would give him no greater reception than an interview in the Strangers' Hall, a ceremonial banquet, and the gift of a suit of clothes, after which you would have him sent under guard to the frontier to prevent him from misleading your people. There is then all the less reason now that he has been dead so long for allowing this decayed and rotten bone, this filthy and disgusting relic to enter the Forbidden Palace. 'I stand in awe of supernatural beings,' said Confucius, 'but keep them at a distance' . . . ; and to my shame and indignation none of your ministers says that this is wrong, none of your censors has exposed the error.

I beg that this bone be handed over the authorities to throw into water or fire, that Buddhism be destroyed root and branch for ever, that the doubts of your people be settled once and for all and their descendants saved from heresy. For if you make it known to your people that the actions of the true sage surpass ten thousand times ten thousand those of ordinary men, with what wondering joy will you be acclaimed! And if the Buddha should indeed possess the power to bring down evil, let all the bane and punishment fall upon my head, and as heaven is my witness I shall not complain.

In the fullness of my emotion I humbly present this memorial for your attention.   *(Copyright © 1972 by Grove Press, Inc.)*

The Emperor was very displeased. But Han Yu was saved by the Confucian scholars of the day. They rallied behind him on the issue and his sentence was reduced to banishment. He was posted to the South.

Han Yu had behaved responsibly. His outspokenness may have been dangerous in terms of his personal safety and his own career, but it was in the classic mould of the honest Confucian official. It should be remembered that the Censorate was a Chinese institution. The officials of this department had the difficult duty of reporting to the Emperor all cases of misgovernment. Opposition to a court favourite or an unreasonable ruler called for moral courage. Censors, Chinese ombudsmen, often perished.

On his recall to Court Han Yu was to use his resoluteness for the benefit of the tottering T'ang dynasty in 822. As an official of the War Office Han Yu was sent, by a harassed Emperor, to persuade a rebellious governor in Hopeh not to plunge the Empire into another civil war. With only a token bodyguard he went to the rebel's camp and spoke his mind. The officers there wavered when they heard what the eminent Confucian scholar had to say. As a result the rebel leader, uncertain of the strength of his support, agreed to terms and the revolt was over. Discipline in the imperial armies greatly improved under Han Yu's watchful eye. As one common soldier put it: 'A person who is prepared to burn the holy finger of Lord Buddha himself will not hesitate to chop the heads from mere soldiers.'

Other Foreign Faiths
Christianity, Islam and several other religions entered China during the T'ang dynasty. In A.D. 635 a Nestorian monk, in Chinese named O Lo Pen, was granted an audience by the ever tolerant Emperor T'ai Tsung. Afterwards the Emperor issued an edict in which he gave permission for Christianity to be preached freely. For 'the Way has more than one name. There is more than one sage. . . . This religion does good to all men.' And the Nestorian Church flourished despite some persecution under Empress Wu, who was a fervent Buddhist. However, it did not really put a strong root down into the Chinese soil, for it was unable to recover from the proscription of all foreign creeds in 845. The Taoists were jealous of the power of the Buddhists and induced the Emperor Wu Tsung to ban all alien faiths. Possibly the Court was worried about the resources tied up in the numerous monasteries, both in terms of land and people, for the eventual compromise let Buddhism keep only one temple with thirty monks in each city of the Empire. The Christian Church in China faded away. When Jesuit missionaries arrived in 1581, the Chinese had forgotten that the Nestorians had already brought the teachings of Jesus Christ.

Such a lapse of memory is not surprising. The Chinese approach to religion was different from that of the West. There was room for a variety of faiths; 'the Way has more than one name.' Exclusive religions, creeds with a single deity like Christianity and Islam, have never made much headway in China. The inclusive habit of mind coupled with Confucian scepticism has tended to keep religion and the priesthood a minor element in Chinese society. The severe, though short, repression of foreign faiths in A.D. 845 was a symptom of national unease and uncertainty connected with the decline of the T'ang dynasty.

THE T'ANG POETS

While the Han Empire was distinguished for prose, particularly in historical writing, and the coming Sung Empire was to be the era of painting, the T'ang dynasty acted as patron for China's finest poets. The three great names are the two friends, Li Po (699–762) and Tu Fu (712–70), and the later Po Chü-i (772–846). In many respects the T'ang Empire was the romantic age. Confucian scholarship was comparatively weak. The importance of the imperial civil service was qualified by the tolerant atmosphere of the Court, especially during the reign of Emperor T'ai Tsung.

Li Po reciting a poem.
A painting by Liang K'ai,
thirteenth century A.D.

By the middle of the dynasty Taoism was accepted in the civil service examinations: in 742 it was decreed that Chuang-tzu and other Taoist works should be regarded as Classics, like the Confucian Classics. Above all, the long reigns of Empress Wu and Ming Huang, 'the brilliant Emperor,' provided the social stability necessary for the development of refined literature.

Li Po was, in fact, a Taoist. Though his verse is not colloquial like Han-shan's unusual style of writing, Li Po had a similar longing for the wilder aspects of Nature, vast mist-filled valleys, tumbling waterfalls, bare mountains, deep gorges and jagged cliffs. To the dismay of his relatives the young poet did not proceed to the civil service examinations and high official rank, but dwelt for a couple of years with a Taoist recluse before taking to a wandering life on the road. During his travels he met the other writers of the day, making a lifelong friendship with the younger poet, Tu Fu.

Imperial notice of Li Po's poetry came when he was summoned to the Court in 742. For three years Li Po enjoyed a sinecure given to him by Ming Huang, composing verse by command and recording his own feelings about life in Chang-an, but Court intrigue made him resign the post and travel again. In the capital his drinking may have caused difficulties, but wine often was, and still is, a part of creativity for the Chinese calligrapher, poet and painter. The long years of training and discipline necessary for accomplished brushwork—twenty years would not be considered as much more than a moderate preparation—tended to induce self-consciousness. The wine cup relaxed the heart and hand. After leaving Chang-an Li Po studied Taoism at the residence of the current T'ien Shih, in Shantung, till the rebellion of An Lu-shan drove him southwards to the Yangtze valley. There he became entangled with another rebel group and on the T'ang restoration only escaped the death sentence through the intercession of the loyal general Kuo Tzu-i, whom Li Po had helped on his early travels. Li Po was banished to the South, not far from his own native Szechuan. Several years later a general amnesty allowed him to return along the Yangtze River, in which he is supposed to have drowned in 762. Not far from Nanking a temple to Li Po marks the place where legend says the poet was drowned when trying to embrace the reflection of the moon in the water.

The following poem brings into focus the conflict Li Po must have known so well during his stay in Chang-an. It is that ancient

dispute between Taoism and Confucian philosophy concerning
the naturalness of urban life.

My friend is lodging high in the Eastern Range,
Dearly loving the beauty of valleys and hills.
At green spring he lies in the empty woods,
And is still asleep when the sun shines on high.
A pine-tree wind dusts his sleeves and coat;
A pebbly stream cleans his heart and ears.
I envy you who far from strife and talk
Are high-propped on a pillow of grey mist.

Again his rendering of an old song in *Fighting South of Ramparts*
places human destructiveness in a universal context, Time. The
poet's vision of the futility of war, his civilized detachment and
resigned quietness, rests on Taoist belief in the value of non-
action as much as Li Po's personal experience of civil strife.
The final lines are a quotation from the *Tao Teh Ching*.

Fighting South of the Ramparts

Last year we were fighting at the source of the Sang-kan;
This year we are fighting on the Onion River road.
We have washed our swords in the surf of Parthian seas;
We have pastured our horses among the snows of the T'ien Shan.
The King's armies have grown grey and old
Fighting ten thousand leagues away from home.
The Huns have no trade but battle and carnage;
They have no fields or ploughlands,
But only wastes where white bones lie among yellow sands.
Where the house of Ch'in built the Great Wall that was to keep
   away the Tartars,
There, in its turn, the House of Han lit beacons of war.
The beacons are always alight, fighting and marching never stop.
Men die in the field, slashing sword to sword;
The horses of the conquered neigh piteously to Heaven.
Crows and hawks peck for human guts,
Carry them in their beaks and hang them on the branches of
   withered trees.
Captains and soldiers are smeared on the bushes and grass;
The general schemed in vain.
Know therefore that the sword is a cursed thing
Which the wise man uses only if he must.

A Golden Age

As a final example of Li Po's verse here is a poem of his about drinking:

On Wine

Have you not seen
How the Yellow River, which flows from heaven and hurries
    toward the sea, never turns back?
Have you not seen
How at the bright mirrors of high halls men mourn their
    white hairs,
At dawn black silk, by evening changed to snow?
While there is pleasure in life, enjoy it,
And never let your gold cup face the moon empty!
Heaven gave me my talents, they shall be used;
A thousand in gold scattered and gone will all come back again.
Boil the sheep, butcher the ox, make merry while there is time;
We have never drunk at all till we drink three hundred cups.

    Master Ts'en,
Friend Tan-ch'iu,
Here comes the wine, no standing cups!
I have a song to sing you,
Kindly turn your ears to me and listen.
It is nothing to feast on jade to the sound of bells and drums.
I ask only to be drunk for ever and never wake!
They lie forgotten, the sages of old;
Only the great drinkers have left us their names.
In time gone by, when the Prince of Ch'en feasted in the hall of
    Peace and Joy,
At ten thousand a quart he never stinted the revellers.
Why must our host say he is short of money?
Send to the shop at once, keep the cups filled.
My five-flower horse,
My fur which cost a thousand,
Call the boy, send him out to change them for good wine,
And let me forget with you the sorrows of ten thousand ages!

Tu Fu, the contemporary and friend of Li Po, is regarded by many Chinese as the greatest poet of all. His poetry is stricter, paying more attention to conventional forms; it has a Confucian outlook too. Unsuccessful as a career official, Tu Fu held a number of minor posts in the capital and the provinces. His much appreciated *Autumn Meditation* was composed when he was away from Chang-an. In this poem many aspects of T'ang Empire were fixed forever in the imagination of succeeding generations of Chinese readers. These three stanzas give an impression of Tu Fu's undoubted quality as a poet:

Autumn Meditation

Gems of dew wilt and wound the maple trees in the wood:
From Wu mountains, from Wu gorges, the air blows desolate.
The waves between the river-banks merge in the seething sky,
Clouds in the wind above the passes meet their shadows on the ground.
Clustered chrysanthemums have opened twice, in tears of other days;
The forlorn boat, once and for all, tethers my homeward thoughts.
In the houses winter clothes speed scissors and ruler;
The washing-blocks pound, faster each evening, in Pai Ti high on the hill . . .

The thousand houses, the circling mountains, are quiet in the morning light;
Day by day in the house by the river I sit in the blue of the hills.
Two nights gone the fisher boats once more come bobbing on the waves,
Belated swallows in cooling autumn still flutter to and fro.
K'uang Heng writing state papers, which earned me no credit,
Liu Hsiang editing classics, my hopes elsewhere . . .
Yet many of my school friends have risen in the world.
By the Five Tombs in light cloaks they ride their sleek horses.

Well said, Ch'ang-an looks like a chessboard—
Won and lost for a hundred years, sad beyond all telling.
The mansions of princes and nobles all have new lords,
And another generation wears the caps and robes of office.
Due north on the mountain passes the gongs and drums shake,
To the chariots and horses campaigning in the west the winged dispatches hasten.
While the fish and dragons fall asleep and the autumn river turns cold
My native country, untroubled times, are always in my thoughts . . .

(Copyright © 1972 by Grove Press, Inc.)

Po Chü-i, the son of a minor provincial official, hailed from the northern province of Shansi. Unlike Li Po and Tu Fu, the later poet had a distinguished career in the imperial civil service and rose to high rank. He retired in 831, settling at Lung Men, a Buddhist shrine in the country near Loyang, where he had had his official residence as governor of Honan province. As a

116

thorough-going Confucian scholar, Po Chü-i wrote a number of sharp political poems, like *The Spin-dance Girl*.

The Spin-dance Girl

Spin-dance girl! Spin-dance girl!
She danced to the music of drums and stringed instruments;
She lifted her sleeves as the music sounded;
And, revolving like whirling snow and floating blades of grass,
She turned this way and that, untiring,
In seemingly endless gyrations.
Nothing in the world could equal her speed,
Not even fast-moving wheels and the whirlwind.
When the music ended, she bowed to the Emperor,
Who responded merely with a faint smile.
'Spin-dance girl, born in Sogdiana,
Your eastward trip covering over ten thousand *li*
Was a waste of time. Here spin-dancers abound.
You may not know that they have vied with one another
Since the end of T'ien-pao, when times began to change,
Ministers and concubines have sought to learn
The art of revolving smoothly.
Of these there were two—T'ai-chen and Lu-shan,
Who succeeded best of all. The one was made
Imperial concubine in the Garden of Pear-Blossoms;
The other became Lady Yang's adopted son.
Lu-shan, revolving, deceived the Emperor's eyes;
His revolt was not suspected even after
His troops advanced past the Yellow River.
The Lady, revolving, beguiled the Emperor's heart;
Her death at Ma-wei made his recollections more poignant.
Since that time heaven and earth have changed places;
And for fifty years no ban has fallen on the whirling.
Spin-dance girl, do not dance in vain;
Sing this song often to stir the well-meaning ruler.'

The purpose of the appeal is plain; China needs an Empire undisturbed by violent alterations of policy and changes of powerholders. Po Chü-i is looking at a weakened T'ang dynasty, still recovering from the rebellion of An Lu-shan, mentioned as Lu-shan in the same line as T'ai-chen, or Yang Kuei Fei. T'ien-pao is Ming Huang, whose heart was beguiled by Lady Yang. But the tremendous popularity of Po Chü-i's poetry in his own lifetime did not entirely please him. The lines he had written were 'on the mouths of kings, princes, concubines, ladies, plough-boys and grooms,' but usually they were not those with the really serious meaning. For as a poet Po Chü-i favoured content above form; his style is deliberately simple and direct. He thought he had something to say to his contemporaries, as this satire shows:

The Chancellor's Gravel Drive
(A Satire on the Maltreatment of Subordinates)

A Government-bull yoked to a Government-cart!
Moored by the bank of Ch'an River, a barge loaded with gravel.
A single load of gravel,
How many pounds it weighs!
Carrying at dawn, carrying at dusk, what is it all for?
They are carrying it towards the Five Gates,
To the West of the Main Road.
Under the shadow of green laurels they are making a gravel-drive.
For yesterday arrived, newly appointed,
The Assistant Chancellor of the Realm,
And was terribly afraid that the wet and mud
Would dirty his horse's hoofs.
The Chancellor's horse's hoofs
Stepped on the gravel and remained perfectly clean;
But the bull employed in dragging the cart
Was almost sweating blood.
The Assistant Chancellor's business
Is to 'save men, govern the country
And harmonize Yin and Yang.'
Whether the bull's neck is sore
Need not trouble him at all.

As a member of the Censorate, he tells us in another poem, his 'bluntness did not suit the times.' Firm memorials had caused his banishment to Hangchow in 822. Po Chü-i was a 'loyal' *shih* and, like Han Yu, his career was marked by a series of ups and downs. Yet his personal poems do communicate to us today as they must have moved his contemporaries.

On His Baldness

At dawn I sighed to see my hairs fall;
At dusk I sighed to see my hairs fall.
For I dreaded the time when the last lock should go. . . .
They are all gone and I do not mind at all!
I have done with that cumbrous washing and getting dry;
My tiresome comb for ever is laid aside.
Best of all, when the weather is hot and wet,
To have no top-knot weighing down on one's head!

I put aside my messy cloth wrap;
I have got rid of my dusty tasselled fringe.
In a silver jar I have stored a cold stream,
On my bald pate I trickle a ladle full.
Like one baptized with the Water of Buddha's Law,
I sit and receive this cool, cleansing joy.
Now I know why the priest who seeks Repose
Frees his heart by first shaving his head.

*Emperor Ming Huang teaching Yang Kuei-fei to play the flute, by
Ch'ien Hsuan (1235–90).*

CHINA

The period of division between the T'ang and Sung Empires is known as the 'Five Dynasties', after the short-lived military dictatorships which controlled the provinces of North China. The length of the longest of these dynasties was seventeen years.

● In the North only three events during this period of instability were to have lasting significance.
1 The capital was moved down-river from Loyang to K'ai Feng, outside the Land within the Passes. This shift may well have been a recognition of the economic changes which had been in progress during the T'ang dynasty. The site was closer to the Yangtze valley.
2 There was an exodus of many T'ang officials to the South, which weakened even more the remaining central administration. They chose not to serve the Northern Emperors who were mostly adventurers of barbarian stock.
3 The cession of large tracts of Hopeh, including the gates in the Great Wall and what is now Peking, by the first ruler of the Later Tsin (936) to the Kitan nomads. In this key strategic area, these people established the Liao kingdom (936–1168); the region was to remain outside China for four hundred years, and through it foreign invaders, the Mongols, were to conquer all China.

● In the South the traditions of the T'ang Empire were preserved. The influx of scholars considerably advanced the culture of the region. Nan T'ang and Shu were particularly distinguished. Being weak the Southern kingdoms were not able to inflict much damage on each other. Printing became widespread.

960 ended fifty-three years of division. General Chao Kuang-yin seized power in the North, then conquered the South, like the earlier Sui reunification. When one king begged independence, the first Sung Emperor asked, 'What wrong have your people done to be excluded from the Empire?'

INDIA and WEST ASIA

ISLAM (Turks)

ISLAM (Arabs)

SIND

Tibet

Rajputana

900 onwards

EUROPE

● The westward sweep of Muslim arms was halted at the Battle of Poitiers (732). Spain remained the frontier until Italian fleets beat off attacks from Sardinia (1016) and, gaining control of the Mediterranean, allowed a counter-attack. This was to be 'The First Crusade', launched to aid a struggling Byzantine Empire, now reduced to an eighth of its original size, and free the Holy Land from Islam. Although Pope Urban II found a useful outlet for restless warrior nobles in the Crusade, its success was transitory. A feudal army of quarrelling barons had taken on a sophisticated civilization. Charlemagne (768–814) had failed, like Justinian, to restore Roman power; the Crusader kingdoms, an alien growth in the Holy Land, soon fell through the disunity of Christendom.

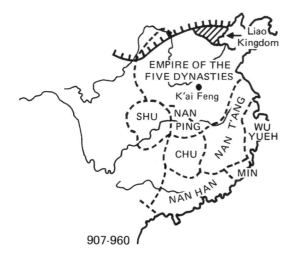

EMPIRE OF THE
FIVE DYNASTIES
K'ai Feng
SHU NAN
PING
CHU
WU
YUEH
MIN
NAN HAN
NAN T'ANG
Liao
Kingdom

907-960

● The Hindu Kingdoms of North India were dominated by the Rajputs, who had kept the Arabs at bay since their occupation of Sind (712). But new Muslim forces were building up in Central Asia: the Turkish tribes made serious inroads after 1000. Hindu India was under siege. Only the far South was to maintain the tradition when Islam conquered the sub-continent.

● In the West the Muslim world passed on to Christendom the Greek heritage and, by transmission, Chinese achievements. Spain and Norman Sicily were the points of cultural interchange.

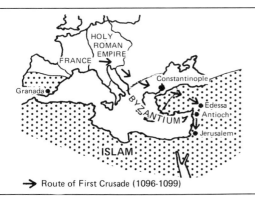

HOLY
ROMAN
EMPIRE
FRANCE
Granada
Constantinople
BYZANTIUM
Edessa
Antioch
Jerusalem
ISLAM

→ Route of First Crusade (1096-1099)

4 A Second Golden Age

The Northern Sung, A.D. 960–1126, and the Southern Sung Dynasties, A.D. 1127–1279

HISTORICAL OUTLINE

The founder of the third Empire, the Sung, was a northern general named Chao Kuang-yin, whose mutinous troops forced him to don the yellow gown, the colour reserved for Emperors. Such a military revolution was an unusual beginning for a successful dynasty in Chinese history. But the reluctant Emperor was a shrewd ruler. He spared the fallen imperial family, gained the goodwill of the *shih* by restoring the civil service to its dominant position, and, not least, rid himself of those military leaders who had put him on the throne. An early historian has recorded how the vicious circle of suspicion and mutiny that had raised and degraded the five brief dynasties in the North was broken:

> In the first year of his reign the new Emperor summoned all his military officers—the men responsible for the mutiny to which he owed his throne—to a banquet. When the company had drunk deeply and were in cheerful mood, the Emperor said:
> 'I do not sleep peacefully at night.'
> 'For what reason?' inquired the generals.
> 'It is not hard to understand,' replied the Emperor. 'Which of you is there who does not covet my throne?'
> The generals made a deep bow, and all protested:
> 'Why does Your Majesty speak thus? The Mandate of Heaven is now established; who still has treacherous aims?'
> The Emperor replied:
> 'I do not doubt your loyalty, but if one day one of you is suddenly roused at dawn and forced to don a yellow robe, even if unwilling, how should he avoid rebellion?'
> The officers all declared that not one of them was sufficiently renowned or beloved for such a thing to happen, and begged the Emperor to take such measures as he thought wise to guard against any such possibility. The Emperor, having brought them to this point, promptly made his proposals known:
> 'The life of man is short,' he said. 'Happiness is to have the wealth

and means to enjoy life, and then to be able to leave the same prosperity to one's descendants. If you, my officers, will renounce your military authority, retire to the provinces, and choose there the best lands and most delightful dwelling-places, there to pass the rest of your lives in pleasure and peace until you die of old age, would this not be better than to live a life of peril and uncertainty? So that no shadow of suspicion shall remain between prince and ministers, we will ally our families with marriages, thus, ruler and subject linked in friendship and amity, we will enjoy tranquillity.'

The officers and generals immediately vowed to follow the Emperor's wishes, and the next day, pretending imaginary maladies, all offered their resignations. The Emperor accepted their offer, and carried out his part of this strange bargain. All were given titles of honour and richly endowed with wealth and land.

The Northern Sung Dynasty

The southern kingdoms watched these developments with interest and sympathy. Nan P'ing and Shu submitted to the Sung dynasty through diplomatic arrangement. Nan Han (971) and Nan T'ang (975) surrendered after short wars, while the last independent state, Wu Yueh, held out only till 979. Except for the Liao kingdom, China was reunited for the third occasion as 'one Empire under Heaven.' There was an overwhelming consciousness among the Chinese that unity was natural and deserved the sacrifice of local autonomy. The early part of the tenth century A.D. had witnessed a revolution in communications. Block-printing made the Classical Books of China generally available for the first time. Not only did the number of scholars greatly increase but the cultural heritage contained in literature became more widely spread through society. To be a Chinese meant— even for the illiterate *nung* who listened to some one read from the newly available books—belonging to a great cultural tradition as well as an Empire.

The second Sung Emperor attempted without success to recover the territory occupied by the Liao kingdom. Defeat and a long war ended when the third Emperor agreed to tolerate the Kitan presence and pay a large annual subsidy to Liao (1004). Unlike the Han and the T'ang dynasties, the foreign policy of the Sung was never imperial in design. Containment of the nomad peoples, the *status quo*, not expansion, was the fundamental rule. Foreign invasion remained the perpetual threat and was the cause of final overthrow of the Sung Empire. Apart from the Kitans on the northern frontier another group, the Tungus, Tibetan tribesmen, had secured in Hsia a power-base

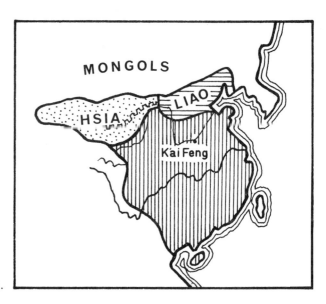

Empire of Northern Sung Dynasty (till A.D. 1126).

from which to exploit any Chinese weakness for southern expansion (1032).

The Sung administration was modelled on the T'ang. The civil service reached its zenith, completely overshadowing the military arm of government. Organization and recruitment procedures were perfected. At Court two groups of officials vied with each other for power, the Conservatives and the Innovators. During the reign of Emperor Shen Tsung (1068–85) a revolutionary economic policy was introduced by Wang An-shih, the leader of the Innovators. Although it did not outlast the ministry of Wang An-shih, the new measures seem to have been beneficial to the *nung*, as was intended. Political failure brought banishment to a distant provincial post, nothing worse. Indeed, the pacific atmosphere of the Sung Empire, particularly from 1004 till 1126, has led not a few people to regard this period as the climax of Chinese civilization. Philosophy, painting and science reached levels before unknown, while the pattern of urban life became the envy of later ages.

Disaster struck the Sung Empire in the form of the warlike Kin. These untamed nomads were originally vassals of the Kitans, but ten years of conflict with the Liao kingdom gave them mastery of the region and direct contact with the Chinese. The Emperor Hui Tsung, the painter and patron of art, misjudged the strength of the Kin army and tried to recover the Liao territories by force. In 1126 the Kin besieged and captured K'ai Feng; they took prisoner three thousand of the *shih* as well as the Emperor, who died in captivity.

124

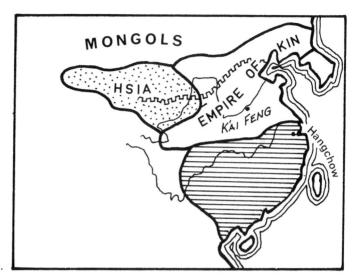

Empire of Southern Sung Dynasty (after A.D. 1126).

The Southern Sung Dynasty

Kin cavalry crossed the Yangtze in 1129 and captured the city of Hangchow, where new Sung Emperor Kao Tsu had established his capital. The situation looked grave but the Empire rallied, finding in Yo Fei a general capable of defeating the Kin (1131). When fighting had restored Sung control over the Yangtze valley and the southern provinces, Emperor Kao Tsu decided to come to terms with the Kin (1141). To the anger of Confucian historians, Yo Fei was secretly executed and China divided between two powers, the Sung and Kin Empires. Their frontier was almost identical to the line drawn across China during the Tartar partition (316–590). It was the northern boundary of the wet, rice-growing valleys of southern and central China, country unsuited to the military tactics of nomad cavalry.

Despite a further Kin invasion in 1161, which was repulsed, the Sung Empire continued on its pacific course, at home and abroad. Painting and philosophy came into their own, though Chu Hsi (1130–1200) found his ideas neglected by the Court. His re-interpretation and development of Confucian ideas bear the stamp of the concern that a 'loyal' *shih* must have felt when he reflected upon the reduction of the Empire. Since he died before Genghiz became the Great Khan of the Mongols (1206) and started his nation on their world-shattering course of conquest and destruction, Chu Hsi was spared seeing the agony of civilization savaged by the Mongol horde. The Kin Empire fell first (1210) amid scenes of appalling ferocity. But it was the cold-blooded extermination of the Hsia kingdom, in 1224, that proclaimed the inhumanity of the Mongols. So thorough was that

125

devastation the region became a permanent wasteland, while the language and culture of the Hsia was lost forever.

In 1235, after Genghiz Khan's death, the Mongols turned their attention to the Sung Empire. Nearly half a century of war was necessary before the last member of the Sung dynasty perished in a sea battle off what is now Hong Kong (1279). The terrain of the South, valleys, forests, mountains, hindered the Mongols. And, though a pacifist dynasty, the Sung was technically the best equipped for warfare in the world. Gunpowder had been adopted by the imperial armies. Explosive grenades and

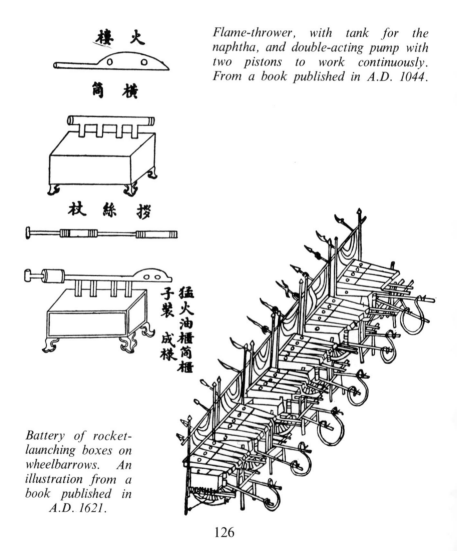

Flame-thrower, with tank for the naphtha, and double-acting pump with two pistons to work continuously. From a book published in A.D. 1044.

Battery of rocket-launching boxes on wheelbarrows. An illustration from a book published in A.D. 1621.

bombs were launched from catapults; rocket-aided arrows and flame-throwers were in service; poisonous smokes could be deployed too. Yet there was another factor involved. The Kin Empire had provided the Mongols with scholar-statesmen like Yelu Ch'u-ts'ai, a Kitan admirer of Chinese culture. He did what he could to temper the furious determination of the Mongols, converting an urge to destroy into a desire for a regular empire. The absolute hatred of sown lands typical of Genghiz Khan was transformed into Kubilai Khan's great foundation, the city of Peking (1263). The grandson of Genghiz and the first Yuan, or Mongol Emperor (1279), had transferred his people and his capital from steppe to sown lands.

NEO-CONFUCIANISM

> The educated believe nothing,
> the uneducated believe everything.
> —*Chinese saying*

The names of Chu Hsi and Confucius are always linked together because the Sung philosopher recast the sage of Lu's teaching in a form that has been accepted as orthodox ever since. The Sung Empire was a time when Confucian philosophy was debated, re-interpreted and transformed into a more modern system of ideas. Perhaps the continued development of Buddhism caused this rethinking of Confucius, though it seems likely that scientific discoveries and applications may have influenced Chu Hsi too. His views have been called 'a kind of scientific humanism.' The traditional Confucian contempt for popular religion, whether Taoism or Buddhism, was taken a stage further by Chu Hsi, who denied that there was a personal deity. 'There is,' he said, 'no man in heaven judging sin.' Instead a moral force, an impersonal power, ruled the universe; the duty of mankind was cooperation with its workings, since they were the laws of Nature.

The Confucian Classics contained few references to divine powers so that Chu Hsi had little difficulty in removing the supernatural realm altogether. The good life, proper conduct as a citizen, was to be expected because the nature of man was good. Decent behaviour did not need to depend on a sense of sin and fear of punishment. Evil was simply the result of neglect and the absence of a proper education. These ideas were to impress profoundly the European scholars of the Enlightenment who first became aware of Chinese thought at the end of the seventeenth century. They responded to a morality that managed without supernatural sanction. The social emphasis pleased them too. According to Chu Hsi, there was no real reason why human society could not become perfect. It was a question of attunement to *li*, or the moral law. A favourite comparison used by Chu Hsi was between man in society and a pearl in a bowl of dirty water. Although the pearl appears grey and spoilt, it has lost nothing essential. Taken from the bowl it shines forth in all its original brilliance. Should man seek his true nature and live in harmony with it, then his original goodness will become clear likewise. His natural purity has become clouded through the false values of social life. The way is to follow the Mean, a balanced style of living. The idea that men have been led astray by the distortions of the society in which they live is not far from present-day Chinese Communism, which has adopted a policy of re-education for those 'who have taken the capitalist road.' After the 'Hundred Flowers' episode in 1957, when Mao Tse-tung relaxed censorship and encouraged the educated classes to voice their views, those 'rightists' who did criticize the government from mistaken viewpoints were sent to the country districts for re-education among the revolutionary *nung*.

Despite Chu Hsi's considerable reputation in his own lifetime the relation between the Sung Court and the philosopher was often strained, even antagonistic. He experienced the inevitable ups and downs in the series of official appointments that were forced upon him. For Chu Hsi was loath to serve in a capacity which compromised his philosophy. The tone of a memorial he addressed to Emperor Hsiao Tsung in 1180 concerning the Court favourites was less than tactful:

> As the power of these people waxes and as their prestige becomes established, throughout the land everyone bends before them like grass before the wind, with the result that Your Majesty's edicts, promotions, and demotions no longer issue from the Court, but from the private houses of these one or two favourites. Ostensibly these acts are Your Majesty's individual decisions, but in fact it is this handful of men who secretly exercise your power of control.

What Chu Hsi wished to see was an Emperor surrounded by true and virtuous *shih*. A memorial of 1188 stated: 'Know those who are worthy and employ them.' His role, as that of all 'worthy' *shih*, was teacher to the Emperor. Scholarship and moral character were required in those who would serve the Empire. They had to follow the Mean. To register protest against things he disliked at Court, Chu Hsi would decline official posts. But it was a negative gesture and he failed to find ways of applying his philosophy. In fact, Chu Hsi's influence was on succeeding generations of Confucian scholars.

SUNG PAINTING

When you are planning to paint, you must always create a harmonious relationship between heaven and earth.
—Kuo Hsi

China's tradition of painting, like much else in her civilization, differs considerably from what we are used to in the West. Artists were not professional in the sense that they did nothing else apart from painting. Just as good handwriting, or calligraphy, and the ability to compose verse became an expected accomplishment of the *shih*, so painting was added by Emperor Hui Tsung to the minimum qualifications of would-be officials of his Court. A good painter himself, the Sung Emperor introduced painting in the Palace examinations, those designed to select candidates for the most senior posts in the imperial civil service. The examination question consisted of a line or phrase taken from the Classics or a well-known poem, which had to be illustrated in an original way. Thought, the idea behind the composition, was more important than fidelity to natural objects. One year Emperor Hui Tsung chose for illustration the line:

When I return from trampling flowers,
the hoofs of my horse are fragrant.

The candidate judged to have produced the best work offers an insight on what is valued in Chinese art, for his painting showed a horse walking along a path with a pair of butterflies fluttering around its hoofs. Neither field nor flowers could be seen—Spring was implied. The observer had to discover for himself the artist's intention. Like a great deal of Chinese poetry, paintings were appreciated for their inexplicit quality, a reticence on the part of the artist.

129

In the Sung Empire Chinese art found its perfect mode of expression, namely landscape painting. Later dynasties, the Ming especially, were to be patrons of famous artists but the surviving scrolls of the Sung masters have rarely been equalled. T'ang painters tended to prefer figure painting but the period of the Five Dynasties and the Northern Sung witnessed the rise of

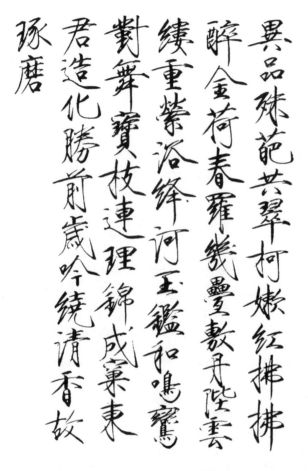

A poem written by the Sung Emperor Hui Tsung. He called this style of calligraphy 'Slender Gold.'

landscape as the pre-eminent form. The shift from human subjects to Nature continued with the growing interest in birds and flowers. From Emperor Hui Tsung's brush came a number of much prized bird paintings as well as fine examples of calligraphy, before the unfortunate ruler was carried off as a Kin prisoner (1126).

Sung landscape painting grew from the spontaneous delight Chinese people took in the splendid natural scenery with which the Empire abounded. The popular Chinese proverb 'Mountains make great trees' expresses the idea that significant landscape moulds men of great character. T'ang poets had put into words the traditional pleasures of the hermit, remote from the bustle of cities, so that a romantic appreciation of landscape became a general sentiment among the literate classes. Religion contributed to this movement; the Ch'an school of Buddhism had no small influence on individual Sung painters.

Kuo Hsi (1020–90) was one of the founding masters of Sung landscape painting. Not only did he paint numerous large-scale scrolls and wall paintings, but he left a record of his views on the purpose of such art. His *Advice on Landscape Painting* explains how he hoped his own works would be used:

> It is human nature to resent the hustle and bustle of society, and to wish to see, but not always succeed in seeing, immortals hidden in the clouds. In times of peace, under a good Emperor and kind parents, it would be wrong to go off alone and try to find oneself. For there is duty and responsibility which cannot be ignored. . . . But the dream of a retreat to forests and springs and finding the company of saints in retreat is always there. We are usually excluded from the sights and sounds of Nature. Now the artist has reproduced it for us. One can imagine oneself sitting on rocks in a gully and hearing the cries of monkeys and birds; while in one's own sitting-room the light of the mountains and the colours of the water dazzle one's eyes. Is it not a joy, a fulfilment of one's dream? That is why paintings of landscapes are so much in demand. To approach such paintings without the requisite state of mind would be committing a sin against such natural beauties. . . .

It should be noticed that we are expected to prepare ourselves, to acquire 'the requisite state of mind,' as much as the artist had to prepare himself in order to catch and record the unique character of a landscape. Kuo Hsi tells would-be painters that they must study every aspect of the natural world, for true vision should transmit the life within all things. Two landscapes by an older contemporary, Fan K'uan (990–1030), could serve as illustrations here. One depicts the immensity of rugged mountain peaks, while the other has a winter landscape softened by a covering of snow.

131

Fan K'uan (c. 990–1030): Travelling Among Mountains and Streams. *Ink on silk.*

Winter landscape by Fan K'uan.

Perhaps the perspective seems odd, but Western eyes have been trained to see things from a single point. The Chinese artist imagines himself to be looking from the top of a small hill so that he has a total vision of every part. Another surprise may be the restricted palette, the sparse use of colour. But the Chinese saying 'Black is ten colours' indicates the importance of the brush, whose strokes give vitality to the composition. Skill with the brush had become an art in calligraphy since the Han Empire, and its techniques were transferred into painting. Notice the variety of brushwork in the following painting by Ma Yuan (1190–1224): it is simply ink on silk.

Landscape by Ma Yüan.

Indian ink was condensed to a solid state in China. Then it was rubbed on an ink-stone with the required amount of water in order that the artist could obtain a range of colour strengths.

The most celebrated Sung landscape painter was Hsia Kuei (1180–1230). In his scrolls, often long panoramas measuring several metres, the romantic spirit of Chinese art finds full expression. His brushwork has remained the admiration of later generations of painters and connoisseurs.

Distant View of Rivers and Hills *by Hsia Kuei. Large panoramic scroll, another part of which is reproduced in the Introduction.*

Finally, Mu-chi (early thirteenth century A.D.), a monk, represented the Ch'an school of Buddhism in painting, for which reason most of his works are to be found today in Japanese temples and collections. Traditional Chinese critics have consistently underestimated Mu-chi's paintings because the outlook they embody did not remain central to either Chinese thought or Chinese Buddhism, whereas the Japanese who turned Ch'an into Zen prize his work.

135

SCIENCE AND TECHNOLOGY IN THE T'ANG AND SUNG EMPIRES

Whenever one follows up any specific piece of scientific or technological history in Chinese literature it is always at the Sung dynasty
that one finds the major focal point.

—Joseph Needham

The freedom and stability afforded by the T'ang and Sung
dynasties was responsible for a great expansion in scientific and
technical knowledge, which culminated in a minor 'Industrial
Revolution' by the twelfth century. Enquiring minds were not
suppressed and new, or alien, ideas were not rejected. An increasing flow of knowledge between East and West was facilitated
by the tolerant attitude towards foreign travellers in China.
Neo-Confucianism rejected the idea of a deity being responsible
for earthly phenomena and sought 'down to earth' empirical
explanations of them. The resulting spirit of scientific enquiry,
permeated to the West only slowly, but technological developments travelled faster. Even so, some Chinese inventions such as
the 'magazine' crossbow were never used outside China.

Printing
Between the invention of paper in the first century and the
emergence of block-printing in the eighth century little written
material survives. The origins of block-printing were in the stone
and bronze seals and rings engraved with raised inscriptions
which could be reproduced on wax. Larger inscriptions on stone
tablets could be copied by rubbing techniques (cf., brass rubbing
in churches). As early as the fifth century B.C. records were
being engraved on stone and Confucian and later Buddhist works
were recorded in this way to avoid distortion in their retelling,
and to popularize them. After the invention of paper, books
could be made by binding together a number of rubbings.

Although the first reference to printing comes in A.D. 593,
hand copying was most common until the ninth century. In 932
the government ordered the printing of nine Confucian classics
consisting of 130 volumes. This took twenty years to complete
for block-printing was slow and expensive. Each page had to be
carved on to a separate piece of wood or stone. In the mid-
eleventh century movable type was introduced by Pi Sheng.
Each Chinese character was represented on a separate piece of
clay (later porcelain and tin). To print a page, the type was

glued together on an iron plate. Subsequently, the pieces could be removed by heating the plate. Block and movable type printing existed side by side until the twentieth century.

This rubbing comes from a monument of A.D. 1107 and shows Confucius and a disciple. The stone carving was a copy of a famous eighth-century painting.

Mechanical Engineering

The development of mechanical engineering was closely tied to the harnessing of water power, initially in the metallurgical industries.

The earliest use of water power was probably in the *spoon-tilt hammer*. Water would be channelled into a succession of spoons which on filling would tilt, empty and operate a hammer which could be used for forging metal or operating an air blast. The spoons could be arranged side by side or as a continuous bucket wheel. References to this technique go back to A.D. 20. Gradually such machines were adopted for milling purposes, such as grinding corn or hulling rice. A twelfth-century poem by Lou Shou gives a beautifully apt description of them in operation.

The graceful moon rides over the wall,
The leaves made a noise 'sho, sho, sho' in the breeze;
All over the country villages at this time
The sound of pounding echoes like mutual question and answer;
You may enjoy at your will the jade fragrance of cooking rice
Or watch the water flowing in and out of the slippery spoon
Or listen to the water-worn wheel industriously turning.

137

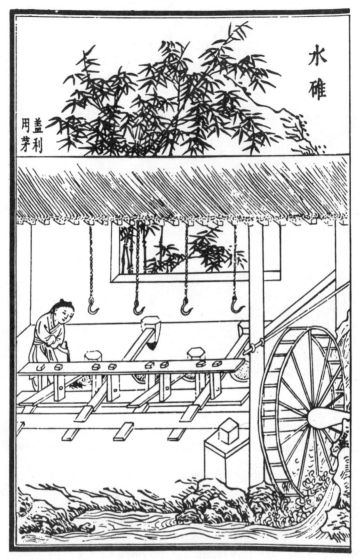

Water powered trip hammers.

The bucket wheel developed into the *water-wheel* as we know it. In China they were often arranged horizontally not vertically. By the thirteenth century water power was being applied to textile machinery for throwing silk and spinning hemp.

Such machines combining crank or eccentric, connecting rod and piston rod, and depending on toothed cogs and gearing apparatus, contained many of the features of later western steam-powered engines.

Mill on a river. This system of milling by interconnecting cogs had been invented by the early fourteenth century.

Clockwork

Water power was the basis of mechanical timekeeping devices in the absence of weighted pulleys and springs. In the twelfth century four methods of timekeeping were recorded:

- clepsydra or water clock;
- the burning of incense sticks;
- the sun-dial;
- the 'revolving and snapping springs.'

The first and last of these were connected. The simple clepsydra had developed beyond recognition by the tenth century. The principle of regular and controlled water flow had been linked

139

with the armillary sphere, a model of the heavens used in astron-omy. It allowed the sphere to turn slowly keeping pace with the apparent movement of the heavens. This obviously necessitated accurate timekeeping but the machine was not regarded as a clock. In 1090 an astronomical clock tower was constructed in K'ai Feng powered by water-flow. This actually struck a gong to indicate the hours by the system of bamboo 'revolving and snapping springs.'

Marine Developments
It is highly relevant to move from the field of astronomy and mechanical engineering to that of shipping and navigation developments.

In A.D. 118 Chang Heng, the astronomer, said 'there are in all 2 500 stars, not including those which the sea people observe.' By sea people he meant sailors who relied on astronomy for navigation. By the tenth century the *magnetic compass* had been perfected, though it had been around in various forms since Han times. The first clear description comes in *The Dream Pool Essays* of Shen Kua in 1080.

While the Chinese were initially a continental rather than a maritime nation, the significance of inland waterways and coastal trade was so great by the T'ang Empire that many marine developments ensued. The Chinese craft, typified by the 'sampan and junk,' were very different from western craft. They had no keel, no stern or stern post, no framework of ribs, and they were flat-bottomed. The junk's side planking ended at the stern with a solid transom of planks. Rigidity was maintained by solid bulkheads, of which the bow and stern transoms were the terminal ones. These could be made watertight thus establishing a principle not found in western vessels until much later.

The origins of these vessels may derive from observation of split

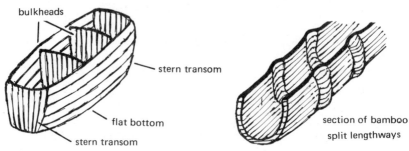

Key features of hull of Chinese junk.

bamboo which contains many parallels. Also, some features may have developed from the large ocean-going bamboo sailing rafts still found in South East Asia.

Methods of propulsion were far ahead of the West. Three important developments were:

- the self feathering 'propeller' or sculling oar;
- the use of multiple masts as early as the third century A.D.—usually of mat and batten, their arrangement and shape were so developed by the ninth century as to be aerodynamically very efficient;
- treadmill-operated paddle warships. Their origins lay in the mounting of water wheels in ships which were moored in river currents. Such ship-mounted mills were known in Europe by A.D. 500 but already the Chinese had man-powered paddle boats. The Sung navy developed warships with up to twenty-three wheels (eleven on each side and one stern wheel). These carried crews of 200–300 men, a complement of marines and crossbow-men, and an artillery of catapults for throwing bombs and grenades. From 1100 to 1230 the Yangtze was successfully defended by these vessels from the Kin.

Shantung freighter exhibiting classical features of multiple mat and batten sails and abrupt termination at stern transom.

The stern-post rudder has been mentioned in Chapter 2. By 900 it had ousted the steering oars, which were up to fifteen metres long on even the small sea-going and lake vessels. The steering oar maintained its use on the rivers as it was useful in countering strong currents and rapids. In a rough sea its use was very limited. In 940 one of the earliest specific references to the stern-post rudder was made thus: 'The control of a ship carrying 10 000 bushels of freight is assured by means of a piece of wood no longer than one fathom.'

Cartography

Just as the scientific cartography of the Greeks was disappearing from Europe, to be replaced by religious and symbolic inspiration, the same science was being developed in China. From the first century to the seventeenth, Chinese cartographical development was uninterrupted. Chang Heng (A.D. 78–139), the astronomer and seismologist, was said to have 'cast a network about heaven and earth, and reckoned on the basis of it.' The first principles of scientific cartography were laid down by P'ei Hsiu (224–71) who was Minister of Works in A.D. 267. In drawing up a map of the short-lived Tsin Empire he established six principles:

1 the use of scale based on graduated divisions;
2 the use of a rectangular grid to 'depict correct relationships between different parts of the map';
3 the pacing out of the sides of a right angled triangle to determine the length of the third side where the terrain made it impossible to do a physical measurement;
4 the measuring of the high and the low;
5 the measuring of right angles and acute angles;
6 the measuring of curves and straight lines.

These principles were passed down to later mapmakers such as Chia Tan who in 807 completed a map nine metres long and ten-and-a-half metres high entitled *Map of both Chinese and Barbarian Peoples within the Four Seas*. At a grid scale twenty-five millimetres to 100 *li* this map must have been of the whole of Asia. The T'ang period also contributed early contour maps and the adoption of a mercator-type projection borrowed from astronomy. The application of celestial co-ordinates to the world may have provided the first evidence of a spherical Earth. Moreover, the Chinese put North at the top of their maps unlike the Arabs who placed South at the top. The oldest printed map in the world was of Western China in 1155.

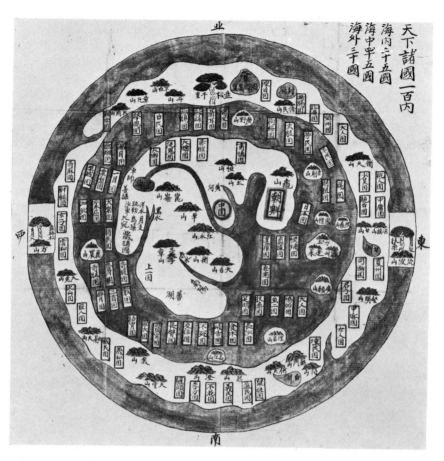

An ancient Chinese view of the World. China is at the centre—the outer ring of land has such names on it as 'Country of the Giants.' The inscription says: 'There are 100 Nations in the World, 25 surrounded by the 4 Seas, 45 on the 4 Seas, and 30 beyond the 4 Seas.'

The knowledge accrued in the T'ang and Sung periods was inherited by Chu Ssu-pen (1273–1337). He added to it the products of cross-fertilization with Arabs and Persians and the Mongol knowledge of West Asia. His work was the basis of the Chinese view of the Asian continent until the nineteenth century. By the time the *Enlarged Terrestial Atlas* was printed in 1555 the shape and alignment of Africa was known. The Atlas was based on a two-metre map divided into sheets as follows: 16 on various provinces; 16 on border regions; 3 on the Yellow River; 3 on the Grand Canal; 2 on sea routes; 4 on Korea, Annam, Mongolia and Central Asia.

143

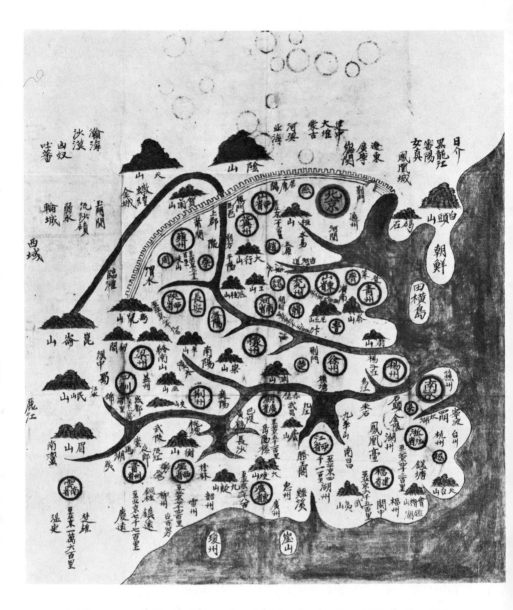

A Ming map of North China showing clearly the Great Wall, the Yellow River and the Yangtze River.

Although at this point China's geographical knowledge became fused with Western knowledge it was not until the work of the intrepid field geographer Hsu Hsia-kho (1586–1641) that the source of the West River was discovered; it was proved that the

144

Chin Sha Chiang River was the upper reaches of the Yangtze, and that the Mekong and Salween were separate rivers.

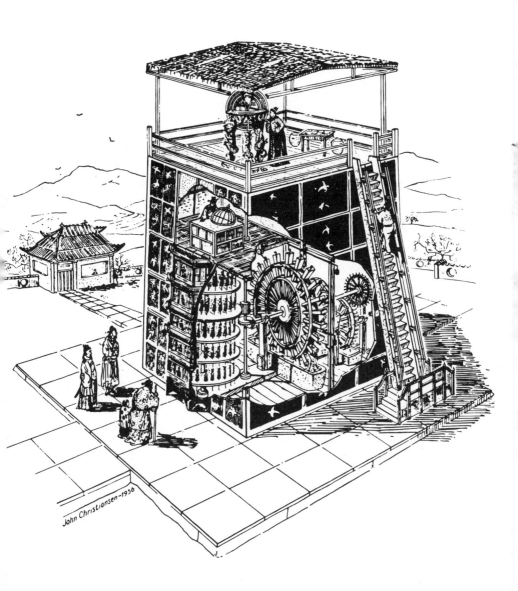

Su Sung's astronomical clock at K'ai Feng (built 1088–92). This reconstruction shows clearly a celestial globe and an armillary sphere. The striking mechanism is to the left: there was no outside dial.

145

ECONOMY AND SOCIETY

The Growth of a Cash Economy

Before the tenth century the amount of cash in circulation was limited for three basic reasons:

- most taxes and dues were paid 'in kind';
- metals such as copper were generally in short supply;
- there was a problem of maintaining a coinage free from debasement and counterfeiting.

The basic unit of money, the circular copper 'cash' coin with a central square hole, was of very low value (equivalent to about ·028 of a gram of silver). State accountants only dealt with units of one thousand 'cash,' while in everyday trading one hundred was a standard unit. By the eleventh century the 'hundred' was still the common unit but in fact its value had fallen to about seventy-seven 'cash' and by the end of the dynasty was worth only fifty 'cash.' (Just as the Pound Sterling maintains its name but falls in value.) Metal-based, low value, money was very inconvenient, since a 'thousand cash' weighed over half a kilogram.

The Sung dynasty saw a great increase in currency mainly in the form of paper money. Merchants who stored their copper 'cash' with wealthy families received receipts in exchange. These could be cashed in other towns by other members of the wealthy family or their friends. This system was called 'flying money.' The state extended this service in the eleventh century, initially by accepting receipts in exchange for its monopoly products of salt and tea. By the twelfth century the number of notes issued in a single year amounted to twenty-six million strings of 'cash.' Notes were only valid for a certain length of time and in certain areas. But from 1265 to 1274 the government put out notes backed by gold and silver; they were valid throughout the Empire. The great increase of money in circulation led to general price rises and reduced even further the value of 'cash.' The penalty for counterfeiting notes was death.

The Economic Reforms of Wang An-shih

Wang An-shih was Chief Minister in the reign of Emperor Shen Tsung (1068–85). He saw the dangers of disintegration in the Empire as the affluence of K'ai Feng increasingly contrasted with rural poverty. His measures were unpopular with his court rivals, the conservative *shih*, on the grounds that they were 'new.' Despite their fears of peasant rebellion similar to that

146

which overthrew another reformer, Wang Mang, a thousand years before, his measures tended to unify and strengthen the Empire.

The key points of his 'New Laws' were:

● *'Equalization of Loss.'* State granaries were established throughout the provinces to store grain tribute. This was then resold to the population in times of need at low prices. The money was then forwarded to the capital. Prior to this grain was transported to K'ai Feng. Not only did this add to its price, but also there were often great surpluses there when the provinces were starving.

● *'Young Shoots' Law.* State loans to farmers were introduced at low interest rates. This reduced the power of local money-lenders and merchants, thus encouraging farmers to extend the area of land under cultivation.

● *'Remission of Services' Law.* Forced labour (the *corvée*) was commuted for money payments.

● *Rationalization of Court Expenditure.* 40 per cent of the national budget was saved.

● *Control of Trade.* Taxation was reformed. Hoarding of commodities by merchants was reduced and production of luxury goods restricted. Prices were fixed and profits limited.

● *'Pao Chia System.'* Families were grouped in units of ten, all members being responsible for the misdeeds of any one. Each group was forced to provide conscripts to the army. Wealthy families had to maintain a standing supply of cavalry mounts for army use. By increasing the military reserve, Wang An-shih was able to reduce the size and power of the standing army.

● *Reform of Examination System.* The Classics and poetry were replaced by more practical subjects including geography, economics, law and medicine.

The criticisms aroused by these reforms stemmed from the growth of bureaucracy and policing of the population. The existing administration had neither the ability nor experience to organize the New Laws. Furthermore, there was popular opposition to conscription and the Pao Chia system. When Wang An-shih died in 1086 his policies had not caused rebellion and most of his measures were continued by his successors.

The Growth of Trade and the Rise of Merchants
The Sung Empire was a great period of trade expansion. As the key economic area of China shifted to the Yangtze valley and the South-East coast a 'national' market was developed based

on 3200 kilometres of the navigable Yangtze river, the Grand Canal, and ever increasing coastal traffic. The great southern ports of Canton, Ch'uan Chou, and Fuchow had contact with Africa, Arabia, India, the Pacific Islands and the South-East Peninsula. Chinese porcelain and 'cash' of the period have been found in Cairo, Bengal, Annam and South India.

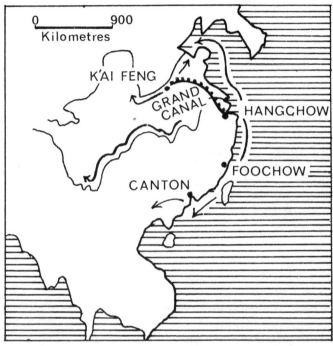

Expansion of a national market in the Sung dynasty.

The government monopoly on the trade of tea, salt, liquor and incense did not prevent the actual transportation and warehousing of these goods from being in the hands of private merchants. Merchants traditionally were entrenched in the lower orders of society, but by the Sung Empire their growing wealth could neither be controlled nor ignored. Increasingly, wealthy merchants were allowed to buy titles to join the ruling *élite*. Mercantile activity, theoretically forbidden to individuals in government service, was undertaken by civil servants on a large scale in Hangchow. The same administrators leased warehouses, shops and dwellings. Nepotism and patronage were common. It even became respectable for well-to-do families to buy businesses for their sons who failed the imperial examinations.

Retail and wholesale organization in Hangchow was highly organized and controlled by guilds. Each trade, such as rice, jewellery, or even medicine, had its own guild. Some parts of the city were areas of specialized trades. The 'Pearl Market,' a jewellery centre, was located between the 'Sweet Harmony District' and 'South-of-the-Market.' The money-changers were to the north between 'Five Span Pavilion' and 'Official's Lane.'

Despite the Chinese desire to prosper, the merchants were regarded as being scrupulously fair in payment of debts and other financial transactions. The guilds enforced standards of quality and behaviour. The determination of merchants to be accepted socially led them to distribute great sums of money on charity, on outward signs of culture like painting, and on great banquets.

Rural Peasantry to Urban Proletariat

The rapid growth of southern cities was characterized by two features:

- a growing inability for the city to support itself;
- a great immigration of poverty stricken peasants from rural areas.

Being dominated by the desires and needs of a wealthy *élite* the economy of the city was based on expansion of luxury trades at the expense of necessities. In short, cities consumed more than they produced. The difference was increasingly made up by the flow of money and foodstuffs from the great estates in the North. The increased demands of the landowners put increasing pressure on an already impoverished peasantry. Similarly, government expenditure was being financed by higher taxes and increasing pressure on the large numbers of employees in state industries. 280 000 families in the salt marshes of Huai lived in semi-slavery and perpetual debt. Interest rates were as high as 20 per cent per month. Men were forced to sell their own land to pay debts and became landless labourers. One eye-witness account runs:

> The man is hired for the season, generally from the first moon [February] until the ninth [October]. His wage is one 'load' [about 8 bushels] of cereals [corn and millet] per month. His employer undertakes to furnish him with free clothing, a 'spring' outfit, a shirt and trousers for summer, and a pair of leather shoes. In exchange he must work without stopping, from morning until evening. . . . If he falls ill, payment for the days when he is not at work, is deducted from his wages. If he loses or damages the agricultural goods entrusted to him [wicker baskets, sacks, knives, hoes and spades] he has to see that they are replaced.

149

The final alternatives for men who had sold their land, sold their children as servants, and not committed suicide or become hired labourers, were to become brigands or to migrate to the city.

The cities swarmed with the poor searching for freedom and employment. Many were homeless. Labour, being plentiful, was extremely cheap. A man or woman could only survive by a mixture of cunning and intense specialization. The main areas of occupation available were:

● *Servants and employees of wealthy families.* These families maintained large retinues of dependants, including jewellers, tutors, private soldiers, and a whole range of services to maintain a large household. Such employment was relatively secure as long as the family maintained its wealth.

● *Street vendors and labourers.* These lived from 'hand to mouth' and were their own bosses. 'Poor and honest' pedlars collected a few cheap goods, such as sweets, from 'factory workshops' in the morning, and received a 10 per cent commission on their sales. The labourers included navvies, water-carriers, scavengers and night-soil removers.

● *Entertainers.* A vast number of mimics, comedians, jugglers, animal trainers, singers and dancers were found in covered bazaars, known as 'pleasure grounds.' Also a large number of tea-houses provided singing-girls and the amount of prostitution in Hangchow amazed visitors, Marco Polo included.

● *Vagrants and thieves.* Petty crime was common throughout the cities, so that many gangs of vagabonds were openly able to defy the police.

The urban proletariat had no feeling of unity. Many were totally dependent on the continuing wealth of their employers. While everyone belonged to a guild, even beggars, they were too numerous and diverse to present a common face on their members' behalf. Occasional crises such as the fire which destroyed 50000 houses in Hangchow in 1201 prompted officials and wealthy members of society to increase their charity in an attempt to reduce panic and unrest.

THE CHINESE CITY

Development of Walled Settlements
Walled settlements developed as early as the Shang dynasty. They were the most efficient means of protection from marauding

nomads. They also allowed easy collection and storage of grain taxes and helped reduce the impact of famine. The permanent residents were largely administrators, civil servants, the military and those providing food and services for them. Intensive agriculture was carried out within the walls and immediately around them for the residence population.

Among the earliest settlements in the 'Land within the Passes' were the cave dwellings of the loess country. These were photographed in Honan province.

Such settlements were most numerous in areas of high population density, namely the most fertile parts of the river valleys. However, numerous garrison towns were 'planted' along the almost deserted northern boundaries.

Distribution of the chief cities referred to in this section.

Craft industries developed as winter occupations of farmers but the larger settlements soon had permanent segregated industrial and commercial sectors. The administrators imposed strict controls on these for fear of the growing power of the merchants. Shih Huang Ti was to use the city to hold the Empire together. He centralized power at the capital Hsien Yang and instituted thirty-six provincial capitals and hundreds of prefectures called *hsien*. The hsien were miniature capitals controlling the small towns and large villages. By Han times the number of settlements recorded indicates that most of the population lived in one of these types of settlement for at least part of the year. Some settlements became cultural centres, places of worship or education, and trade, but all were dominated by their function as administrative centres. Each carried the stamp of government

152

uniformity, from Anyang and Cheng-chow up to the nineteenth-century growth of the Western commercial Treaty Ports. Where they grew around mining, industry or fishing, government control was obtained by nationalizing the industries and recruiting the powerful entrepreneurs into government service.

Today's pattern of Chinese cities was largely established by the fourteenth century A.D. when Kubilai Khan finally organized forty-five hsien in the previously independent area of Yunnan. The coast was relatively neglected until the eighteenth century and the Chinese have remained a continental people as the vast majority of present sites indicates, with a preference for river valleys.

Town Planning

The ancient Chinese considered that heaven was round and the earth square. Human organization of space was supposed to repeat this cosmic pattern. Thus, the basic unit of the classical Chinese settlement was the square. It had to be surrounded by four walls facing the points of the compass. Each wall was identified with the changing position of the sun or with the four seasons. As the Polar Star dominated the universe so the Palace or Official Residence should dominate the city, being centrally located with its rear facing the North Wall, allowing the ruler or his representative to look southward down the main north/south avenue leading to the main gate. This pattern was followed, with allowances for natural conditions, in all sizes of settlement.

The settlement was a microcosm of the natural order. The Chinese were determined to ally themselves with Nature rather than oppose it and to reach this end the initial siting of any settlement involved complex calculations by geomancers, whose knowledge of *Feng-Shui* (Wind and Water) would ensure that evil spirits in the form of flooding or attack would be repelled. 'Without harmony nothing lasts,' according to an old Chinese adage. (The north/south axis of the city and the south-facing main gate had a logic in North China considering the major climatic and barbarian onslaughts came from the north.) The ceremony involved the accurate measurement of sun and shade and the direction of running water. The final decision would be checked by consulting an oracle. Once a site was chosen the construction would be done with great speed during the winter months from October to January, when labour was available. The walls were built first, followed by gates and towers, sometimes a moat, then the ancestral temple and altar of the soil, and, last of all, the official residence at the centre. The places of worship were located south of the Palace and the market place to the north; thus the sacred and profane were separated.

Selection of a city site.

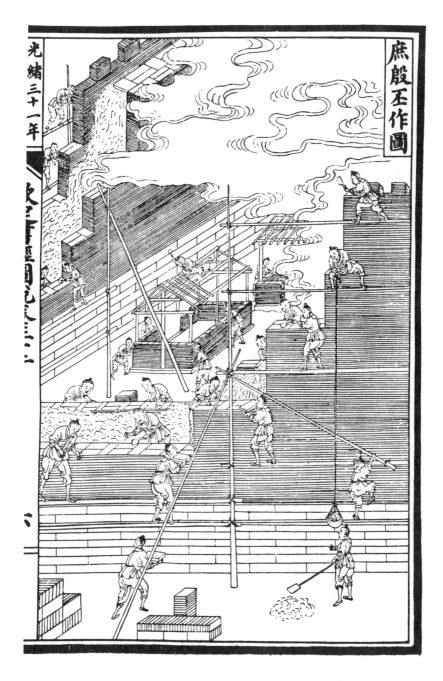

The construction of the walls of the capital of the Chou Dynasty. An illustration from the Ch'ing period. Note the solid foundations and tamped earth walls contained by brickwork.

155

A royal city's outer walls contained twelve gates to represent the months of the year. Smaller cities had four gates. Gates were of great importance in controlling the urban population. The Han city of Chang-an was divided into 160 *li* or wards, each containing up to 100 households. Each ward was surrounded by a wall controlled by a single gate. Each household in turn was surrounded by a smaller wall with one gate. Each of the three sets of gates was guarded and closed at night, thus a close watch was kept on the movement of the population.

A royal tomb of the Shang built in the fourteenth century B.C. Excavated in the area of the capital Anyang.

The rigidity of the Han system was later relaxed as a result of population expansion, less totalitarian régimes, and the enforced movement of large numbers to less typically Chinese cities in the South, as the North collapsed under Mongol attack. By the Sung dynasty the fastest growing cities were south of the Yangtze and were largely commercial centres. Even so the Mongol capital of Khanbaluc (Peking) in the North, despite being designed by a Muslim architect, displayed all of the classical Chinese features although construction did not begin until 1267.

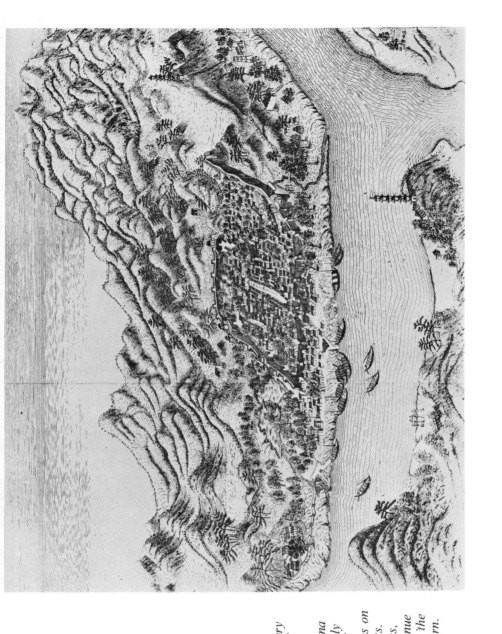

This
eighteenth-century
illustration of
a small town
in Southern China
illustrates clearly
the impact of
planning traditions on
later settlements.
The walls, gates,
towers, main avenue
are all clearly in the
traditional pattern.

The City as a Centre of Change

Cities in Europe have been great centres of social change. Through trade and industry they have been wealthy enough to maintain their independence and have rejected established political, legal and religious ideals. The Chinese city is obviously different. Western university towns have traditionally been centres of provincial dissent against metropolitan ruling. Chinese universities have acted to support centralization by feeding their graduates into the civil service, via the examination system. Chinese rulers have seldom relied on the support of wealthy urban merchants. If anything they discriminated against them, particularly in the sphere of taxation, and absorbed the most able and influential into government service. Change in China could only be obtained by successful peasant rebellions and even then it was not the nature of the political social and economic system that was attacked, only its administrators.

Traditionally, craftsmen and merchants were segregated, often being forced to live outside city walls. Their position was relaxed with the shift of the national centre of gravity to the South, the growth of population in the eleventh century, and the overall expansion of trade in the T'ang and Sung dynasties. An increasing number of cities developed as 'break-of-bulk' points and transport termini on rivers and coast. The rigid-grid pattern was neglected and suburban sprawl became common. In some areas commercial cities developed as twins to existing administrative cities, like: Chengtu and Chungking in Szechuan, K'ai Feng and Chengchou in Honan and Peking and Tientsin in Hopeh.

Chang-an and Hangchow

Chang-an

The site of Chang-an has been developed as a strategic city location from early Chou times to the present day. Hsien Yang, Shih Huang Ti's capital, dominated the fertile Wei Valley which could then be easily defended from attacks from the east. Hsien Yang was razed to the ground to be replaced by Liu Pang's seat, Chang-an. The new city had ramparts over 24 kilometres long, 18 metres high and up to 15 metres thick. The centre and south of the city were occupied by Emperor and Court while the craft and service quarter lay to the north-west and the rest of the population to the north-east. The 160 *li* were served by 9 markets located on each side of the main north/south thoroughfare.

City life in Ka'i Feng about A.D. 1125. The painting emphasizes the bustle of commercial areas of the cities with numerous refreshment houses to the foreground. The painting celebrates the Spring festival and gives a great feeling of merrymaking. The bridge is of bamboo with a multi-angular cantilever construction no longer found in China.

Chang-an was sacked in A.D. 25 and Emperor Kuang Wu chose Loyang in the east as his capital. In the sixth century the Sui reunified the Empire which had collapsed in A.D. 220 and again chose Chang-an as the capital. The architect, influenced by barbarian adaptation of traditional planning built the Royal Palace against the North Wall with government offices directly to the south. These were entirely separated from the rest by walls. The residential and market areas were split by a main north/south highway over 145 metres wide, into two administrative sections each with its own police force. One-hundred-and-eight separate wards were defined, each with its own brick-paved, tree-lined avenues up to 36 metres wide.

159

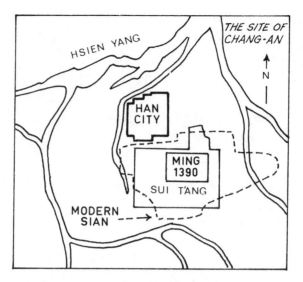

Chinese city sites in the vicinity of modern Sian.

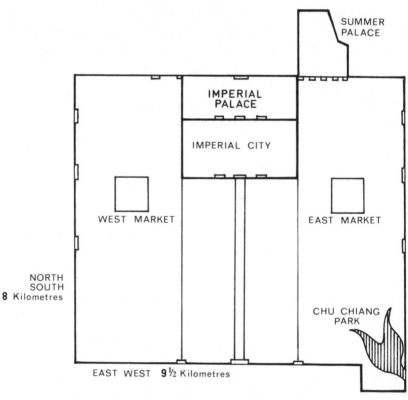

Chang-an during the T'ang dynasty.

The market occupied 9 squares, the central one being used by government officials for checking weights and measures, fixing prices and collecting taxes. Each market had 220 trading units and each market street had its own specialized merchandise. 300 drum beats heralded the opening at noon while 300 bell chimes gave warning of closure nearly 2 hours before sunset. Population distribution was uneven. Hence the largely middle-class eastern sections could not maintain sufficient support for their market which gradually declined. The densely populated western section supported a very lively and cosmopolitan market.

About one million people lived in the 77 square kilometres of Chang-an by the seventh century A.D. Large areas were devoted to parkland and open space and the city was used as a model for many others including Nara, an early Japanese capital. The present city of Sian shares the same site as Chang-an.

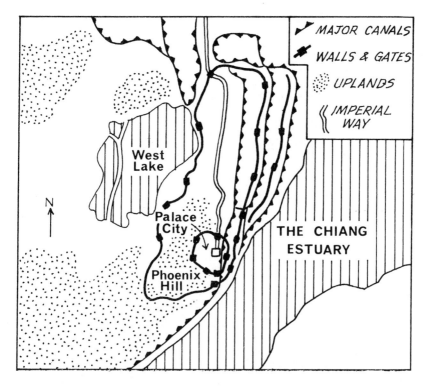

Hangchow, capital of the Southern Sung dynasty in the thirteenth century. Note the irregular form and the contravention of many classical town planning traditions.

Hangchow

K'ai Feng was the capital of the Northern Sung dynasty from 960 to 1126. Attacks from the Kin, coupled with a continued southward movement of surplus population led to the adoption of the southern city of Hangchow as the new capital. Hangchow failed to follow any of the major planning precepts of classical China but came to symbolize a golden age in Chinese history.

Life along the river *by Chang Tse-tuan, a Sung artist.*

Why Hangchow differed from the northern cities:
- Its shape was irregular and the walls were pierced by thirteen equally irregular gates.
- The palace was located to the south while the centre was occupied by a pig market.
- Commerce was uncontrolled and spilled out of its allocated quarters.
- There was great freedom of movement for all and the streets were alive with people and entertainment well into the night.
- Increasing use was made of multi-storeyed dwellings through lack of space. These faced directly on to the street rather than into courtyards.
- Great fortunes were made by individual merchants who were increasingly influential.

Houses adjoining waterway, a typical city scene in South China. Population growth and the shortage of land are reflected in the crowding of dwellings along the brinks.

A street in K'ai Feng, shortly before its fall to the Kin.

Hangchow substituted irregularity and human charm for the order and grandeur of the cosmicized cities of the North. The city walls enclosed 10 square kilometres compared to Chang-an's 77 square kilometres. The population of $1\frac{1}{2}$ million was crowded into 26 square kilometres including the immediate suburbs. There were few open spaces. The ten markets were not large enough to cope with all the trade created. Marco Polo was astonished at the city which he called Kin-sai. Life in the capital could be hectic and exciting. There was a continual danger from fires in the densely populated sectors but also a continuous and large selection of entertainments available from music halls to tea houses and state-run taverns. The charms of its singing girls were one of the reasons why it obtained its nickname of the City of Heaven.

Gardens
Poetry, painting and garden art have always been closely inter-related in China. Appreciation of Nature led to attempts by all three at expressing the beauty of the landscape as well as the contrasts to be found in it. Rocks and gnarled stones are often juxtaposed with the soft leaves of plants, like bananas. Because of Taoism water has been a fundamental element in the garden, while water lilies remain one of the favourite subjects for painters today.

Snowscene at the Five Dragon Pavilion, Peihoi Park, Peking. Notice how the formal style of architecture is softened by the snow.

165

During the Sung Empire both landscape painting and the garden reached a high point, which has rarely been equalled again.

Snow at the Ye Ho Garden, Peking.

But the country house had been a favourite resort, a kind of 'hermitage,' for the *shih* from the Han period onwards.

Opposite is the house and garden of the T'ang painter and poet Wang Wei (609–759), probably by his own hand.

Flowers have always fascinated the Chinese too. Either seeking cherry blossoms in the snow or gazing on chrysanthemum flowers at home the scholar has taken delight in the delicate beauty of the living world around. Failure to do so would have been regarded as a serious shortcoming in the 'cultured' person.

The Japanese garden is a development of the Chinese model, though it may not have been a direct import. Korea could have acted as a half-way stage for its transfer.

Enjoyment of the Chrysanthemum Flowers *by Hua Yen, 1753.*

The Chinese House

The House. The house below is typical of a prosperous family of the Sung period. The connecting courtyards were arranged in accordance with the classical pattern. Regional variations in house-type varied from caves on the loess plateau to stilt houses in the South-East. The poor often had to dispense with courtyards. As population pressure increased in towns an increasing number of dwellings became multi-storeyed.

The Courtyard. Passing through the outer gate from the street, a visitor entered the first courtyard, which might contain shrubs and a goldfish pond. Into this 'public' yard traders might be invited. The rooms along the side might be used as libraries, rest

169

rooms, or guest rooms. The inner courtyard was reserved for the family, side rooms being allocated to in-laws, concubines and other relatives. The main building contained five rooms for the head and his first wife. Behind this were the kitchens and servants' quarters. Gardens would surround the building within the confines of the outer wall. Circular doorways and terracotta reliefs added visual effect to the whole household unit.

The Walls. The buildings were characterized by a rigid wooden structure which supported the whole of the roof weight. The walls could be completely remodelled without danger of collapse Inner walls were usually of pounded earth or bamboo wattle, sometimes plastered with clay and white-washed. Outer walls might be of sun-baked brick. Wood was often in short supply but stone was not favoured in construction as it was an 'unnatural' pillar between earth and heaven. Wood was also more likely to withstand earthquake tremors. Houses were not built as monuments. 'One can create something, it is true, which will last a thousand years, but no one can tell who will be living after a hundred.' Great stability was derived from the use of the corbel bracket, allowing a slight wooden framework to support a heavy roof. Eventually these became a great source of ornate decoration.

The Roof. Most Chinese houses had ridge-pole roofs, overhanging eaves, and gable ends. Curved roofs originated in the South where split bamboo was used as roofing material. The natural sag in these long bamboo strips was incorporated into roof design when curved tiles provided a more durable agent. Poorer houses were often thatched with cereal straw, but this was a great fire hazard in towns. Tiles were colourful, safe, durable, but expensive in comparison.

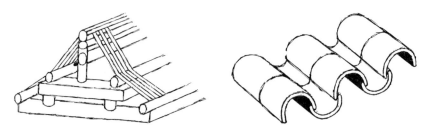

A Land of Bridges
In a country dominated by waterways and mountains it is easy to exaggerate the number of bridges. However, their military and economic importance could not be overrated. Marco Polo estimated that Hangchow alone had over 12 000 bridges, mainly of stone.

Bridge at the Summer Palace, Peking.

The earliest bridges were of wooden planks on semi-submerged pillars but by the early Han dynasty stone was the major material. The style was a direct copy of the wooden plank bridge although the stone trusses were up to fifteen metres long. By the later Han dynasty the stone-arch bridge was seen more frequently in North China. These were both ornamental and functional as they allowed junks to pass along the canals. The stone trusses were used mainly for ornamentation and light traffic, over shallow water not used for transport.

The oldest extant stone-arch bridge in China was built in A.D. 605–16 at Chao-hsien in Hopeh. The An-chi bridge has a span of thirty-seven metres but rises only seven metres from foot to crown. This gave a very flat crown which was not emulated in Europe until the sixteenth century. It was in use until 1954 and is the earliest segmental arch bridge in any civilization. The arch bridge reached a peak of perfection in the Sui dynasty and has been adopted for the ornamentation of lakes in major cities such as Peking.

The stone-truss bridge was developed for commercial purposes in the south-east particularly during the Sung period. These were up to 1 200 metres long, composed of twenty-one-metre sections each weighing up to 200 tonnes.

The oldest segmental arch bridge in the world. The An-chi bridge at Chao-hsien, Hopeh.

A suspension bridge across the Mekong.

In western China, mountain gorges demanded bigger spans at greater heights and the arch was replaced by the cantilever and suspension bridges. Wooden cantilever bridges were tunnels with resting houses at each end. Suspension bridges were initially supported by cables of twisted bamboo hung from towers on opposite sides of a gorge. The towers contained winding gear to keep the cables tense. Iron-chains were used as early as the sixth century and were extended into the south-west throughout the Sui and T'ang dynasties. Such mountain bridges became important market and communication centres.

Ornamental marble bridge at the Summer Palace.

A Moon bridge in the Summer Palace at Peking.

Pavilion bridge at Wan Hsien.

Daily Life in Hangchow
The inhabitants of thirteenth century Hangchow were early risers. Monastery bells and the cries of the monks touring the streets shouting details of the day's weather would waken them between four and five o'clock. The city would already be busy. The rice wharves operated continuously to provide the 200 tonnes and more of rice needed to feed the population each day. The abattoirs would be killing and preparing the day's meat. Shopkeepers arranged the day's displays by six o'clock and the Imperial Way was thronged with farmers and street traders coming in from the suburbs. The aroma of fried tripe and other breakfast delicacies would emanate from the large number of kiosks and the portable stoves of the food vendors. By seven o'clock the whole city, from refuse collectors to the officials of the Imperial Court, would be well into their day's work.

The running of the individual households would be supervised by the elders of the family. Servants would be commissioned to buy and prepare the day's food. Cleaning and housecare would be aided by the simplicity of interior decor and furnishings. Beds were of wooden planks, covered in rush mattresses and covers lined with silk floss. The pillows were cylinders of plaited rushes,

The pillow of wicker, wood or porcelain.

lacquered wood or porcelain with a hollow in the centre for the head. Curtains were used to screen the bed. Wealthy homes made use of black lacquer to cover furniture which might also be engraved or inlaid with precious stones or metal. Chairs were an innovation from India. In the T'ang Empire people sat on them crosslegged. By Sung times lighter 'barbarian seats' with crossed legs were common, as were circular stools. Tables were low and rectangular for dining, but circular pedestal tables were used for flower arrangements and antiques such as vases. Flowers were a common form of decoration and great prestige was obtained by the growing of delicate and fragrant blossoms. The walls of wealthier homes were covered with scrolls and paintings of landscapes, or examples of fine calligraphy.

In summer the houses could be stifling, although the waxed-paper windows could be removed. The wealthier families moved to cooler altitudes outside the city. In winter the thin partition walls gave little protection from the cold and there was great heat loss from the charcoal fires. Coal was very expensive and the main protection from cold was probably obtained from thicker quilted clothes. In rural districts hollow brick seats and beds (*k'ang*) were heated with hot air from the cooking stove.

Water was delivered daily from the freshwater lake to the west. Bathing was very popular in Hangchow unlike the northern cities. Liquid soap made from peas and herbs, and perfumes, was available. The poor who did not own bathing facilities could use one of the hundreds of bathing establishments open to the public for a small fee. Hot water was always on sale in the streets. The city was hygiene conscious. The wealthy had their own cesspits and all refuse and excrement were collected in vessels and carried to the suburbs by the night-soil man. Most visitors were impressed with the cleanliness of both the city and its people but Arab traders found the Chinese use of toilet paper as early as the ninth century quite distasteful.

Mosquitoes were a common pest in the house, particularly in summer, but fumigants could be purchased along with incense. Cats kept down the rodents. The markets had stalls specializing in toys and other goods as well as pets, like Pekingese lapdogs and crickets which were kept in cages.

The kitchens of the houses contained charcoal stoves and

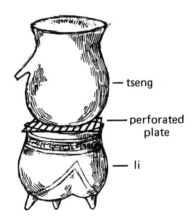

cooking implements of copper and porcelain such as the three-legged li and the tseng. Cooking by steam heat was recognized as being rapid and effective in preserving the goodness of food-

177

stuffs. There were few taboos on foodstuffs. In Hangchow specialized restaurants provided foods as diverse as snakes, dogs and snails. Little beef was eaten for the simple reason that oxen were too valuable as draught animals and there was little tradition of consuming milk or dairy products. Pork was the main meat together with poultry. The wealthy could afford venison or game birds, while the poor consumed large amounts of offal or horse flesh. Per capita consumption of rice in the city was about a kilo per day. Both freshwater and saltwater fish were commonly available. Water was seldom drunk on its own. It had to be boiled to avoid contamination and tea was usually made. Many varieties were known. Vying with tea as the most popular drink was rice wine flavoured with spices. Drunkenness was quite common.

In the evening the wealthy family might entertain friends, relatives or guests. A large number of courses would be served over several hours. Food would be presented on the low tables in many dishes. All meat was cut up in advance, allowing the guests to eat with chopsticks and spoon. Entertainers would be hired to amuse the company. Meanwhile, the streets would be teeming with the evening's pleasure seekers as they visited the numerous tea houses and restaurants until the early hours.

5 The Mongol Conquest

The Yuan Empire, A.D. 1279–1368

Although the date of the beginning of the Yuan or Mongol Empire is considered to be 1279 by Chinese historians—that is, the year in which the last member of the Sung dynasty was killed—there had been a Mongol Empire in China since the accession of Kubilai Khan. From 1263 Peking, not Karakorum in Mongolia, was the centre of Mongol world power.

The Mongol Terror

The Mongol Terror was unleashed on the world by Genghiz Khan, who laid down the rule that any resistance shown to Mongol arms should be punished by total extermination. Whenever a city put up a defence or delayed its surrender, the fate of the inhabitants was certain death—every man, woman and child. Genghiz Khan was a man incapable of feeling pity. On occasions his fury even extended to animals and plants. During a campaign in 1222, Mutugen, the favourite grandson of Genghiz Khan, was killed laying siege to a fortress in Bamiyan, a valley within the folds of the Hindu Kush. To appease the grief of the boy's mother, he took an oath to put to death every living soul in that rich and populous valley. Accordingly, Genghiz Khan set out with his army, devastating villages and towns, until Kakrak, the chief city, had been reduced to rubble. The present-day obscurity and unimportance of Bamiyan is an impressive monument to Mongol ruthlessness. Yet the Mongols exulted in such ferocious actions. 'The greatest joy,' Genghiz Khan said, 'is to conquer one's enemies, to pursue them, to seize their property, to see their families in tears, to ride their horses, and to possess their daughters and wives.'

Every Mongol male was a soldier. Hunting and battle were his sole occupations. Slaves performed the few domestic duties the restless Mongols considered necessary. When these fierce

179

A portrait of Genghiz Khan by a Central Asian artist.

horsemen fell on the Kin Empire in 1220, their physical appearance struck terror into the Kitans, for they were unkempt. In fact, Mongols were expressly forbidden to wash themselves, or have anything washed in running water.

What the Mongol conquest represents is the greatest clash in Asian history between the nomadic culture of the steppe and the civilization of intensive agriculture. There is a revealing incident recorded in *The Secret History of the Mongols*, commissioned by Genghiz Khan's son Ogodei around 1240. After one of his campaigns in Central Asia, Genghiz Khan summoned to his court two people from the city of Khiva, Turkestan, to explain to him 'the sense and significance of the cities.' To the Mongol emperor, the city was something alien, an encroachment upon a world which once belonged to the nomads alone, a world which during the thirteenth century for the first and last time came very close to being dominated by a nomadic empire. But to Genghiz Khan understanding was not condoning: cities were plundered and laid waste by his hordes.

Yelu Ch'u-ts'ai

When the Mongols overran those areas of China under the control of the Kin Empire and the Hsia kingdom, the nomad fear and hatred of settled life was indulged to the utmost. The brunt of this fury fell on the 'Land within the Passes,' whose ancient importance as the centre of Chinese civilization was eclipsed forever. The decimated *nung* were no longer able to maintain the extensive hydraulic works, and many northern frontier towns had to be abandoned. One man, however, spoke out against the Mongol devastation and, fortunately for China and the world, his words convinced Genghiz Khan. Here is an account of the discussion leading up to this momentous alteration of policy:

When Genghiz invaded the western countries, he did not have in his stores a single measure of rice or a single yard of silk. When [they came to the first Chinese provinces] his advisers said 'Although you have now conquered the men of Han, they are no use to us; it would be better to kill them all and turn the land back to pasture so that we can feed our beasts on it.' But Yelu Ch'u-ts'ai said 'Now that you have conquered everywhere under Heaven and all the riches of the four seas, you can have everything you want, but you have not yet organized it. You should set up taxation on land and merchants, and should make profits on wine, salt, iron, and the produce of the mountains and marshes. In this way in a single year you will obtain 500 000 ounces of silver, 80 000 rolls of silk and 400 000 piculs of grain. How can you say that the Chinese people are no use to you?' . . . So Genghiz agreed that it should be done.

Yelu Ch'u-ts'ai, a Kitan, had been summoned by Genghiz Khan to Mongolia in 1218. The Mongol Emperor expected that such a nobleman from the old kingdom of Liao would welcome service in Mongol cause. When Genghiz Khan met Yelu Ch'u-ts'ai for the first time in his court, he said: 'Liao and Kin have been enemies for generations; I have taken revenge for you.' To which Yelu Ch'u-ts'ai replied: 'My father and grandfather have both served Kin respectfully. How can I, as a subject and a son, be so insincere at heart as to consider my sovereign and my father as enemies?' Pleased by the frankness of this reply as well as the demeanour of Yelu Ch'u-ts'ai, the Mongol Emperor found a place for him in his retinue. The Kitan nobleman became secretary-astrologer to Genghiz Khan and, finally, Chief of the Secretariat under Ogodei Khan.

The attitude adopted by Yelu Ch'u-ts'ai in his initial interview with the Mongol Emperor and expressed in his later advice on state affairs was the direct result of a Confucian training. As in the earlier period of the Tartar partition, the Kitans and the Kin had been profoundly influenced by Chinese culture. Through Chinese sympathisers, like Yelu Ch'u-ts'ai, there was a constant attempt to mitigate the harsh Mongol rule in North China as well as to provide an administration for the unwieldy nomad empire. While Yelu Ch'u-ts'ai was prepared to play on Mongol cupidity in an emergency, he hoped that wisdom and learning would triumph at last. In his diary we find this entry:

> The teachings of the Three Sages are all of benefit to mankind. When I read the book of Lao-tzu, my admiration was deeply roused. I wished to make Our Sovereign [Genghiz Khan] tread loftily in the footsteps of the ancient worthies. This is the reason why I supported Ch'an-ch'un, who, of course, I also intended to be an advocate of Confucianism and Buddhism.

Ch'ang-ch'un, a leading Taoist, had been called to the Mongol court because of a rumour that he had found the elixir of life. But at this time in China there was a general belief in the common origin of the Three Ways, the teachings of Buddha, Lao-tzu and Confucius. To follow all of them meant 'to stand firmly in the world like the three legs of a tripod.' Although Ch'ang-ch'un proved a disappointment by using his relationship with Genghiz Khan to further the fortunes of his own sect in China, Yelu Ch'u-ts'ai achieved other successes in the Mongol court. At the election of Ogodei Khan he introduced a number of Chinese practices designed to stabilize the dynasty, but, more important, he opened the civil service to Chinese scholars by having examinations re-established in 1237. This measure alone freed more than a thousand *shih* from being Mongol slaves. Yet agitation from the anti-Chinese faction at Court soon stopped the practice and the influence of Yelu Ch'u-ts'ai on government came to an end in 1239 when tax-farming was permitted by Muslim business men. Yelu Ch'u-ts'ai died of a broken heart in 1243. The Mongol dynasty, which he believed had the Heavenly Mandate, went on to become an entirely non-Chinese régime, supported by a civil service recruited from foreign adventurers. Had the wish expressed in the diary come true, the Mongols might have saved themselves from the great Chinese rebellion that was to drive out the last Mongol Emperor in 1368.

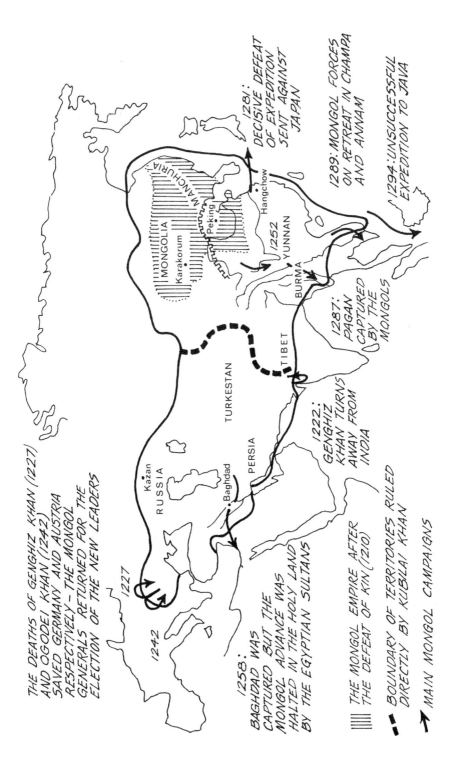

THE DEATHS OF GENGHIZ KHAN (1227)
AND OGODEI KHAN (1242)
SAVED GERMANY AND AUSTRIA
RESPECTIVELY – THE MONGOL
GENERALS RETURNED FOR THE
ELECTION OF THE NEW LEADERS

1227

1242

Kazan

RUSSIA

Baghdad

TURKESTAN

PERSIA

1222:
GENGHIZ
KHAN TURNS
AWAY FROM
INDIA

1258:
BAGHDAD WAS
CAPTURED BUT THE
MONGOL ADVANCE WAS
HALTED IN THE HOLY LAND
BY THE EGYPTIAN SULTANS

MONGOLIA

Karakorum

MANCHURIA

Peking

1252

YUNNAN

Hangchow

TIBET

BURMA

1287:
PAGAN
CAPTURED
BY THE
MONGOLS

1281:
DECISIVE DEFEAT
OF EXPEDITION
SENT AGAINST
JAPAN

1289:MONGOL FORCES
ON RETREAT IN CHAMPA
AND ANNAM

1294:UNSUCCESSFUL
EXPEDITION TO JAVA

||||| THE MONGOL EMPIRE AFTER
       THE DEFEAT OF KIN (1210)

▬ ▬ ▬ BOUNDARY OF TERRITORIES RULED
       DIRECTLY BY KUBILAI KHAN

↑   MAIN MONGOL CAMPAIGNS

The Mongol World Empire on the death of Kubilai Khan (1294).

The Mongol World Empire
Kubilai Khan had been on the Mongol throne for twenty years
when the last member of the Sung dynasty died (1279). Nominally
he ruled an empire spanning Europe and Asia, from the Danube
to the Yellow River. Only the death of Genghiz Khan had
recalled the generals for the election of his successor and spared
Germany from invasion. That year English merchants decided
not to sail to Baltic ports: they feared the Mongol Terror might
be there by the time they arrived. But the vast extent of the
Mongol conquests, spread over so many diverse peoples and
places, forced successive Great Khans to appoint rulers for distant
provinces. By 1270 it was beginning to split up into the four
distinct Mongol states of China, Turkestan, Russia and Persia.

A Mongol bowman, as seen by a Japanese artist.

184

Ogodei Khan ruled 1229–41

Ogodei was considered a benign ruler, particularly before the fall of Yelu Ch'u-ts'ai. However, he became addicted to alcohol—he preferred grape wine from the West to kumys, the alcohol obtained from fermented mare's milk that Mongols had always drunk. His wife became increasingly powerful as he withdrew from active leadership before finally dying of drink. Kubilai was more sober and stable, though his successors indulged in women and drink, leaving the non-Chinese Yuan civil service to run the Empire for its own benefit.

The conversion of the western Mongols to Islam in 1295 completed the process of fragmentation, because the Muslim Khans refused to recognize Buddhist Kubilai Khan or his successors.

Despite the steady break-up of the Mongol World Empire, the reign of Kubilai Khan has remained a marvellous image in the mind of West. The chief reason for this very odd view of

185

Kubilai Khan ruled 1260–94

Chinese history is that China during the Yuan Empire was better known to Europe than at any time till the twentieth century. Mongol control of so much of the world ensured that roads were safe and travel easy, while the Mongol prejudice in favour of war meant that foreigners with any useful skill or ability could make a career for themselves in China. Marco Polo served in the Yuan civil service from 1271 to 1297.

Military ventures undertaken from the Yuan Empire had a mixed success. Yunnan and Burma were quickly annexed, but serious reverses were sustained in Indo-China and Japan. The Mongol army sent against Champa, modern South Vietnam and South-east Cambodia, found the guerrilla tactics employed by the Chams utterly exhausting. Fever and jungle warfare forced the invincible Mongols into a difficult withdrawal, not unlike the experience of Western powers since 1945. The invasion of Japan was a complete disaster (1281). A storm wrecked the fleet and those who managed to wade ashore were cut down by Japanese samurai. Little more success was achieved by a sea-borne expedition against Java in 1294, though the Mongols avoided a massacre.

Kubilai Khan ruled an empire already showing signs of decay. The violence of the initial Mongol attacks on China had impoverished whole provinces. The administration was unconcerned with the welfare of the people; the state officials were corrupt and unreliable. The *shih* and the *nung* found themselves steadily coming together as a united opposition to the Yuan dynasty.

The End of the Mongols
In 1315 the reintroduction of the examination system for entrance to the civil service came too late to rally support from the long-excluded *shih*. The Yuan dynasty was clearly in decline with a series of mediocre Emperors. The last ruler, Togan Timur, was advised by his chief minister, Bayan, that the only hope for the Mongols was wholesale massacre of the Chinese. Open rebellion began in 1348 and for twenty years rival groups and secret societies jostled for position in the fight against the struggling Yuan dynasty. Taoism, a politically subversive philosophy ever since Lao-tzu rode off into the West, played a considerable part in the expulsion of the Mongols through the 'White Lotus' secret society. Foreign dynasties such as the Mongols and the later Manchus were always suspicious of Taoism on account of its ancient opposition to the pomp and ceremony of government. At last Chu Yuan-chang, a peasant, assumed the lead of a national movement and the last Yuan Emperor fled from Peking without a fight (1368).

Chu Yuan-chang, later the Ming Emperor Hung Wu, had great ability as a leader. Indeed, his success derived from the way in which he was able to unite both the *shih* and the *nung*, those two pillars of Chinese society. No other peasant rising has obtained the support of the scholars.

A popular festival today incorporates a legend about this rare event. 'Moon cakes,' the chief item of offering in celebrations for harvest, are said to have been used to co-ordinate action against the Mongols. One version of the story runs like this:

It was not easy for a weaponless population, just ordinary citizens, to overthrow the Yuan dynasty, with a fully armed Mongol soldier billeted in every house. A scholar hit on a simple and effective idea. Every Chinese family must act together and at the same moment. To do this a secret message had to be sent to every house without arousing suspicion. Since the harvest festival was approaching in the autumn and one of the celebrations was eating special cakes by all the members of the family as soon as the moon had climbed into the sky, he and his trusted friends decided to get the bakers to put the message inside these cakes. Throughout the cities of China 'moon cakes' were baked with a tiny piece of paper in the middle; not a word was breathed to outsiders.

On the festival night the Chinese families and their unwanted Mongol lodgers gathered round the table. The moon rose and the head of the household picked up the table knife to slice the cake. As each man cut a cake he was amazed to see the paper within. The message was clear, an order: 'Kill the Mongol.' Knife after knife was grasped hard, then plunged into the chest of the unwary soldier. By the morning panic had seized the remaining Mongols and the last Khan fled.

MARCO POLO AND THE WESTERN IDEA OF CATHAY

The Pope sent Franciscan friars to convert the Mongols to Christianity in the middle of the thirteenth century. After the hordes had turned back from the borders of Germany and Austria, Europe began to see the Mongol Terror not as a new 'scourge of God' but a possible ally against its chief foe, the Muslim powers. The missionaries had no success, though Kubilai Khan asked for the assistance of a hundred men of learning. Marco Polo, as a young man, accompanied his father and uncle on the mission dispatched by the Pope in reply to this request (1271). Although the two learned Dominican friars sent with the Polos were faint-hearted and dropped out of the journey at the first sign of danger, Kubilai Khan received the Venetian travellers kindly and found employment for Marco in the Yuan administration. Twenty years' service gave him a unique opportunity for observing and collecting information about the Yuan Empire. *The Travels,* the account of his experiences, provides us with interesting details about Mongol rule but it lacks real insight concerning the situation of the Chinese. He did not learn the Chinese language and seems to have moved only in Mongol social circles. His writings gave Europe a glimpse of another world, the splendour and power of the Yuan Empire. Kubilai Khan is portrayed as a great ruler, presiding over a magnificent court, to which all men of worth were welcomed, regardless of origin, race or creed. While the amazement and praise at this liberal atmosphere expressed in *The Travels* is understandable in the light of the narrow, closed world of Europe at this period, the Yuan Empire was a pale imitation of what had been a general

Chinese practice since Han times. And lost on Marco Polo was the political motive behind the employment of foreign adventurers, namely the Mongol desire to exclude the *shih* after the fall of Yelu Ch'u-ts'ai.

Ignorant of Chinese history and culture, Marco Polo divides the Yuan Empire into two regions: Cathay, or Northern China, where the Mongol capital was situated at Khanbaluc (Peking), and Manzi, the lands to the south of the Yangtze valley. But his description of Hangchow, which he calls Kin-sai, is valuable because this city, the capital of the Southern Sung dynasty, capitulated to the Mongols and so avoided destruction.

OF THE NOBLE AND MAGNIFICENT CITY OF KIN-SAI

At the end of the three days you reach the noble and magnificent city of Kin-sai, a name that signified 'the celestial city,' and which it merits from its pre-eminence to all others in the world, in point of grandeur and beauty, as well as from its abundant delights, which might lead an inhabitant to imagine himself in paradise. . . . According to common estimation, this city is an hundred miles [160 kilometres] in circuit. Its streets and canals are extensive, and there are squares, or market-places, which, being necessarily proportioned in size to the prodigious concourse of people by whom they are frequented, are exceedingly spacious. It is situated between a lake of fresh and very clear water on one side, and a river of great magnitude on the other, the waters of which, by a number of canals, large and small, are made to run through every quarter of the city, carrying with them all the filth into the lake, and ultimately to the sea. This, while it contributes much to the purity of the air, furnishes a communication by water, in addition to that by land, to all parts of the town; the canals and the streets being of sufficient width to allow of boats on the one, and carriages on the other, conveniently passing, with articles necessary for the consumption of the inhabitants. It is commonly said that the number of bridges, of all sizes, amounts to twelve thousand. Those which are thrown over the principal canals and are connected with the main streets, have arches so high, and are built with so much skill, that vessels with their masts can pass underneath them, while, at the same time, carts and horses are passing over their heads—so well is the slope from the street adapted to the height of the arch. If they were not in fact so numerous, there would be no convenience of crossing from one place to another.

Beyond the city, and enclosing it on that side, there is a fosse about forty miles [64 kilometres] in length, very wide, and full of water that comes from the river before mentioned. This was excavated by the ancient kings of the province. . . . The earth dug out from thence was thrown to the inner side, and has the appearance of many hillocks surrounding the place. There are within the city ten principal squares or market-places, besides innumerable shops along the streets. Each side of these squares is a half mile [0·8 km] in length, and in front of them is the main street, forty paces in width, and running in a direct line from one extremity of the city to the other. . . . In each of the market-places, upon three days in every week, there is an assemblage of from forty to fifty thousand persons, who attend the markets and supply them with every article of provision that can be desired. . . . Each of the ten market-squares is surrounded with high dwelling-houses, in the lower part of which are shops, where every kind of manufacture is carried on, and every article of trade is sold; such, among others, as spices, drugs, trinkets and pearls. In certain shops nothing is vended but the wine of the country, which they are continually brewing, and serve out fresh to their customers at a moderate price. The streets connected with the market-squares are numerous, and in some of them are many cold baths, attended by servants of both sexes, to perform the offices of ablution for the men and women who frequent the baths, and who from their childhood have been accustomed at all times to wash in cold water, which they reckon highly conducive to health. . . . All are in the daily practice of washing their persons, and especially before their meals.

In other streets are the habitations of the courtesans, who are here in such numbers as I dare not venture to report; and not only near the squares, which is the situation usually appropriated for their residence, but in every part of the city they are to be found, adorned with much finery, highly perfumed, occupying well-furnished houses, and attended by many female domestics. These women are accomplished, and are perfect in the arts of blandishment and dalliance, which they accompany with expressions adapted to every description of person, insomuch that strangers who have once tasted their charms, remain in a state of fascination, and become so enchanted by their meretricious arts, that they can never divest themselves of the impression. Thus intoxicated with sensual pleasures, when they return to their homes they report that they have been in Kin-sai, or the celestial city, and pant for the time when they may be enabled to revisit paradise. . . .

The inhabitants of the city are idolaters, and they use paper money as currency. The men as well as the women are handsome. The greater part of them are always clothed in silk. . . . Among the handicraft trades exercised in the place, there are twelve considered to be superior to the rest, as being more generally useful; for each of which there are a thousand workshops, and each shop furnishes employment for ten, fifteen, or twenty workmen, and in a few instances as many as forty, under their respective masters. The opulent principals in these manufactures do not labour with their own hands, but, on the contrary, assume airs of gentility and affect parade. Their wives equally abstain from work. They have much beauty, as has been remarked, and are brought up with delicate and languid habits. The costliness of their dresses, in silks and jewellery, can scarcely be imaged. . . . Their houses are well built and richly adorned with carved work. So much do they delight in ornaments of this kind, in paintings, and fancy buildings, that the sums they lavish on such objects are enormous. The natural disposition of the native inhabitants of Kin-sai is pacific, and by the example of their former kings, who were themselves unwarlike, they have been accustomed to the habits of tranquility. The management of arms is unknown to them, nor do they keep any in their houses. Contentious broils are never had among them. They conduct their mercantile and manufacturing concerns with perfect candour and probity. They are friendly towards each other, and persons who inhabit the same street, both men and women, from the mere circumstance of neighbourhood, appear like one family. In their domestic manners they are free from jealousy or suspicion of their wives, to whom great respect is shown. . . . To strangers also, who visit their city in the way of commerce, they give proofs of cordiality, inviting them freely to their houses, showing them hospitable attention, and furnishing them with the best advice and assistance in their mercantile transactions. On the other hand, they dislike the sight of soldiery, not excepting the guards of the grand Khan, as they preserve the recollection that by them they were deprived of the government of their native kings and rulers.

On the borders of the lake are many handsome and spacious edifices belonging to men of rank and great magistrates. There are likewise many idol temples, with their monasteries, occupied by a number of monks, who perform the service of the idols. Near the central part are two islands, upon each of which stands a superb building, with an incredible number of apartments and separate pavilions. When the inhabitants of the city have occasion to celebrate a wedding, or to give a sumptuous entertainment, they resort to one of these islands, where they find ready for their purpose every article that can be required, such as vessels, napkins, table-linen and the like, which are provided and kept there at the common expense of the citizens, by whom also the buildings were erected. It may happen that at one time there are a hundred parties assembled, at weddings or other feasts, all of whom, notwithstanding, are accommodated with separate rooms or pavilions, so judiciously arranged that they do not interfere with or incommode each other. In addition to this, there are upon the lake a great number of pleasure vessels or barges, calculated to hold ten, fifteen, to twenty persons, being from fifteen to twenty paces in length, with a wide and flat flooring, and not liable to heel to either side in passing through the water. Such persons as take delight in amusement, and mean to enjoy it, either in the company of their women or that of their male companions, engage one of these barges, which are always kept in the nicest order, with proper seats and tables, together with every other kind of furniture necessary for giving an entertainment. . . . And truly the gratification afforded in this manner, upon the water, exceeds any that can be derived from the amusements on the land; for, as the lake extends the whole length of the city, on one side you have a view, as you stand in the boat at a certain distance from the shore, of all its grandeur and beauty, its palaces, temples, convents, and gardens, with the trees of the largest size growing down to the water's edge, while at the same time you enjoy the sight of other boats of the same description, continually passing you, filled in like manner with parties in pursuit of amusement. . . .

CHINA AND THE WEST UNDER THE 'PAX MONGOLICA'

The establishment of a World Empire stretching from the Don to the Mekong greatly facilitated overland travel from West to East. A merchant's handbook of the fourteenth century says 'the road which you travel from Tana [at the mouth of the Don] to Cathay is perfectly safe, whether by day or by night, according to what the merchants say who have used it.' The main reasons for safe and speedy communications were:
- the establishment of an efficient system of relay stations about forty-eight kilometres apart on the main routes, where horses could be exchanged and provisions obtained;
- the benevolent attitude of the Khans to Western travellers. At first Genghiz enslaved foreigners to gain their knowledge and craftsmanship, but Ogodei and Kubilai encouraged the free movement of travellers and employed many of them as administrators.

Western Debts to China
But in the two-way flow of information between East and West China gave far more than it received. As Mohammed once said, 'seek for learning though it be as far away as China.' Even before the unification of Asia under the Mongols the Old Silk Road had been a major source of communication. However, little information about Chinese technology had been directly transmitted, possibly because of the self-containment of the Chinese Empire. Only with the breaching of China's isolation by the Mongols did a flow of technical information actually influence the technological development of the West. This may have happened in two ways:
- the records of increasing numbers of literate and knowledgeable western observers such as the Polos;
- information carried by Tartar slaves for domestic service in Italy in the first half of the fifteenth century.
The granting of Venetian citizenship to Peter the Tartar, Marco Polo's own servant, began this influx of people in 1328. Yet Chinese science was largely neglected in this information flow, though for three years Marco Polo had been governor of Yangchow, a regional capital specializing in the production of armaments and military provisions. By the beginning of the thirteenth century Europeans were using the magnetic compass,

the stern post rudder and the windmill, and in the fourteenth century mechanical clocks, blast furnaces, gunpowder, segmental arch bridges, and block printing are all recorded. Although the exact origin of these inventions was unknown to the inhabitants of Europe at this period, their significance as agents of social and economic change was not altogether unnoticed. In the early 1600s Francis Bacon, Lord Verulam, Lord Chancellor to King James I, was aware that the vast transformations of Europe stemmed from the application of these scientific advances. He wrote:

> It is well to observe the force and virtue and consequences of discoveries. These are to be seen nowhere more conspicuously than in those three which were unknown to the ancients, and of which the origin, though recent, is obscure; namely printing, gunpowder, and the magnet. For these three have changed the whole face and state of things throughout the world, the first in literature, the second in warfare, the third in navigation; whence have followed innumerable changes; insomuch that no empire, no sect, no star, seems to have exerted greater power and influence in human affairs than these mechanical discoveries.

This acute observation is interesting. For printing had ended the monopoly of the Church over education. Knowledge became readily available in printed form whereas previously only the very rich layman could afford the long, tedious and expensive process of hand-copied manuscripts. The Renaissance and the Reformation followed. Gunpowder inaugurated large-scale warfare, eclipsing both knight and castle. The Thirty Years' War, which raged shortly after Bacon's death, was the closest experience of total warfare in Europe before 1914. The magnetic compass had sent Columbus to America in 1492 and helped Magellan circumnavigate the globe in 1520. What Bacon was pointing out—his scientific interests provided him with an important clue—was a crucial watershed in European history. Modern times, in fact, were beginning, and Europe was acquiring technological knowledge from China that would give it such an immense advantage over the 'Empire of all under Heaven' in the nineteenth century.

Some Western Travellers to the Orient
Apart from the Polos there were other travellers who were attracted to the Mongol Court. Not all of them have left records

of their journeys, but we know something of the following men and their motives:

● *Friar John of Pian di Carpine*. An Italian Franciscan, he set off in 1245 as an ambassador from Pope Innocent IV. The Catholic Church was worried at the ease with which the Mongols were sweeping westwards, claiming to be both universal and divinely inspired. John was joined by Friar Benedict, a Pole, in Breslau. They passed through Kiev in mid-winter shortly after its devastation by the Mongol horde. On their arrival in Mongolia they discovered that a new Khan, Guyug, was being elected at the Shira Ordo, or the Yellow Camp, near to Kara-korum, where they were amazed to find a large number of Westerners already in residence. These were mainly the envoys of East European rulers, and slaves. Having exchanged gifts and letters with Guyug, they met Cosmos, a Russian goldsmith, who introduced them to some Nestorian Christians. They arrived back in Lyons bearing Guyug's answer on 18th November 1247.

The earliest travellers heading East were really entering the unknown. Legend, folklore, and superstition were the main sources of information on the East. Fabulous monsters and strange men with dogs heads, or single feet, or faces between the shoulder blades, lived there. Oddly enough the Chinese had the same sort of idea of the West as this illustration of a headless Westerner shows (early fifteenth century).

● *Friar William of Rubruck*. He travelled as a missionary, not as a political ambassador, and his aim was to obtain converts and establish contacts with the groups of enslaved Catholics known to exist in the East. He reached Karakorum in late December 1253. Guyug had just died and been replaced by Mongke who interviewed the Friar shortly after his arrival. William was amazed at the international nature of court society, recording the presence of an Englishman named Basil. After contacting Boucher, a famed Parisian artist and architect, one of the involuntary army of technicians employed at Karakorum, he was able to record more comprehensively the life of the tented city. (Boucher's adopted son spoke Mongolian.) He recorded that Chinese craftsmen were esteemed for pottery manufacture and building and made the first report of their use of paper money and calligraphy. He co-operated with the Nestorian Church,

Life at the Court of Genghiz Khan.

195

celebrating joint masses, in the hope of gaining court support for Christianity. However, competition for favour was strong as Buddhists, Taoists and Mohammedans were all attempting the same. The Mongol leader always encouraged any faith that would contribute its prayers to his spiritual well-being but found William too zealous and uncompromising. At one point a debate between the Christians, Buddhists and Moslems was arranged as an entertainment, the only rule being that no abusive language was to be used. Few converts were made and William returned to France in 1255.

● *John of Montecorvino.* An Italian Franciscan, he set off for Cathay in 1290, before the Polos returned. He knew the Khan gave protection to Christians but all that was known of China itself was that it was the ancient Seres (from Serica, Latin for silk). He departed from Venice to preach for several months in Tabriz, where he was joined by a Dominican, Nicholas, and an Italian merchant Peter of Lucalango. They left Persia by sea to avoid the war between Kubilai and his cousin in Central Asia. After preaching in Southern India, where Nicholas died, and surviving a hazardous journey round what is now West Malaysia, they arrived at Peking in 1294, just after Kubilai's death. The new ruler's son-in-law, Prince George of Ongut, was converted to Catholicism, to become the first Catholic ruler of East Asia. Two churches were opened, one paid for by Peter of Lucalango out of his profits, and forty slave boys were bought and trained as choristers in Latin. John of Montecorvino became first Archbishop of Khanbaluc (Peking), dying as first Patriarch of the Orient (1328).

● *Odoric, the Roving Friar.* He reached Peking in 1325 and, while fulfilling less of a political or religious function, was the keenest observer of the Chinese. He mentioned for the first time the binding of women's feet, the long nails of Chinese gentlemen, and the use of cormorants for fishing. On his return to Europe many of his stories were greeted with incredulity and ridicule.

● *Ibn Battuta* (1304–77). He was the greatest traveller of Islam and his reports on China were more perceptive and influential on technological changes than his predecessors'. He described the construction of Chinese ships, the making of porcelain, machinery for raising water, and even old-age pensions. Zaiton (Ch'uan Chou) had a large Moslem community largely from Persia and it contained the oldest Mosque in China.

6 The Chinese Revival

The Ming Dynasty, A.D. 1368–1644

HISTORICAL OUTLINE

The Mongols were thrown back to their homeland. In 1372 general Hsu Ta crossed the Gobi desert, sacked Karakorum, and pursued what Mongol forces remained into the fastness of Siberia. By the time the first Ming Emperor, Hung Wu, died (1398) the Chinese Empire had enjoyed thirty years of peace at home and successful conquest abroad. Ming armies annexed Yunnan and Liaotung, besides re-establishing Chinese authority over much of Central Asia, while Annam and Korea became tributaries. 'Rule like the T'ang and the Sung' was the advice Emperor Hung Wu had carved on his tomb. His successors did restore Chinese unity and tradition but the Ming Empire was bright rather than golden. The administration was neither as efficient as the T'ang nor as enlightened as the Sung. The harsh punishments meted out to rebels during the Ming Empire suggests that a legacy of the Mongol invasion was a less humane standard of war and politics. Entrance for the civil service examinations was still theoretically open to all candidates, though the development of costly associated customs made advancement the privilege

日月 *Ming* means bright, clear or brilliant. Chu Yuan-chang chose this name for the dynasty he successfully established in 1368. Usually an ancient name connected with the first emperor's birthplace or background was adopted—Liu Pang had called his house the Han from territories held by him at the downfall of the Ch'in dynasty—but the Ming Emperor Hung Wu departed from the traditional practice. It has been suggested that his obscure origins may have prompted this innovation, but the need to revive China and recreate the civilization so badly mauled by the Mongol invasion could be responsible for the choice. The Ming period was a time of brightness for Chinese culture, an era of restoration in which efforts were directly concerned with reviving the glories of the T'ang and Sung Empires.

of the rich. As estimate for 1469 seems to show there were over 100 000 civil and 80 000 military officials in the imperial service. Moreover, the use of eunuchs eventually led to serious clashes within the administration, though the *shih* made vigorous attempts to check the growth of eunuch influence through the permitted criticisms of the Censorate, and a number of child emperors gave unscrupulous eunuchs ample scope to repeat the worst experiences of the Court at the close of the Han Empire.

Emperor Yung Lo

The Emperor Yung Lo, uncle of the second Ming ruler, was commander of the northern armies at Peking when he usurped the throne (1402). Nanking, the capital of Hung Wu, was badly damaged in the civil war and Yung Lo decided to transfer the Court to Peking, where he felt most secure. The present imperial palace, or Forbidden City, is his work. Building the new capital and deepening the Grand Canal took immense resources in terms of both manpower and materials.

LANGUAGE AND THE MOVEMENT SOUTH
Old Forms   Present day

YUEH, meaning to speak, to tell. The mouth ⼝ exhales ∟ a breath, a word.

TA, meaning piled up or crowded together. It also means flow. A flow 沝 of words 曰. So 沝 is used to denote a babbling flow of talk.

The process by which Chinese civilization absorbed the indigenous peoples of the South was a natural extension of the economic penetration that had been in progress since earliest times. During the Kin and Mongol periods large-scale population movements were common, but the southern expansion of the Chinese people is an historical event that has lasted several thousand years. The Chinese trader was followed by his family and their language gradually converted the native tongue into a semi-Chinese dialect. The wealthier natives became bilingual, and later their children started to speak Chinese as a first language. Speech and custom are closely bound together, hence the assimilation of these people into 'the hundred families'. An important function of the Chinese language, with its neutral script, has been this capacity to accommodate non-Chinese peoples: it has maintained the ecosystem.

One million workmen are said to have completed the Forbidden City in just ten years, so that it has been likened to the 'Great Leaps' undertaken in the People's Republic. The northern site of the capital was to prove a grave disadvantage towards the end of the dynasty. Peking, forty miles from the Great Wall, was unnecessarily exposed to attack from the steppes and an extreme distance from the now dominant South. Preoccupation with the defence of the northern frontier may have been a cause of the cessation of naval operations (1433), which has left China vulnerable from the sea for the last four centuries. Opposition from the *shih* was certainly another factor—Cheng Ho, appointed admiral of the fleets by Emperor Yung Lo, was a eunuch.

Although there were many military and naval expeditions—Emperor Yung Lo died on the way back from a campaign in Mongolia (1424)—the reign was a period of internal peace and prosperity. Building activity was conspicuous: city walls, paved roads, bridges, temples, shrines, tombs, villas, palaces, gardens and other monuments were built throughout the provinces of the Empire. Writers and painters flourished, their works form today a major part of the Chinese heritage. China seemed to have not only recovered but reached new heights of achievement. However, it is during the Ming dynasty that for the first time China lagged behind the progress made in other countries, and particularly Western Europe. Marco Polo had taken back tales of wonder about the Yuan Empire, but the final hundred years of the Ming Empire were marked by a steady decline, a fact not lost on the Europeans, who sailed along the Chinese coast; the Portuguese came first in 1514, the Dutch in 1622, and the English in 1637.

The Decline of the Ming Empire
The disaster of Huai Lai (1450) was the turning point for the Ming Empire. The eunuch Wang Chin had gained the confidence of Emperor Cheng T'ung during his youth and he used this influence to persuade the inexperienced ruler that a Mongolian expedition was necessary, despite protests from senior generals. Wang Chin wanted to display his power by entertaining the Emperor in his hometown, Huai Lai, near the northern frontier. The eunuch was given command of the forces raised for the campaign and his generalship proved disastrous. A nomad host destroyed the Chinese army outside Huai Lai and Emperor Cheng T'ung was carried off as a prisoner. Though the nomads were not strong enough to exploit this sudden victory, they had gained the military advantage over the Ming Empire. In 1644 another northern tribe, the Manchus, were to find an entrance through the Great Wall and found a new foreign dynasty.

199

Cheng Ho, the eunuch admiral, had been a loyal supporter of the imperial house. His skill as a naval commander and a diplomat became legend. Unfortunately, the rise and fall of Wang Chin was a sign that the times had changed. In 1510, when Liu Chin, another favourite, was disgraced, officials discovered that the greedy eunuch had amassed an immense fortune. His private stock of precious metal included the equivalent of 251 583 600 ounces of silver in unminted pieces of gold and silver. Corruption had become a widespread feature of the administration, an activity that not all of the *shih* could resist as well. The old ways were breaking down. Ineffectual government was aggravated by a series of economic crises, partly the result of pressure upon the land by a rising population of about two hundred millions. Famines began to recur, accompanied by popular rebellions. The long reigns of Emperor Chia Ching (1520–66) and Emperor Wan Li (1572–1620) helped the declining Empire, though the improvement in administration was due to the work of 'loyal' *shih* like Chang Ku-ching.

The Shun Dynasty and the Manchu Invasion
In 1618 the Manchu tribes united and invaded Liaotung. Ming armies remained continually engaged against the growing Manchu power, which reached the Great Wall itself by 1629. That vast fortification might have been sufficient to have withheld the Manchus, had not internal discord given them an entrance. For the Manchus were not the same kind of people as the Mongols. Their proximity to Chinese culture had begun the process of conversion from nomads to settled agriculturalists even before Nurhachu made them a single nation. What provided the Manchus with their chance of conquest was the civil war that ended the Ming dynasty in 1644, when Li Tzu-ch'eng, an ex-bandit, had captured Peking with his rebel army, whose numbers were increased by famine refugees, and proclaimed himself the first Emperor of the Shun dynasty. But general Wu San-kuei, the commander of the Ming army defending the Great Wall, refused to acknowledge that the Mandate of Heaven had passed to the Shun. Repeating the error of the Tsin dynasty in the third century A.D., Wu offered the Manchus an alliance against Li and opened the gate at Shanhaikuan. Perhaps he intended to gain time by this policy of friendship with the Manchus, thereby using his forces to defeat the usurper and gain the throne himself. Li was soon vanquished but the complicated struggle that followed gave the Manchus the opportunity

to make themselves masters of all the Empire (1682). In this they had greater success than the Hsiung Nu, called in by the Tsin Emperor.

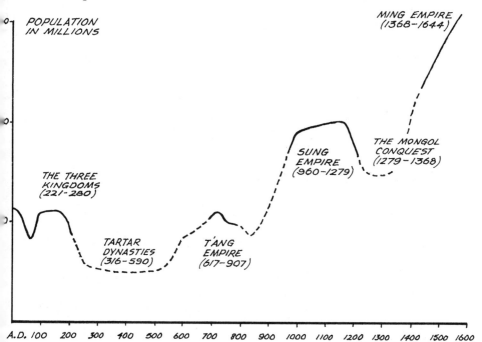

A Han census figure for A.D. 2 gives the population of the Empire as 58 million, which may be somewhat overlarge as a figure. Civil strife, floods and disease soon reduced this number, though during the stability of the Later Han just over 50 million was maintained. Tartar invasions (316–590) reduced the numbers of Chinese people living in Chinese-controlled territories by half, though the reunification under the Sui (589–618) led on to the T'ang Empire and a stable population of over 50 million. In the same way the Sung Empire permitted population growth, which was only arrested, temporarily, by the Mongol Conquest (1279–1368). The Ming Empire topped 150 million. However, the T'ang and Sung figures may prove an underestimate because only those people liable to tax were included in the census.

ECONOMY AND SOCIETY

The Ming dynasty began in a strong, purposeful and ruthless spirit and for a hundred years or more provided an efficient framework for economic advance, particularly in trade and

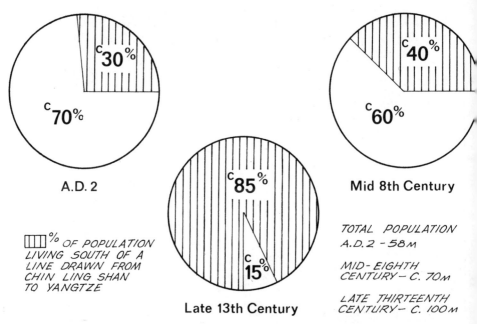

A.D. 2

Mid 8th Century

Late 13th Century

^{c}30%
^{c}70%

^{c}40%
^{c}60%

^{c}85%
^{c}15%

▥ % OF POPULATION
LIVING SOUTH OF A
LINE DRAWN FROM
CHIN LING SHAN
TO YANGTZE

TOTAL POPULATION
A.D. 2 - 58M

MID - EIGHTH
CENTURY - C. 70M

LATE THIRTEENTH
CENTURY - C. 100M

agriculture. After 1500 it was increasingly affected by conservatism, nepotism and corruption in which increased wealth was achieved not by innovation and improvement but by extortion and parasitical exploitation of the rural masses, the *nung*.

Agricultural Development
The Khans had recognized the danger of having a capital in the north which was dependent on southern grain supplies. Sea transport was affected by pirates and storms. The Grand Canal was a great engineering feat but was frequently damaged by floods and changes in the course of the Yellow River. Frequent attempts were made during more stable periods to increase the agricultural efficiency of the North. The harsher climate of the North with the frequent catastrophes of drought, flooding and continuous erosion, combined with its frequency as a theatre of war, had led to a continuous movement southward of its population. To counteract this and to try to make Peking self-supporting, government land was distributed as a reward to Ming supporters. Free seed, oxen and tools were made available and plantations of Chinese settlers reached as far north as the fertile South Manchuria plain. These measures successfully increased output but also stimulated a rapid population increase which nullified its impact.

Rice provided about seventy per cent of China's grain needs and the Ming sought to diversify grain production to reduce this reliance. Contact with the Western countries, who were familiar with the crops of the Americas, led to the introduction of groundnuts, the sweet potato and maize in the sixteenth century. However, these did not become widely accepted until the eighteenth century. Groundnuts were particularly suited to sandy soils unfit for rice and they were most easily adopted in the newly developing territories of Yunnan and western Kwangtung. Maize entered by the ports and also overland via India and Burma; before 1650 it was largely found in the South West. The sweet potato had similarity to existing Chinese crops, yams and taros. Being drought-resistant and high yielding the sweet potato was assimilated more rapidly and widely.

Early European visitors in the sixteenth century were impressed with the efficiency of Chinese agriculture. A Portuguese merchant-writer Pereira wrote: 'Not one foot of ground is left untilled' and 'the dung farmers seek in every street by exchange to buy this dirty ware for herbs and wood. The custom is very good for keeping the city clean.' He also called the 'Chins' the 'greatest eaters in the world.' Fish formed a substantial part of the diet in South China. Tame, trained cormorants were used to catch fish in rivers and at sea, while many artificial ponds had been created where the fish were 'farmed.' Mendes Pinto, another Portuguese who was captured as a pirate and transported from Nanking to Peking along the Grand Canal, noted the hard working peasantry, the careful use of manure, and the extremely common activity of duck raising.

Population Growth and the Movement South
Whether agricultural improvement stimulated population growth or population growth stimulated agricultural development is still debated. What is certain is that population rose rapidly from around 80 to 150 million and that a great amount of land was brought into cultivation for the first time. A conscious policy of colonization was carried out particularly in the south-western areas of Yunnan, Kwangsi and Kweichow.

The south-west had been controlled by the Kingdom of Nanchao which developed its strength thanks to an early alliance with the T'ang. Having come to dominate other kingdoms of the area, it took on and defeated the armies of its former ally and turned westwards to invade Burma. The people of Nanchao were mixed tribal groups dominated by the advanced rice-

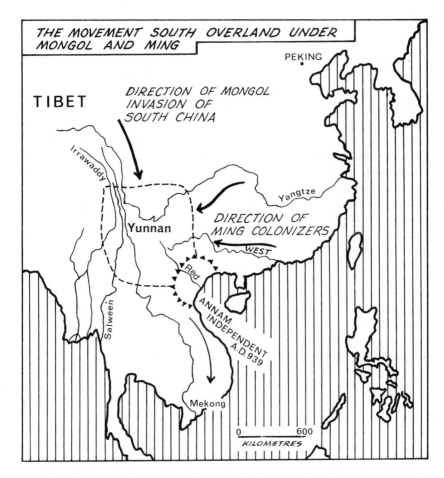

growing Pai of the Tali plain. Tali was an important strategic site and lay on a fertile plain which seldom suffered drought or flood and whose tropical latitude was modified by the altitude of 2000 metres. They expanded their territory eastwards absorbing areas of Chinese settlement and gradually became increasingly sinicized. In the tenth century the kingdom was overthrown by a grandee of Chinese descent who formed the Tali Kingdom. Tali maintained an allegiance to the Sung dynasty, which left it largely alone. Gradually the kingdom consolidated itself in Yunnan. The Mongols invaded South China in 1252, through Tali, taking it by surprise after marching 960 kilometres over difficult terrain. A hundred years later it was the last Mongol stronghold to hold out against the Ming. It was reduced and incorporated officially into China in 1382.

With the inflow of troops came many settlers from the Yangtze valley. They rapidly established themselves on the plains and fertile river valleys, driving the more primitive shifting cultivators on to upper slopes and forcing the stone-age hunters and collectors into the highest and most inaccessible areas. Cities developed as miniatures of Peking. The region was connected to the capital by paved roads, and iron-chain bridges crossed the valleys of the Salween and Mekong. Emperor Yung Lo had great slabs of marble transported by road and river from Tali in 1405, for the construction of the Imperial Palace at Peking.

Not all the settlers were voluntary pioneer farmers, many were forced exiles from many parts of China. As they would tend to go to areas occupied by others from their own home provinces they maintained their own dialect and regional customs. The inhabitants of K'unming, the provincial capital, speak with a close affinity to Peking colloquial speech, while those of Paoshan,

THE STRATEGIC LOCATION OF TALI

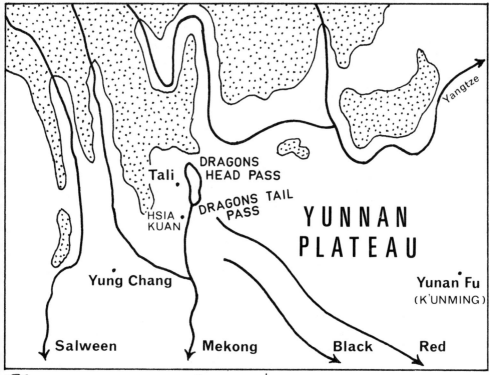

LAND OVER 3000 M (10 000 FT)
THE TALI PLAIN LIES AT 2000M (7000 FT) WHILE THE
YUNNAN PLATEAU FALLS TO 1200M (4 000 FT) IN THE EAST

between the Mekong and Salween rivers, speak the dialect of Nanking. The people of Tali have strong native Pai or Tai accents. Little attempt was made to integrate the 'raw' or uncivilized tribes of Yunnan but those which were considered 'ripe' for improvement were allowed employment and acceptance after receiving some Chinese education.

The settlement of Yunnan by the Chinese ensured that it remained part of the Empire. Wherever territories were merely administered by imperial officials there was always a danger that independence movements would form. Vietnam, centred on the Red River Basin, was a Chinese province for a thousand years but in the tenth century freed itself. It was peopled by the fiercely nationalistic Yüeh peoples who had been decimated or pushed southwards from Chekiang, Fukien and Kwangtung. Since the Chinese were busy colonizing the Yangtze Valley and the coastal areas, they never really sinicized the Red River Basin. Emperor Yung Lo's invasion and occupation from 1407 to 1427 was the last attempt to incorporate Vietnam as a province of China. After this the Vietnamese continued to pay tribute, while beginning their own southward policy of colonization which excluded Chinese from directly controlling the south-east peninsula.

Decline in the North
By the mid-sixteenth century the Ming dynasty was in decline.
- Pirates were virtually controlling the sea coast south of Hangchow.
- Corruption was increasing as more power was placed in the hands of the eunuchs. Offices were created or maintained after the need had passed. Some superintendents of rivers had no rivers to supervise since they had changed course.
- Taxation was increasing to support the wasteful bureaucracy.
- Famine was increasingly common, particularly in the North.
- Tenant farmers were increasingly exploited by the great landlords.

Ming supporters had been rewarded with estates or 'plantations' at the beginning of the dynasty and subsequent Emperors adopted this means of reward. The plantations varied from around 400 hectares to nearly 40000 hectares at a time when a farmer owning 6 hectares was considered prosperous. The landlords used threats to expand their plantations at the expense of small surrounding farms and were able to use their influence to abuse the protection offered in law. They often lived in the major cities, squandering the wealth of the countryside on luxurious living and leaving a manager to extort the highest profit from the labouring *nung*. The Emperors were given warning as early as 1489 when the Minister of Finance, Li Min, in a memorial to the Emperor wrote:

> Within the capital area there are five royal plantations with a total area of 12 800 *ch'ing* [c. 77 500 hectares]. Besides these, there are 332 plantations with a total acreage of 33 000 *ch'ing* [c. 199 700 hectares] owned by royal relatives and eunuchs. Plantation managers and their subordinates hire hoodlums and ruffians to do their bidding. They forcibly take over people's land, extort their money and other valuables, and debauch their wives and daughters. If people dare to make the slightest protest, they find themselves being sued on fabricated charges. The sheriff comes to arrest them, and their whole families tremble with fear. This is why people hate the plantation managers to the marrow of their bones.

Taxes were so crippling, even in the richest parts of the Yangtze Valley, by the mid-seventeenth century that people were being forced to sell their children to meet tax payments. In assessing taxes the government made sure to include all land owned by a tenant even where used for ditches and roads and therefore non-productive. In 1628 a terrible famine in Shensi was recorded in this memorial to the Emperor:

> Your humble servant was born in Anse subprefecture, Shensi province. I have read many memorials submitted by Your Majesty's officials in connection with the present state of affairs. They say that famine has caused fathers to desert their children and husbands to sell their wives. They also say that many people are so starved that they eat grass roots and white stones. But the real situation is worse than that which they have described. Yenan, the prefecture from which your humble servant comes, has not had any rain for more than a year. Trees and grasses are all dried up. During the eighth and the ninth moon months of last year people went to the mountains to collect raspberries which were called grain but actually were no better than chaff. They tasted bitter and they could only postpone death for the time being. By the tenth moon month all raspberries were gone, and people peeled off tree bark for food. Among tree bark the best was that of the elm. This was so precious that to consume as little as possible people mixed it with the bark of other trees to feed themselves. Somehow they were able to prolong their lives. Towards the end of the year the supply of tree bark was exhausted, and they had to go to the mountains to dig up stones as

food. Stones were cold and tasted musty. A little taken in would fill up the stomach. Those who took stones found their stomachs swollen and they dropped and died in a few days. Others who did not wish to eat stones gathered as bandits. They robbed the few who had some savings, and when they robbed, they took everything and left nothing behind. Their idea was that since they had to die either one way or another it was preferable to die as a bandit than to die from hunger and that to die as a bandit would enable them to enter the next world with a full stomach. . . .

The starving *nung* were joined by mutinous troops from South Manchuria whose pay had not been forthcoming, and also a large number of redundant coolies who suffered from the disbanding of the Imperial posting system. This made the North more vulnerable than ever and the Manchus were able to sweep down towards Peking with little opposition.

MARITIME EXPANSION IN THE EARLY MING DYNASTY

The Background to Expansion

We have stressed the 'continental' and anti-commercial nature of early Chinese culture and yet by the Southern Sung dynasty China was obviously the home of the world's largest mercantile and maritime cities. This dualism had developed for many reasons:

● the continual and accelerating movement of Chinese to the once sparsely populated and hostile south-east coast (Yüeh);

● a high level of nautical technology and science;

● a decline in prejudice against trading as an occupation when its profitability was realized. Kao Tsung, accredited founder of the Chinese navy, said in 1143: 'Profits from maritime commerce are great; if properly managed they can amount to millions. Is this not better than taxing the people?'

Long before Kao Tsung, Chinese vessels had plied the Indian and China Seas. The Persian Gulf and the Red Sea were frequented before the eighth century A.D. From this time until the fourteenth century Arabs dominated these routes, establishing settlements in the Chinese ports and monopolizing the spice trade to the West. But the fifteenth century saw a Chinese recovery that was both spectacular and short-lived.

Cheng Ho's Mission to the Western Oceans

'In the third year of the Yung Lo reign period (1405) the Imperial Palace Eunuch Cheng Ho was sent on a mission to the Western Oceans.' Thus, a Chinese historical work of 1767 introduces a chapter of Chinese history that fully indicates the potential of the fifteenth-century Chinese mercantile marine, which, if it had been backed by a 'crusading mentality,' might have put the Chinese in Europe before da Gama reached India.

Cheng Ho was a Muslim from Yunnan who became an admiral, ambassador and explorer responsible for seven major voyages between 1405 and 1433. These voyages were made on behalf of the Emperor and the reasons were manifold.

● It was commonly thought that the Emperor was searching for his predecessor who had supposedly fled westward in 1403.

● More likely the voyages were designed to magnify and extend the grandeur and prestige of the Imperial Court both at home and abroad.

● They may have been an attempt to counteract a reduction in overland trade with the West following the break up of the Mongol Empire.

Each voyage combined diplomatic functions, such as the exaction of 'tribute,' with commercial enterprise and scientific discovery. Local rulers felt little compunction about giving tribute to the distant Chinese Emperor when they received in exchange much wanted gifts of porcelain, jade, lacquer, silk and cotton.

The voyages of the Imperial Fleet were as follows:

1   1405–07 to Champa, Java, Sumatra, Ceylon and Calicut;
2   1407–09 to Siam and Cochin;
3   1409–11 to Malacca, Quilon and Ceylon;
4   1413–15 to Bengal, Maldive Islands and Hormuz;
5   1417–19 to Java, Brunei, Hormuz, Aden, Somaliland and Malindi;
6   1421–2 to South Arabia.

The Emperor then died and his successor, Hsia Yuan-chi, reversed this policy with the following statement in 1424: 'If there are any ships already anchored in Fukien or Thai-tshang they must return at once to Nanking, and all the building of sea-going ships for intercourse with barbarian countries must cease at once.' His early death provided a short reprieve for Cheng Ho and the seventh voyage was commissioned between 1431 and 1433 going to Java, Nicobar, Mecca and Al Zaij.

Cheng Ho's initial fleet of 62 treasure-ships contained the

largest ships known to the world. They were over 134 metres long and 55 metres in their broadest beam. They had 3 super-imposed decks and up to 9 masts. The upper decks and poop

A seventeenth-century European view of junk construction at Kowloon. Hong Kong is in the background. By this time junks were much smaller than Cheng Ho's.

could override the beams by up to 30 per cent. The rudder was about 6 metres long. (In 1962 a rudder post 10 metres long was discovered from one of these ships.) They carried cannon, and a crew of over 400.

Chinese and Portuguese Voyages Compared
While the 'Three-Jewel Eunuch' was exploring the east coast of Africa, the Portuguese were edging southwards down the west coast. Diaz rounded the Cape in 1488, about sixty years

after the Chinese. There were fundamental differences in the voyages of the Europeans and the Chinese.

● The Chinese voyages were an extension of a pattern which had occurred before (even if a long time before). The Portuguese voyages were unprecedented.

● The Chinese vessels were larger versions of traditional craft. The Portuguese were experimenting with triangular, lateen sails borrowed from the Arabs, with the marine compass and stern-post rudder which had originated in China, and multiple masts which were a common feature of Asian craft.

● The treasure-ships of Cheng Ho weighed up to 1 500 tonnes compared with 300 tonnes for da Gama's ships.

● The Portuguese maintained a 'conquistador mentality' with large-scale slaving and warring. Although Chinese fleets were armed and threats were commonly used to exact tribute, they had few skirmishes. They established no forts and founded no colonies.

● Portuguese mercantile activity was based on a private enterprise search for personal fortune; the search for the mythical El Dorado. The Chinese voyages were an extension of state bureaucracy with incidental, if somewhat large, trading. Portuguese hopes lay in the slave trade and the breaking of the Arab spice monopoly. Chinese ambitions lay in the collection of drugs and medical knowledge and materials such as rhino horn, and exotic beasts like giraffes and zebras.

● The Portuguese were in the position of wanting goods from the East but of having nothing the East wanted in exchange; thus, they had to pay in gold bullion which was not very satisfactory. On the other hand, China had lots to offer the countries to the West but found little it needed there, and so never had the same bullion problem.

● Except where an alliance with heretics suited them, the Portuguese extended the reign of terror associated with the Inquisition into their colonies and trading ports. The Chinese were 'all things to all men,' distinguishing the different religions, and making gifts to leaders of all.

Why the Chinese Voyages Ceased

Thirty-six countries in the Western Ocean sent tribute to China, acknowledging the Mings' overlordship. These included eight from the East Indies, eleven from India and Ceylon, five from Persia and Arabia, and five from the east coast of Africa.

However, such returns were not sufficient to placate the Confucian scholar-landlords who felt the Emperor was devoting too much attention and money to the ventures of the eunuchs. Confucianism was losing its scientific humanism to an anti-scientific idealism which was to encourage lethargy and conservatism, particularly under the next dynasty, the Ch'ing.

East–West maritime exploration in the fifteenth century.

212

Furthermore, the northern frontier was under attack from the Mongols and Tartars, making Peking very vulnerable. By 1474 only 140 warships out of 400 survived after a long period of neglect and hostile legislation. In 1500 it became illegal to build a sea-going junk with more than two masts and in 1551 it became treasonable to go to sea in a multiple masted ship. It was decided that the Chinese lost more than they gained through such maritime contacts and a period of withdrawal from maritime intercourse ensued until the Europeans prised China open. One effect of this was to weaken the south coast defences, virtually handing over the seas to an increasing number of Japanese pirates. At the same time there was a reversal of migratory trends towards that area. The further development of the Grand Canal reduced the amount of coastal traffic and tended to reinforce the role of the North as the focal point for Ming internal development.

A Ming carved lacquer cup-stand of the type highly valued in the West. The arrival of such treasures in the West stimulated a whole range of copies known as 'Chinoiserie' which became extremely fashionable.

213

THE COMING OF THE EUROPEANS

By 1440 the Ming dynasty was reducing contact with barbarian merchants by the force of law. At the same time the Renaissance spirit was sweeping Europe, stimulating a desire for knowledge, and bizarre luxury. Coupled with this in southern Catholic Europe was the Inquisition with its fanatical desire to convert all to the Church of Rome. These two forces conspired to put the Portuguese in Canton harbour for the first time in 1514.

Since they were dealing with pagans the Portuguese and Spaniards had no scruples about using violence in the interests of profit. They had no wish to return from such hazardous voyages empty-handed. Naturally the Chinese came to the conclusion that Westerners were merely marauding pirates. As the barbarians had no manners or understanding of Chinese etiquette it was difficult for them to be accepted as 'bearers of tribute,' which had become virtually a euphemism for traders.

The Portuguese established themselves as intermediaries between Malacca, their colony in the southern archipelago, and South China. They were also involved in smuggling. Since the cities of the Southern coast were dependent on trade for their survival they increasingly argued for a relaxation of government restrictions. In 1557 Macao was allocated to the Portuguese as a base for their 'factories' or warehouses. It was hoped that this would confine their activities and keep them out of the other ports such as Canton and Ch'uan Chou.

The growing wealth of the Portuguese encouraged rivalry from other European states. The Dutch were twice refused permission to trade in the early seventeenth century and operated as smugglers from Taiwan. In 1636 the first British China expedition began as a rival to the East India Company. They arrived at Canton a year later to be rebuffed by the governor of the city. The captain of the fleet, John Weddell, was determined not to return empty-handed. Naturally, they received no co-operation from the Portuguese at Macao and when the Chinese made the mistake of firing a few badly aimed cannon balls at them, they landed and took the city without much trouble. The Chinese garrison's feeble defence amazed the sailors. A compromise was achieved after two English merchants were captured. One cargo of ginger, silk and porcelain was allowed to be loaded on condition that the fleet left rapidly.

While the traders were considered ignominious barbarians, many Jesuit missionaries who accompanied them became

Sketches from the notebooks of Peter Mundy, a Cornish sailor who visited China in 1634.

accepted. Matteo Ricci landed in China in 1583 at the age of 31. He had studied mathematics, astronomy and cartography and took the trouble to learn the language, philosophy and customs of China. He preached near to Canton, dressed as a Mandarin, until he was allowed to go to Peking in 1607. His gifts to the Emperor included a crucifix and paintings of Christ and the Virgin Mary—they were not well received. However, two clocks sufficiently impressed the court to grant him a favoured position as a scientist and translator rather than as a preacher. Some influential converts were made, and increasingly Jesuits were entrusted with the preparation of maps, translations of such books as encyclopaedias and Galileo's writings. In 1611 Father Adam Schall headed a team of priests in revising the Imperial Calendar. Before Ricci died in 1610 he had observed

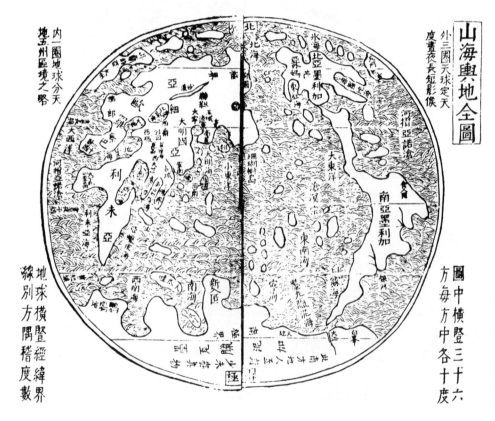

Matteo Ricci's map of the world sensibly placed China at the centre and thus overcame their prejudices against it.

that the Chinese army was underpowered. Although gunpowder was a Chinese invention dating back several hundred years, its main use was for fireworks. Their cannon were inefficient and small in number. Later Jesuits designed and cast better cannon after European models. An order for 500 was placed with Schall in 1640, only four years before the Ming dynasty fell. It was obviously too late.

Father Adam Schall as a mandarin of the first class.

217

The success of the Jesuits and the privileges of movement they obtained from the Court, encouraged other missionary groups from Europe. However, the Dominicans and Franciscans failed to appreciate the need for pragmatism and compromise over deep rooted cultural traits and criticized the Jesuits for doing so. The long debates and increasing rivalry between the different orders did little to encourage the Chinese to change their views and overall few converts were made (perhaps 200 000 in the seventeenth century).

Foreign devil, 1839:
Chinese sketch of a
fire-breathing English sailor.

YANG KUEI TZU or 'Ocean Devils' was the nickname the Ming Chinese used for Europeans. It has been unfortunate for international relations that the first impressions of people from Western Europe gained by China were so uniformly bad.

Albuquerque, the second Portuguese viceroy in the East, who captured Goa (1510) and Malacca (1512), told the Sultan of Calicut that he had come 'for Christians and spices.' Possibly the Ming Court was warned by Arab traders—whose activities had been tolerated for over 700 years—but the piratical behaviour of Portuguese visitors at Canton, Ningpo and Ch'uan Chou (1549) only served to confirm Chinese suspicions. It was not until 1598 that Ricci was permitted to travel to Peking and explain the Catholic faith. But the Protestant nations behaved in much the same way. The Dutch and the English were quick to seize opportunities for plunder.

218

PEKING

Under the Ming rule there was a definite reaction against the unplanned, sprawling, mercantile cities of the South, such as Hangchow and Ch'uan Chou. Traditional town-planning concepts were re-introduced and the walls of 500 cities were entirely reconstructed by the New Ministry of Public Works. The centre of gravity in political and economic terms shifted north and inland towards the cradle of Chinese civilization. Symbolic of this change was the choice of Peking as capital to replace Nanking in 1409.

Peking was on the site of Khanbaluc, the Yuan capital. Kubilai had followed the classical chessboard pattern on a north–south axis when he commissioned the city. The walls were over 25 kilometres long and up to 12 metres high. While the Ming had little to do but extend this existing pattern little now remains of the Yuan city. The Bell Tower which lay at the centre of Khanbaluc today lies to the north of the Imperial Palace which indicates a southward expansion of the city under the Ming.

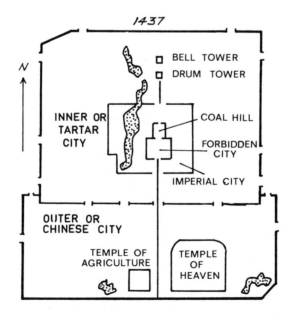

Peking in the Ming Dynasty.

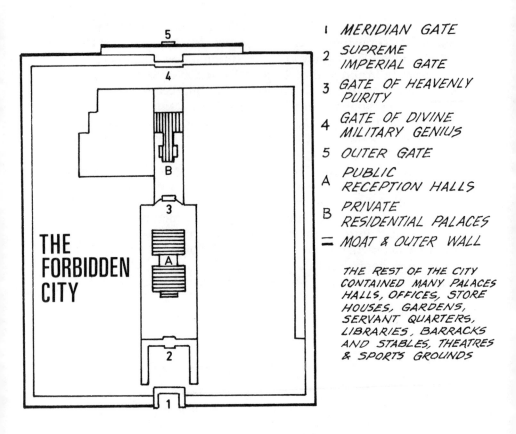

1	MERIDIAN GATE
2	SUPREME IMPERIAL GATE
3	GATE OF HEAVENLY PURITY
4	GATE OF DIVINE MILITARY GENIUS
5	OUTER GATE
A	PUBLIC RECEPTION HALLS
B	PRIVATE RESIDENTIAL PALACES
=	MOAT & OUTER WALL

THE FOREST OF THE CITY CONTAINED MANY PALACES HALLS, OFFICES, STORE HOUSES, GARDENS, SERVANT QUARTERS, LIBRARIES, BARRACKS AND STABLES, THEATRES & SPORTS GROUNDS

THE FORBIDDEN CITY

The city walls enclose four distinct sections. *The Inner, Tartar, or Northern City*, enclosed in 1437 by a wall 24 kilometres long. This in turn surrounds the *Imperial City* with its wall 10 kilometres long. Within this section lies the *Purple Forbidden City* containing the Imperial Palace, again protected by its own wall. The growth of suburbs to the south led to the incorporation of *the 'Outer' or Chinese* city in 1544 by a wall 22 kilometres long. The latter contained the important Temples of Agriculture (from 1422) and Temple of Heaven (1420). These temples were parks containing halls and altars for prayers and sacrifice. The Outer city was very congested particularly along the avenues from the main gates. The noise, smell, and volume of traffic, amazed visitors. Commercial activity was as intense as one would expect in a city of 500 000.

The Temple of Heaven This has been called the 'noblest example of religious architecture in the whole of China.' It lies within a 300-hectare walled enclosure just inside the southern Gate. To the south is the Altar of Heaven where each winter solstice the Emperor offered sacrifice. This was the only time the Emperor faced north to worship instead of facing south to be worshipped. At the northern end lay the Hall of Prayer for Good Harvests where the Emperor prayed on a spring day chosen by the astronomers. This is a magnificent temple with a triple tiered roof covered in blue tiles. The walls, beams and pillars are richly painted in red, blue, gold and green. The three terraces on which it stood were of marble. Both buildings were circular and were surrounded by square courtyards. This symbolized the journey from earth to heaven as one approached the Altar.

221

The Imperial Gardens and menageries on Coal Hill, protecting the Palace from evil northern influences.

If the main north–south avenue was taken from the outer wall the visitor would pass from the Outer to Inner City and be headed directly for the Imperial City. The Inner City appeared just as busy, but away from the main avenues lived the *shih* and the *kung* who worked in the Imperial City. The public were not allowed access to the latter unless on business. Having crossed a moat and passed through the Gate of Heavenly Peace the whole pace of life changed. Few people were about, it was quiet and there was a spacious distribution of classically arranged parks, lakes, halls, pagodas and pavilions. Here the officials and scholar bureaucrats would be at work. At the northern end of the main avenue was the Meridian Gate. Here the Emperor sometimes received tribute from foreign ambassadors.

Within the Forbidden City few were allowed. The southern part was dominated by three aligned halls. First came the Hall of Supreme Harmony where the Emperor gave his audiences; behind this was the Hall of Middle Harmony which was a waiting chamber; the third, the location for state banquets, was the Hall of Protecting Harmony. Beyond these lay the Offices of State, palace workshops and gardens and finally the private quarters which were accessible only to the royal family and their eunuchs. This area contrasted sharply with the rigidity of form elsewhere;

222

Inside the Imperial Palace. Behind the Hall of Supreme Harmony (see below) lay the Hall of General Harmony. In the northern wall of the public part of the Palace was the Gate of Heavenly Purity leading to the private quarters.

Ambassadors at the Meridian Gate in the seventeenth century.

it contained a complex and informal maze of courtyards, alleys and gardens—a perfect setting for palace intrigue.

It is considered that Ming architecture was less adventurous and experimental than that of the Sung. Buildings were plain rectangles, rigidly laid out. However, some features were very striking:

- the sheer scale of construction;
- the increasing use of durable materials such as marble;
- the great increase of colour, particularly through the use of porcelain tiles, the painting of eaves, and the use of gold leaf, while marble bridges and steps contrasted with the pink, red and gold walls, yellow and blue-tiled roofs, and blue, red and gold eaves;
- widespread use of curved roofs in which all four faces of the roof swept down to the eaves thus eliminating the east- and west-facing gable ends typical of the Sung;
- the corbel brackets were increasingly decorative rather than functional in the largest buildings.

Ming architecture was far more durable than its predecessors. Even where fire or age created a need to replace an official building the increasing conservatism of later Chinese architects preserved the styles and techniques of the period.

PLAYS, NOVELS AND POTTERY

The exclusion of the *shih* from the imperial civil service during the Yuan dynasty stimulated the development of two new forms of literature, the play and the novel. Preoccupation with the Confucian Classics was relaxed while the examinations were discontinued. Scholars found themselves free to venture beyond

Papercut of an opera character.

the confines of history, philosophy and poetry and they took up the popular play and novel. In a similar way the potter's art so outstripped painting that the European importers of Ming wares called all porcelain china, after the country that made the finest products. A kind of creative split appeared in Chinese culture, which lasted till 1911. The Ming and Manchu Courts became traditional, antiquarian, backward-looking, as the *shih* wistfully

225

A noble character of the opera, and (below) the opera's version of a mother-in-law.

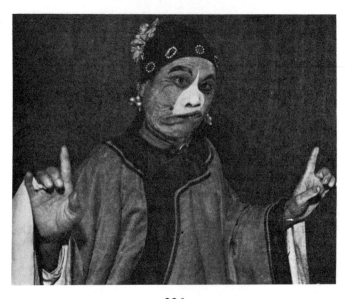

recalled the lost splendours of K'ai Feng and Chang-an, while the more vital and exciting artists worked without imperial patronage.

A fine example of Chinese porcelain.

During the T'ang Empire the manufacture of porcelain was perfected. China clay and china stone were fused at high temperatures to give a hard but translucent ware. Coloured glazes became common as copper, iron and cobalt were added to the colourless lead silicate in order to produce reds, yellows and blues. The North was the major area of innovation.

The fall of K'ai Feng to the Kin (1127) caused refugee potters to set up kilns in the South. Imperial factories were dotted around the Yangtze and associated canals, allowing easy transportation, internally and for export. In the Ming period cobalt blue was the most popular colour. From late Ming times mass production methods steadily reduced the individuality of the potter's art.

Monkey by Wu Ch'êng-ên (1505–80) illustrates the colloquial power of both new forms, since it is a novel that draws on the folk stories and plays that had collected around Tripitaka's pilgrimage to India. The historical Tripitaka, Hsuan Tsang, was greeted by the T'ang Emperor T'ai Tsung in A.D. 645 when he returned to Chang-an with the Buddhist scriptures. By the Southern Sung dynasty (A.D. 1127–1279) a whole cycle of fantastic legends was in existence and the various episodes from the pilgrimage were constantly represented on the Chinese stage. Possibly, *Monkey* is the most widely read book in Chinese literature. Below is a comic extract relating the worsting of the dominant Taoists in Cart Slow Kingdom, where Tripitaka and his three companions, Monkey, Pigsy and Sandy, are not well received. Ingenious and resourceful, Monkey devises a plan to disconcert the religious opponents of the Buddhists and have the pilgrims' passports stamped with travel visas. The knock-about humour may surprise Western readers, though the wisdom of laughter was appreciated by Chuang-tzu long before the foundation of the First Empire and the sceptical tradition of Confucian thought discovered in ridicule a potent weapon against religious fanaticism. Indeed, the humorous story is something close to the Chinese heart.

'Get up and come with me,' said Monkey. 'We're all going to have a treat.' 'Who wants a treat in the middle of the night,' said Sandy, 'when one's mouth is dry and one's eyes won't stay open?' 'The Taoists are celebrating a Mass in their great temple,' said Monkey, 'and the whole place is littered with offerings. There are dumplings that must weigh a quart, and cakes weighing fifty pounds, and all kinds of dainties and fruits. Come and enjoy yourself.' Pigsy, hearing in his sleep something about things to eat, at once woke with a start. 'Brother, you're not going to leave me out of it?' he cried. 'If you like the idea of something to eat,' said Monkey, 'don't make a fuss and wake up the Master, but both of you come quietly with me.'

They dressed quickly and followed Monkey. As soon as they came into the light of the torches, Pigsy wanted to rush in and get to work. 'There's no hurry,' said Monkey. 'Wait till the congregation disperses; then we'll go in and set to.' 'But they're praying for all they're worth,' said Pigsy. 'They have evidently no idea of dispersing.' 'I'll see to that,' said Monkey; and reciting a spell he drew a magic diagram on the ground. Then standing upon it he blew with all his might. At once a great wind rose, which blew down all the flower-vases and lamp-stands and smashed the ex-votos hanging on the walls. The whole place was suddenly in darkness. The Taoists were frightened out of their wits. 'I must ask the congregation to disperse,'

228

said the Tiger Strength Immortal. 'The wind will no doubt subside, and tomorrow morning we will recite a few more scriptures, so that the prescribed number may be reached.'

As soon as the place was empty, the three of them slipped in, and that fool Pigsy began to stuff himself with victuals. Monkey gave him a sharp rap over the knuckles. Pigsy drew back his hand and retreated, saying, 'Wait a bit. I've hardly had time to get my tongue round the things, and he begins hitting me!' 'Mind your manners,' said Monkey. 'Let's sit down and enjoy ourselves decently.' 'I like that,' said Pigsy. 'If we're to sit down and behave ourselves decently when we are stealing a meal, what pray should we do if we were invited?' 'What are those Bodhisattvas up there?' asked Monkey. 'If you don't recognize the Taoist Trinity,' said Pigsy, 'what deities would you recognize, I wonder?' 'What are they called?' asked Monkey. 'The one in the middle,' said Pigsy, 'is the Great Primordial, the one on the left is the Lord of the Sacred Treasure, and the one on the right is Lao Tzu.'

'Let's take their places,' said Monkey. 'Then we can eat decently and comfortably.' The smell of the offerings made Pigsy in a great hurry to begin eating, and scrambling up on to the altar he knocked down the figure of Lao Tzu with a thrust of his snout, saying, 'You've sat there long enough, old fellow. Now it's Pig's turn.' Monkey meanwhile took the seat of the Great Primordial, and Sandy that of the Lord of the Sacred Treasure, pushing the images out of the way. As soon as he was seated Pigsy snatched at a big dumpling and began to gobble it down. 'Not so fast!' cried Monkey. 'Surely, brother,' said Pigsy, 'Now that we've taken our places, it's time to begin.' 'We mustn't give ourselves away just for the sake of a small thing like a bite of food. If we leave these images lying there on the floor, some Taoist monk may come along at any minute to clean the place up, and trip over them. Then he'll know at once that there is something wrong. We had better put them away somewhere.' 'I don't know my way about here,' said Pigsy. 'There may be a door somewhere, but I shouldn't find it in the dark. Where am I to put these images?' 'I noticed a small door on the right as we came in,' said Monkey. 'Judging from the smell that came from it, I should think it must be a place of metabolic transmigration. You had better take them there.' That fool Pigsy was uncommonly strong. He hoisted the three images on to his back and carried them off. When he reached the door, he kicked it open, and sure enough it was a privy. 'That chap Monkey finds some wonderful expressions,' he said laughing. 'He contrives to find a grand Taoist title even for a closet!' Before depositing them, he addressed the images as follows: 'Blessed Ones, having come a long way, we were hungry and decided to help ourselves to some of your offerings. Finding nowhere comfortable to sit, we have ventured to borrow your altar. You have sat there for a very long time, and now for a change you are going to be put in the privy. You have always had more than your share of good things, and it won't do you any harm to put up with a little stink and muck.' So saying, he pitched them in. There was a splash, and, not retreating quickly enough, he found that his coat was in a filthy state. 'Have you disposed of them successfully?' asked Monkey. 'I've disposed of them all right,' said Pigsy, 'but I have splashed myself and my coat is all filthy. If you notice a queer smell you'll know what it is.' 'That's all right for the moment, come and enjoy yourself,' said Monkey. 'But you'll have to clean yourself up a bit before you go out into the street.' That fool Pigsy then took Lao Tzu's seat and began to help himself to the offerings. Dumplings, pasties, rice-balls, cakes . . . one after another he gobbled them down. Monkey never cared much for cooked food, and only ate a few fruits, just to keep the others in countenance. The offerings vanished swiftly as a cloud swept away by a hurricane, and when there was nothing left to eat, instead of starting on their way, they fell to talking and joking, while they digested their food. Who would have thought of it? There was a little Taoist who suddenly woke up and remembered that he had left his handbell in the temple. 'If I lose it,' he said to himself, 'I shall get into trouble with the Master tomorrow.' So he said to his bed-fellow, 'You go on sleeping. I must go and look for my bell.' He did not put on his lower garments, but just threw his coat over his shoulders and rushed to the temple. After fumbling about for some time, he succeeded in finding it, and was just turning to go when he heard a sound of breathing. Very much alarmed, he ran towards the door and in his hurry slipped on a lychee seed and fell with a bang, smashing his bell into a thousand pieces. Pigsy could not stop himself from breaking into loud guffaws of laughter, which frightened the little Taoist out of his wits. Stumbling at every step he dragged himself back to the sleeping-quarters and, banging on his Master's door, he cried, 'Something terrible has happened!' The Three Immortals were not asleep, and coming to the door they asked what was the matter. 'I forgot my bell,' he said, trembling from head to foot, 'and when I went to the temple to look for it, I suddenly heard someone laughing. I nearly died of fright.' The Immortals called for lights, and startled Taoists came scrambling out of all the cells, carrying lanterns and torches. They all went off to the temple to see what evil spirit had taken possession there. . . .

Monkey pinched Sandy with one hand and Pigsy with the other. They understood what he meant and both sat stock still, while the three Taoists advanced, peering about in every direction. 'Some rascal must have been here,' said the Tiger Strength Immortal. 'All the offerings have been eaten up.' 'It looks as though ordinary human beings have been at work,' said the Deer Strength Immortal. 'They've spat out the fruit stones and skins. It's strange that there is no-one to be seen.' 'It's my idea,' said the Ram Strength Immortal, 'that the Three Blessed Ones have been so deeply moved by our prayers and recitations that they have vouchsafed to come down and accept our offerings. They may easily be hovering about somewhere on their cranes, and it would be a good plan to take advantage of their presence. I suggest that we should beg for some holy water and a little Elixir. We should get a lot of credit at Court if we could use them to the king's advantage.' 'A good idea,' said the Tiger Strength Immortal. And sending for some of his disciples, he bade them recite the scriptures, while he himself in full robes danced the dance of the Dipper Star, calling upon the Trinity to vouchsafe to its devout worshippers a little Elixir and holy water, that the king might live for ever.

'Brother,' whispered Pigsy to Monkey, 'there was no need to let ourselves in for this. Directly we finished eating we ought to have bolted. How are we going to answer their prayer?' Monkey pinched him, and then called out in a loud, impressive voice, 'My children,' he said, 'I must ask you to defer this request. My colleagues and I have come on straight from a peach banquet in Heaven, and we haven't got any holy water or elixir with us.' Hearing the deity condescend to address them, the Taoists trembled with religious awe. 'Father,' they said, 'you surely realize that for us this is too good an opportunity to be lost. Do not, we beseech you, go back to Heaven without leaving us some sort of magical receipt.' Sandy pinched Monkey. 'Brother,' he whispered, 'they are praying again. We're not going to get out of this so easily.' 'Nonsense,' whispered Monkey. 'All we've got to do is to answer their prayers and give them something.' 'That would be easier if we had anything to give,' whispered Pigsy. 'Watch me,' whispered Monkey, 'and you'll see that you are just as capable of satisfying them as I am.' 'Little ones,' he said, addressing the Taoists, 'I am naturally not keen on letting my congregation die out; so I'll see if we can manage to let you have a little holy water, to promote your longevity.' 'We implore you to do so,' they said, prostrating themselves. 'All our days shall be devoted to the propagation of the Way and its Power, to the service of our king and the credit of the Secret School.' 'Very well then,' said Monkey. 'But we shall each need something to put it into.' The Tiger Strength Immortal bustled off and soon re-appeared carrying, single-handed, an enormous earthenware jar. The Deer Strength Immortal brought a garden-vase and put it on the altar. The Ram Strength Immortal took the flowers out of a flower-pot and put it between the other two. 'Now go outside the building, close the shutters and stay there,' said Monkey. 'For no-one is permitted to witness our holy mysteries.' When all was ready, Monkey got up, lifted his tiger-skin and pissed into the flower-pot. 'Brother,' said Pigsy, highly delighted. 'We've had some rare games together since I joined you, but this beats all.' And that fool Pigsy, lifting his dress, let fall such a cascade as would have made the Lü Liang Falls seem a mere trickle. Left with the big jug, Sandy could do no more than half fill it. Then they adjusted their clothes, and sat down decorously as before. 'Little ones,' Monkey called out, 'you can come and fetch your holy water.' The Taoists returned, full of gratitude and awe. 'Bring a cup,' said the Tiger Strength Immortal to one of his disciples. 'I should like to taste it.' The moment he tasted the contents of the cup, the Immortal's lip curled wryly. 'Does it taste good?' asked the Deer Strength Immortal. 'It's rather too full-flavoured for my liking,' said the Tiger Strength Immortal. 'Let me taste it,' said the Ram Strength Immortal. 'It smells rather like pig's urine,' he said doubtfully, when the cup touched his lips. Monkey saw that the game was up. 'We've played our trick,' he said to the others, 'and now we'd better take the credit for it.' 'How could you be such fools,' he called out to the Taoists, 'as to believe that the Deities had come down to earth? We're no Blessed Trinity, but priests, from China. And what you have been drinking is not the Water of Life, but just our piss!'

No sooner did the Taoists hear these words than they rushed out, seized pitchforks, brooms, tiles, stones and whatever else they could lay hands on, and with one accord rushed at the impostors. In the nick of time Monkey grabbed Sandy with one hand and Pigsy with the other, and rushed them to the door. Riding with him on his shining cloud they were soon back at the temple where Tripitaka was lodged. Here they slipped back into bed, taking care not to wake the Master. 'Now we are all going to Court to get our passports put in order,' Tripitaka announced when he woke.

The king of the country, on hearing that three Buddhist pilgrims sought admittance to the palace, was in a tearing rage. 'If they must needs court death,' he said, 'why should they do it here, of all places? And what were the police doing, I should like to know. They ought never to have been let through.' At this, a minister stepped forward. 'The country of T'ang,' he said, 'is ten thousand leagues away and the road is as good as impassable. If they do indeed come from there, they must be possessed of some mysterious power. I am in favour of verifying the papers and letting them proceed. It would be wiser not to get on to bad terms with them.'

The king agreed, and ordered the passports to be sent in. . . .

7 The Manchu Empire and Western Imperialism

The Ch'ing Dynasty, A.D. 1644–1912

HISTORICAL OUTLINE

The Ch'ing dynasty was a foreign one. This fact was never forgotten by the Chinese, though there were significant differences in attitude to the new government adopted by the North and the South. Since the Manchus had been invited to enter the Great Wall, the experience of people living to the north of the Yangtze valley was a more or less peaceful takeover of power. The North acquiesced, too, because of the relative lack of friction in daily life, caused by the rapid cultural assimilation of the Manchus, which culminated in the disappearance of their own language. The situation in South China was entirely different: several Chinese leaders, including Wu San-kuei, remained almost undisturbed till 1673, when the young Ch'ing Emperor, K'ang Hsi, began reducing the whole Empire to obedience. Only in 1683 when the island of Taiwan was captured by the Manchus had the last Chinese stronghold fallen. That the Ch'ing dynasty sought assistance from Dutch ships for this campaign shows how far from respectability the idea of a navy had slipped in the mind of the Court. The Manchus were powerful on land but their disregard of the sea proved a fatal error of policy for China in the nineteenth century. This dislike of overseas adventure was connected with the hostility of the South to Manchu rule. Fearing that foreign contacts and trade abroad would only encourage further restiveness among the southern Chinese, successive Ch'ing Emperors barred the coast to Chinese and foreigner alike. From 1757 all foreign trade was confined to the one city of Canton.

The Celestial Empire

The Manchus were outnumbered by Chinese, probably as much as thirty to one. This disparity between rulers and ruled obliged the Ch'ing Emperors to make the system of bannermen a permanent element of imperial government. Bannermen, Manchu soldiers sworn by an oath of personal loyalty to the throne, were stationed in large garrisons around the main centres of population. In the wars of expansion conducted by the early Emperors these men proved their worth and maintained a high standard of military efficiency. Mongolia was conquered; Sinkiang was annexed—for the first time since the T'ang Empire; Tibet was brought under Chinese suzerainty; Burma, Annam, Korea and Siam became tributaries; and the Emperor Ch'ien Lung was the only monarch able to subdue the kingdom of Nepal (1792). Yet the very success of these campaigns undermined the Manchu Empire, for with no enemies to fight the army began to decay; failure to modernize gave Western forces an immense advantage when conflicts eventually came, and the inability to meet sea-borne attacks left the country exposed from Peking to Canton. But for the Ch'ing dynasty the main threat seemed the Chinese themselves. Bannermen were kept in idleness for reasons of internal security.

The administration of the Empire provided the Ch'ing Emperors with a headache too. Posts had to be reserved for Manchus, otherwise the *shih* would gain control of the government. Fifty per cent of the places were awarded to Manchus, North China and South China having twenty-five per cent each. As the intellectual centre of the country had shifted southwards during the Sung Empire, this meant that the intense competition for awards in the southern examinations at Nanking ensured that successful candidates from this centre were more learned than their peers. Paradoxically, the hostile South produced the leading Confucianists of the Ch'ing Empire.

From the outside the Ch'ing Empire appeared almost ideal. 'The Celestial Empire' was the name by which China was known to admirers in eighteenth-century Europe. The long reign of Ch'ien Lung (1735–95) was the showpiece of the Manchu Empire. The Empire enjoyed peace at home and victory abroad; the Court was a centre of culture, renowned for its splendid ceremonies. But the Ch'ing dynasty was becoming an elaborate façade, behind which Chinese civilization was undergoing a sweeping transformation. Decline came swiftly in the nineteenth century. Isolated and conservative, the Manchu Court lost contact with the mass of the population and its high officials misused their positions for the sake of personal gain through all kinds of corrupt practices. In desperation, a foreign dynasty

234

The Emperor Ch'ien Lung approaching his tent to meet the British Ambassador.

When in 1793 Lord Macartney tried to negotiate a trade agreement, he received this reply from the Ch'ing Emperor: 'The Celestial Empire possesses all things in great abundance and lacks no product within its borders. There is no need for the importation of any item manufactured by outside barbarians in exchange for our own goods.'

clung to a moribund tradition of thought, a kind of Confucianism that rejected any original idea out of hand as an unnecessary and dangerous innovation, while it exaggerated the 'turning inward' policy of the later Ming Empire into an absurd belief in isolationism. Ostrich-like the Ch'ing dynasty, supported by ultra-conservative officials, Manchu and Chinese, hoped that by not looking at all they would neither see nor encounter anything which might disturb them. The best of the *shih* were alienated from the Manchu Empire.

The Opium War (1840–2)

The 1757 imperial decree by which all foreign trade was restricted to Canton proved less workable every year. Since tea and silk, the main export commodities, were produced in the Yangtze valley, Chinese merchants had to arrange a long overland haul of 800 kilometres to the official trading port, where facilities for the growing international commerce were quite inadequate. At such a vast distance from the capital, trade was out of sight and out of mind in Canton, but problems of regulation could not solve themselves. The Hoppo, always a Manchu of low rank, was in charge of the Canton trade, and during the three-year appointment he was expected to make as much money as he could for his Court patrons who had obtained the post for him. Extortion was normal. Those Chinese scholars in the imperial administration of South China, particularly Kwangtung and Kwangsi, were discouraged from thinking about the implications of commerce by the steady narrowing of Confucian orthodoxy in the Court and the examination system. It is not surprising, therefore, that pressure built up among the European trading nations for a freer approach to Chinese markets.

Financial difficulties caused a crisis. The East India Company found that having to pay in silver for tea and silk was a great strain, and attempts were made to reach a trade agreement whereby goods could be exchanged. Lord Macartney in 1793 and Lord Amherst in 1816 failed to accomplish anything when they visited Peking, while Lord Napier in 1834 was prevented from travelling beyond Canton. Manchu fears of outside influences on the Chinese population were reflected in the deliberately humiliating treatment accorded to these ambassadors, though the general bad impression of Europeans since the Ming period facilitated this propaganda exercise and helped to confirm Chinese suspicions of the Ocean Devils.

But there was an even stronger reason for the people of China to look upon our ancestors with distaste. To the lasting shame of Britain, India was used to grow opium for export to China after 1773. The British Empire became the world's largest grower, processor and exporter of the drug in order to reduce the outflow of silver in the trade with China. An imperial edict of 1800 sought to prohibit this dangerous import, but the British authorities replied that they were unable to prevent the trade as private vessels carried the opium. To the Manchu Court, the centre of all authority in the Empire, this answer seemed very hypocritical. What grated even more was the not-so-unjust British suggestion that the Manchu Empire was more concerned with the loss of the silver than the harm opium smoking might do to its people. In 1839 the Emperor sent an honest official, Lin Tse-hsu, to Canton to end the opium trade. British merchants were shut up

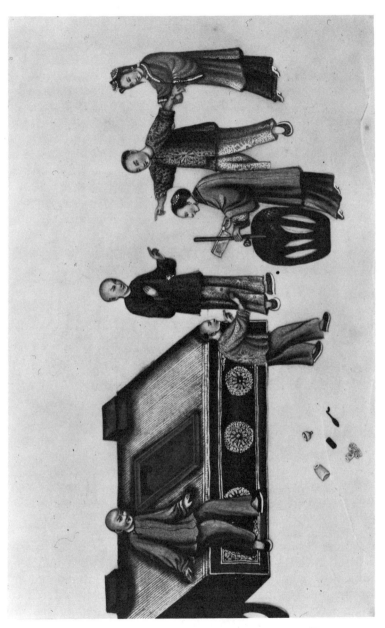

A woman drags her husband home; his friends urge him to enjoy his pipe. An illustration from a Chinese book on the evils of opium smoking.

in their factory and the opium stock destroyed—without compensation. Chinese junks clashed with two British warships at Hong Kong and in 1840 the British were formally excluded from Canton.

An American cartoonist's view of Europeans grabbing land in China. Russians and Germans carve large slices, while France waits vulture-like. Britain, lordliest bully of them all, demands 'the lion's share.'

The Opium War startled the world. A brigade of British troops from India and a small naval squadron were sufficient to humble the Manchus. The bannermen were annihilated by superior weaponry and no resistance at all could be offered to the British navy. Three imperial commissioners had to sue for peace on the deck of a British warship; the Treaty of Nanking, 1842, which legalized opium trade, ended the Canton monopoly, opened up other ports, made the island of Hong Kong a British base, freed British subjects from Chinese law and gave them concession areas to live in, was the first of what the Chinese call the 'Unequal Treaties.' It was something of a model for later

A sea-battle during the Opium Wars, when the Chinese learned that their slow-moving, cumbersome wooden junks were no match for European cannon.

agreements which Western nations imposed on China. With the seclusion policy of the Tokugawa Shoguns after 1640, which had reduced the sea power of Japan at the same time as China turned inwards, there was nothing to stop this 'gunboat policy.' Britain and France actually captured Peking in the Second Opium War (1858–60) and the Franco-Chinese War (1883–5) wrung suzerainty of Indo-China from a dynasty unwilling to face up to the desperate need for modernization. But, unlike China, under the Emperor Meiji (1868–1912) Japan became an industrial power soon capable of defending its sovereignty.

'If the Chinese must be poisoned by opium, I would rather they were poisoned for the benefit of our Indian subjects than any other exchequer,' Sir George Campbell said in the House of Commons in 1880.

The T'ai P'ing Rebellion (1851–64)

Taoism and Buddhism were losing their hold on the mass of the Chinese people at the very time that the Ch'ing Empire was in decline. Protestant Christianity, introduced to China by the British, Dutch and American missionaries, provided momentarily spiritual succour and political direction for a popular movement against the Manchus and their misgovernment of the country. Missionary activity by Protestants was directed at the Chinese man in the street, so from the very beginning the Christian inspired T'ai P'ing rebellion was opposed by both the Court and the *shih*. Hung Hsiu-ch'uan, the leader of the movement, was a southerner who had failed in the civil service examinations.

A portrait of Hung Hsiu-ch'uan, the leader of the Tai P'ings. The characters—t'ien teh—mean 'heavenly virtue.'

Visions and religious conviction followed his reading of a translation of the Bible during an illness. The T'ai P'ing rebellion, or the Great Peaceful Heavenly Kingdom, began in Kwangtung and its armies, reinforced by numerous oppressed *nung*, captured Nanking (1853).

Hung was an embarrassment. The European missionaries were split over his interpretation of the Gospels; the Catholics saw him as a dangerous heretic, while the Protestants felt he led an unorthodox crusade against a corrupt and pagan régime. The European imperialist governments used the civil conflict to increase the dependence of the Manchus on their support: a Chinese national revival was not in their interests. Military advisors, including the British general Gordon, were sent to help suppress the rebels. Again, the Ocean Devils had done little to endear themselves to the Chinese people. Eye-witness accounts of the T'ai P'ing rebels are entirely favourable. They mention the self-discipline of the soldiers and the honesty of the officials, a startling contrast to conditions prevailing in provinces still in the Manchu Empire. The social policy of the T'ai P'ings was liberal and modern—opium and foot binding were outlawed, the status of women was raised, and sensible encouragement was given to trade and industry. Because the North did not join the rebellion and the *shih*, bound to Confucian tradition, were obliged to raise Chinese armies for the defence of the throne against an alien system of thought, the T'ai P'ings were defeated. The long struggle left the Manchus weak and destroyed forever the chance that China might be converted to Christianity. For the T'ai P'ing movement was unusual in that it looked outside Chinese civilization for its inspiration. In this sense it pointed the way to future national renewal, in the twentieth century.

Reform—too little, too late

The unchecked encroachments of Western countries on the Empire forced the *shih* as a class to reconsider their belief in isolationism, which had been fostered so carefully by the Ch'ing dynasty. A reform movement gathered strength from the 1870s and K'ang Yu-wei, a Cantonese scholar whose family had raised loyal bands during the T'ai P'ing rebellion, emerged as its spokesman. The young Emperor Kuang Hsu gave his confidence to the southern reformer and in 1898 a programme of sweeping reforms was announced. China was to be modernized within the context of the Manchu Empire. The recent Sino-Japanese War of 1894–5, after which Korea, Taiwan and parts of Manchuria were ceded to Japan, had shown the advantage an oriental country could gain from Western technology. The modernized Japanese armies had inflicted a crushing defeat on China's forces.

But the Empress Dowager Tz'u Hsi, who had been the power behind the throne since the death of Emperor Hsien Feng (1861), feared that such changes would threaten her influence and she determined to stop the programme. Hearing of her plans, Emperor Kuang Hsu ordered Yuan Shih-k'ai, commander of a modernized unit in the imperial army, to arrest Tz'u Hsi. But Yuan betrayed the Emperor, who was imprisoned in the Palace at Peking. More fortunate, K'ang Yu-wei and other leading reformers of the Hundred Days escaped abroad.

The Boxer Rebellion and the Fall of the Chinese Empire
The Empress Dowager Tz'u Hsi, old but resolute, used her eunuchs to keep a check on any innovation, while the Manchu Empire fell apart. In 1900 'The Society of the Harmonious Fist,' or the Boxers, became active in Shantung. This violent agitation was directed against the growing power of Western nations in China and involved attacks on foreigners, foreign importations and Chinese converts to Christianity. Tz'u Hsi foolishly decided to back the Boxers and they were permitted to invest the legation quarter in Peking. The South remained undisturbed by the Boxers, and the war with the 'barbarians' was confined to the North. Peace meant, of course, more concessions and even foreign garrisons, not less interference with Chinese affairs.

When Tz'u Hsi died (1908), the captive Emperor Kuang Hsu was dispatched by her order, so that the Manchu Empire was left with a child Emperor. P'u-yi (Hsuan T'ung) was, in fact, the last Emperor of China, for in 1911 the accidental discovery of a republican plot in Hankow triggered a nation-wide revolution that swept away the Empire and established the Chinese Republic.

EXPANSION AND CONTRACTION UNDER THE CH'ING DYNASTY

By 1683 the Chinese rebels had been defeated or pacified and the rising prosperity of the new régime gained it tacit support from the *nung* who suffered greatly since the decay of the Ming Empire. The last outpost of rebellion was Taiwan, the fertile island 240 kilometres off the coast of Fukien province. The Chinese migrated there in large numbers in the seventeenth century to escape both population pressure and exploitation. After 1623 the Dutch had gained control of the island, defeating Japanese

P'u-yi, the last Emperor of China.

traders and Chinese pirates. In 1661 the Dutch were overthrown by the rebel general Cheng Ch'eng-kung who maintained an independent Chinese state for the next twenty years before the Ch'ing dynasty finally incorporated it as a prefecture.

The North-West
In the period of consolidation following the founding of the dynasty the Ch'ing sought to safeguard their frontiers. Even before they conquered China, they had brought Korea and Inner Mongolia under their control. Now they sought to strengthen the north-west. Mongol tribes were defeated, reducing Outer Mongolia to a vassal state. Further west, however, lay the Mongol kingdom of Dzungaria, occupying Turkestan and the Altai Mountains. It was not finally defeated until the mid-eighteenth century.

Tibet
After moving their capital from Mukden to Peking the Manchus invited the leaders of the Lamaist Church, which dominated Tibet, to send tribute. An opportunity arose to make their presence more concrete when the Dzungars invaded Tibet and captured Lhasa in 1717. The Ch'ing Emperor sent a relieving army which routed the invaders but stayed on first to install the Dalai Lama and then to offer him permanent protection, thus ensuring the maintenance of Chinese influence.

The south-west provinces of China proper were subjected to increasing government control in the early eighteenth century after Oh-erh-g'ai, the governor of Yunnan, successfully abolished indirect rule over the minority tribes, commonly known as the Miao. A large number of tribes in Yunnan, Kwangsi, Kweichow, Szechuan and Kwangtung had formerly ruled themselves. After 1720 the principle of direct rule by Chinese officials spread throughout the south-west.

Attempts to gain the allegiance of Burma had little success until the late eighteenth century. Successive armies were defeated in the heavily forested malaria-ridden valleys of the north-east frontier. Internal problems eventually forced the king to accept Ch'ing protection. The Vietnamese in Annam, on the other hand, readily accepted the payment of tribute to Peking and in so doing kept Chinese intervention to a minimum.

The Erosion of Chinese Authority
European trading activity was restricted to Canton from 1757. With the increase in British companies involved in the China

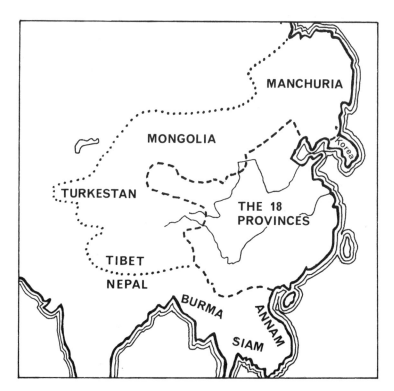

The Ch'ing Empire in 1800 showing 'China proper' and the outlying provinces and countries paying tribute.

trade after 1834, when the monopoly of the East India Company expired, pressure increased for more port facilities. The Opium War of 1839 allowed Britain to increase the number of 'treaty' ports to five (Canton, Foochow, Shanghai, Amoy and Ningpo). Hong Kong was ceded to Britain. 'Gun boat' diplomacy further extended the number of coastal and inland ports licensed for trade. While the British and French were sacking Peking and the T'ai P'ing rebels were ravaging the South, the Russians were advancing eastwards in the North. Early treaties in 1689 and 1727 attempted to control their expansion. In 1858 Count Nicholas Muravier, the governor-general of eastern Siberia presented a new set of territorial demands based on the exploration and gradual colonization of the region north of the Amur River which was nominally Chinese. Two years later the Russians offered to mediate with and influence the Europeans in their treatment of Peking, if the coastal territories west of the Ussuri River were given to them. Vladivostock was founded at the southern tip of this territory.

Territories ceded to Russia by China 1858 and 1860.

France was increasingly interested in Annam and obtained trading and navigation rights in 1862. It was recognized as an independent country by France in 1874 but it continued sending tribute missions to Peking until the 1880s, when the French dominated it. The Chinese sent troops to stop the French expansion but their surprising success on land was nullified by the French naval policy of bombarding China's harbours in retaliation. In 1885 Annam was recognized as a French protectorate. China had already recognized British control of Burma in 1866.

The Rise of Japan
From the sixteenth century onwards the Japanese were increasingly involved in piracy and trade in East Asia. Europeans were encouraged to establish factories there in the early seventeenth century. By 1640 the increasingly conservative and insular Tokugawa Shoguns, the family which ruled Japan in the Emperor's name for over two-hundred-and-fifty years, finally banned most foreigners and established a policy of isolation which lasted until 1850.

The earliest clashes with China came over control of the kingdom of Korea. Traditionally China was stronger and maintained its influence. After 1850 an increased desire for moderniza-

246

tion gave Japan military and technological supremacy. The first show of strength came in 1874 when Japan invaded Taiwan to back its claim to the Ryukyu Islands, which the Chinese disputed. In 1876 two Korean ports were opened to Japanese ships after further hostilities. Korea was the gateway to the fertile Manchurian Plain, the homeland of the Ch'ing dynasty, and China reacted strongly to further Japanese attempts at extending its influence, by annexing Korea. In 1894 a civil war led to the invitation of both armies. Japan gained the support of the new Korean ruler who wanted the Chinese thrown out. Japanese troops penetrated South Manchuria and sank a Chinese fleet. Moving towards Peking they forced China to sue for peace. Under the Treaty of Shimonoseki, China:

- recognized the independence of Korea;
- ceded Taiwan, the Pescadores and Liaotung Peninsula to Japan;
- had to pay reparations of 200 m taels;
- had to open up her ports to Japan on the same terms as those offered to Europeans.

Taiwan was occupied immediately and remained a colony until 1945. Intervention by the European powers, lobbied by Russia, led to the return of the Liaotung Peninsula to China. (They did not wish to see Japan in an area on which they themselves had designs. The Russians were invited to build a railway linking the Trans-Siberian line, via Manchuria, to Vladivostock. Railway building was very limited in China because of the fears of disturbance of the natural elements. Having backed up China against Japan the Europeans now made their claims that:

- the Germans obtained Chiao-Chow Bay and the rights of mineral development in Shantung;
- Russia obtained the southern part of the Liaotung Peninsula including Dairen and Port Arthur;
- the French, having gained the rights of mineral development in the south-west, obtained a lease of Kwangchow Bay for 99 years and the right to build a railway from Tonkin to K'unming;
- Britain guaranteed the safety of her sphere of influence in the Yangtze valley and obtained a 99-year lease on Kowloon.

The Boxer rebellion conveniently gave each of these the opportunity to reinforce its position. Only disagreement among them prevented China from being carved up like Africa a decade before. The USA unexpectedly became an ally of China by suggesting an 'open-door' policy which would maintain trading

Foreign concessions in 1900.

opportunities for all without disturbing the spheres of influence, and thus kept China intact. In 1904–5 Japan soundly defeated Russia in a land war fought largely on Chinese territory and in a sea battle that revealed the true extent of Japan's modernization programme. The resulting treaty gave Japan the Liaotung territory of Russia and confirmed its influence in Korea.

ECONOMIC DEVELOPMENT

Population Growth and Distribution

The initial stability afforded by the Ch'ing dynasty, coupled with the increasing use of New World food crops, created a rapid rise in population from 1750 to 1850 to over 400 million. By 1910 this had fallen to under 350 million. The decline was partly due to natural catastrophes, and partly to civil war and occupation by foreign aggressors. In 1855 the Yellow River's course

248

An early view of foreign ships at anchor off Whampoa Island in the Pearl River, sixteen kilometres downstream from Canton.

changed, through lack of maintenance of the levées, with massive loss of life, through flood and ensuing famine and disease. A four-year drought in the northern provinces of Shensi, Shansi, Honan and Hopei led to over ten million deaths in the late 1870s. The T'ai P'ing Rebellion is estimated to have cost the lives of over 20 million in South and Central China.

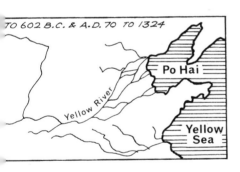

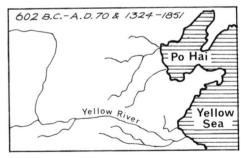

Some changes in the course of the Yellow River. Chinese history records 1500 inundations in the last 3000 years and 26 changes in course.

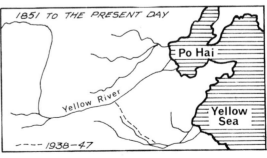

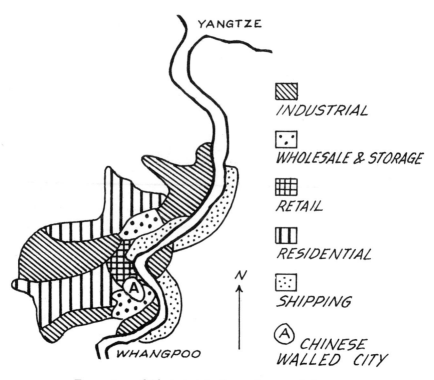

YANGTZE

⬛ INDUSTRIAL

⬚ WHOLESALE & STORAGE

▦ RETAIL

▥ RESIDENTIAL

⬚ SHIPPING

Ⓐ CHINESE WALLED CITY

N

WHANGPOO

Expansion of Shanghai in the early twentieth century.

The frequent annihilation of population in the fertile lowlands stimulated great internal migration. As the population grew so did pressure on land. The peasants of the North China plain and Shantung peninsula increasingly moved into South Manchuria which had been officially 'closed' to migrants in 1668. The Manchus objected to the racial 'pollution' of their homeland but eventually came to depend entirely on the agricultural produce of the Chinese in the Liaotung Peninsula and the basins of the Liao and Sungari Rivers.

There was also increasing migration to the growing centres of trade and industry such as Shanghai. This was transformed from a fishing village into a commercial metropolis after the creation of the International Settlement in 1863. By 1895 it had a population of over 400 000 and in 1900 this had exceeded 1 million. Today it is the largest city in the world. The nineteenth century saw urban growth increasingly divorced from the traditional administrative and protective function and steadily following the Western pattern where growth was based on industry, trade and communications.

Economic Growth

Agriculture In the nineteenth century agriculture inevitably maintained its role as the basis of the economy and the major employer. The economic history of China does not record an agrarian revolution at this time but it must be remembered that farming was already highly efficient in the use of fertilizer, if somewhat restricted by the pattern of land holding. The patchwork of small farms covering the country was increasing continually through sub-division at the death of the owner, among his heirs. Thus, they were almost entirely subsistence holdings subject to crises at the slightest climatic irregularity. Produce from the small farmers did enter the local market because they were forced to sell to pay taxes. In years of bad harvest the taxes had to come before the stomach. The large estates that existed did produce a surplus for the Court, for other non-agricultural inhabitants and for export.

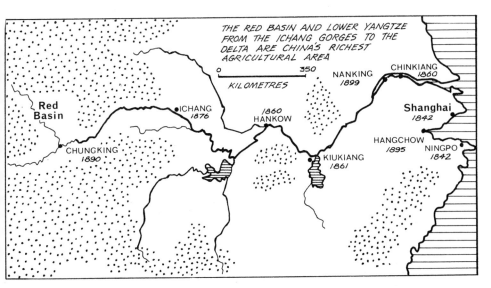

The hinterland of Shanghai showing European concessions and date of opening. The Red Basin and Lower Yangtze were China's richest agricultural areas.

Increasing demand from world markets for tea, cotton and silk stimulated a response often financed by merchants. In the South, beef was introduced to meet the demands of Europeans and dairy herds were maintained around the Treaty Ports. The

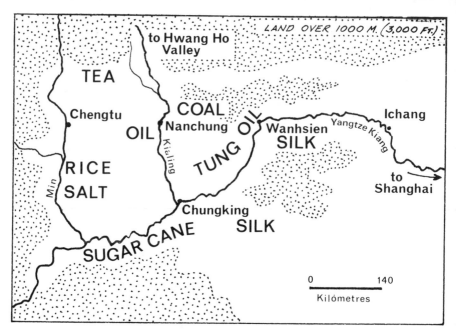

THE RED BASIN OF SZECHUAN, THE MOST DENSELY POPULATED PROVINCE
- Protective mountains create an equable climate, despite being 1 600 kilometres inland.
- Growing season of eleven months per annum.
- Virtually all crops grown in China can be grown here.
- Two-thirds of cultivated land is double-cropped.
- Rice output per hectare is up to twice as high as elsewhere.
- Important commercially for fruit, tea, sugar and silk.
- Chengtu Plain's long established irrigation helps make it the most densely populated agricultural area in the world.

Irish potato and American maize proved adaptable in the southern highlands which were increasingly encroached upon, resulting in destruction of their tree-cover and accelerated soil-erosion. The problem was recognized by the government who ordered a halt to such pioneering, and encouraged the growing of tree crops in plantations.

The pioneer frontiers of Tibet and Mongolia attracted relatively small numbers of migrants, who were forced either to adopt the survival pattern of the indigenous peoples or modify the environment to allow them to maintain traditional Chinese methods. In Tibet house and dress styles were copied, while in Mongolia irrigation was used to increase cropland at the expense of pasture. Chinese 'oases' emerged with whole villages seemingly lifted from the North China plain. The Manchus did not feel the need for protection of the northern frontiers to the same extent as former dynasties, because the nomadic tribesmen were increasingly being controlled by the eastern movement of the Russians, who initially showed little interest in China. The main areas of expansion were Manchuria, where physical restrictions were much less intense, and Szechuan, where the population rapidly recovered from the massacres of the seventeenth century peasant rebellion. In 1786 its population was registered at around $8\frac{1}{2}$ million. By 1850 it was over 44 million.

Industry Industrial expansion in the nineteenth century was closely linked with the impact of the Europeans. Existing industry was small-scale and limited to water, wind and manpower, although the Chinese had devised so many of the techniques and principles on which industrial expansion had been made possible in the West. After the defeat of the Chinese forces by a small number of Europeans with advanced weapons in 1840 and 1856, some Chinese realized the need for modernization. Li Hung-chang, a Governor General of Kiangsu, advised the Emperor in 1864 to acquire the use of modern weapons and to install machinery to make them. By 1865 Shanghai was producing naval vessels, rifles, cannons, gunpowder and cartridges. Following this, many companies were established by the Ch'ing government including the following:

China Merchant Steam Navigation Company, 1872;
Kai Ping Coal Mines, 1877;
Shanghai Cotton Cloth Mill, 1878;
Imperial Telegraph Administration, 1881;
Hanyang Iron Works, 1896;
Imperial Bank of China, 1896.

The British financed the first railway linking the coal of Woosung with the arsenals of Shanghai. In 1876, just two years later, the government broke it up and sent it to Taiwan following agitated opposition from *nung* and *shih* on the grounds that it was disturbing the harmony of the land. Russia was later allowed to build an arm of the Trans-Siberia railway to Vladivostock, across Manchuria, and having entered Chinese territory, manoeuvred successfully to obtain a southward link to its Treaty Ports of Dairen and Port Arthur.

Li Hung-chang also criticized Chinese education as being 'divorced from utility.' Despite Court opposition 120 students were sent to study Western technology. In 1861 a Board of Foreign Affairs had been established to deal with the Western traders. The following year saw the establishment of a school of languages. Such 'modernization' was frowned on by the Court, which was increasingly influenced by the reactionary Dowager

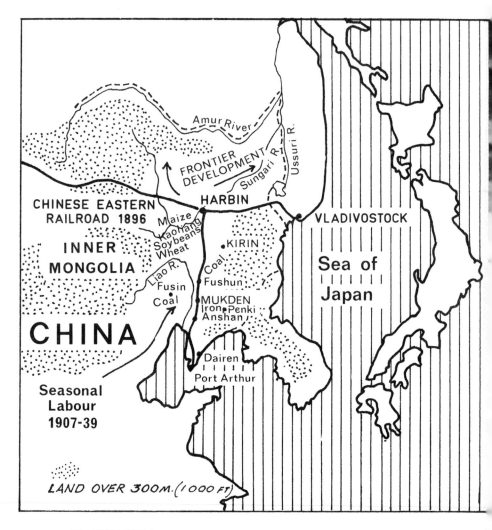

MANCHURIA

1896–1904 Russian Sphere of Influence
1904–45 Japanese Sphere of Influence. The region was developed as a reservoir for food and raw materials for Japan. Agricultural development in the North was limited by the extreme winter temperatures (as low as −40°C) and the short growing season (five months).

Tz'u Hsi. Industrial development was impeded by the imposition of a transit tax initially for goods carried on the Grand Canal. By the 1890s it had been extended to a production tax and a sales tax as the Ch'ing government's indemnity payments to the occupying forces soared.

254

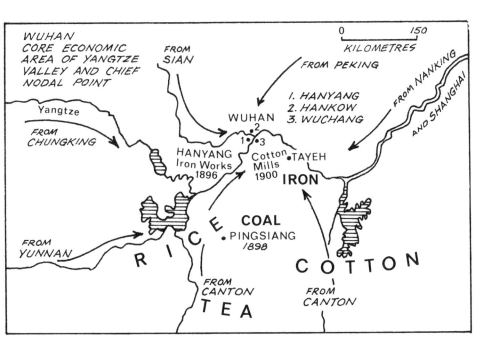

The Hanyang Iron Company, Pingsiang Coal Mines and Tayeh Iron Works amalgamated in 1908 to form the Hanyehping Iron Company.

Following the treaty of Shimonoseki in 1895, foreigners were allowed to develop industries in China and this, coupled with their exemption from the transit tax and other impositions, created China's first industrial boom. Between 1904 and 1908 227 joint-stock companies were registered. However, many of these were small in size. A survey of 'factories' in 1912 noted that only 363 out of 20749 employed mechanical power. The increasing amount of foreign investment gave the outsiders even greater influence in China and increasingly the only government officials who could meet them on their own terms were those involved in similar industrial enterprises, such as the Hanyehping Iron Works founded in 1908. This was an amalgamation of the Hanyang Iron Works, Tayeh Iron Mines and Pingsiang Coal Mines, formed by Chang Chih-tung, governor general of Hupeh and Hunan. Only in the Yangtze valley and South Manchuria did heavy industry prosper. Elsewhere, the growth was confined largely to modernized and enlarged versions of traditional processing industries and textiles, and these were mainly located in the Treaty Ports.

Trade The Treaty of Nanking (1842) gave limitless opportunities for trade to the British, establishing five treaty ports (Canton, Amoy, Foochow, Ningpo and Shanghai) and ceding the island of Hong Kong to Britain. Chinese tariffs (taxes on imports) on British goods were made low and uniform. Yet the British failed to capitalize on these advantages at first. They flooded the market with useless goods such as Sheffield steel cutlery, though the infamous opium trade was maintained, providing an easy and vast source of income for the British. Even with the soaring exports of silk, and tea, the Chinese could never hope to obtain a favourable trade balance. The low tariffs and exemption from transit tax made imported British cotton goods cheaper than Chinese ones with a resulting decline in the domestic industry. Having revealed China's vulnerability, the Europeans pressed for more treaty ports and inland and coastal concessions, at every opportunity. The Peking Convention of 1860 opened up ten new ports to all and virtually carved up China among the European powers. The Chinese had little jurisdiction over the concessions. The 'most favoured nation' concept was introduced to extend any individually negotiated rights with the Chinese, to all other countries. In 1899 at a point in which China was about to be split politically between the European powers, the USA suggested the 'open-door' idea that was to form the basis of American relations with China until 1949. Under this idea all spheres of influence were to remain open to all other traders on the principle of 'equal and impartial trade with all parts of the Chinese Empire.' Thus China was preserved as a territorial and administrative entity.

THE GROWTH OF CHINESE SETTLEMENTS OVERSEAS

One of the earliest references to Chinese communities overseas derives from a thirteenth-century Mongol Embassy to Cambodia. The Chinese settlers were scathingly referred to as 'men of the sea,' implying that they originated as coastal traders or pirates. Another community was recorded at Tumasik in 1349 but this declined until the British revived the port as Singapore in 1819. The longest continual settlement may be that of Malacca which outlasted successive rules by Portugal, Holland and Britain. Among the earliest settlers intermarriage was frequently recorded.

The descendants known as 'Babar' Chinese maintained the culture if not the language of China. As the numbers of migrants increased in the seventeenth century intermarriage became less common.

Origins and Destinations
Migrants to the Nanyang (Southern Ocean) were almost entirely from Kwangtung and Fukien. The reasons for the movement can be summarized as follows:
● ever increasing population pressure on the south-east coastal lowlands;
● increasing alienation between the people of the south-east and successive harsh northern régimes under the Mongols, Ming and Manchu;
● inability of China to extend its southern boundaries overland;
● the availability of both sea-going sailing craft and knowledge of the Nanyang in south-east China.
The people of Kwangtung and Fukien spoke many dialects and when migrating they often chose to go to areas already peopled by those whose dialect they understood. Sibu in Sarawak became known as 'New Foochow' because of the large Chinese settlement from that area. Hokkien speakers from Amoy went to Java and Malaya. Teochin speakers from Swatow went to Siam, Sumatra and Malaya. The Hakka, a people who had fled to the south of China from the Mongol invaders, went in large numbers to Borneo. A major exception were the Cantonese traders who were found wherever commercial opportunities presented themselves.

The Role of the Migrants
It would be wrong to categorize all Chinese in South-East Asia as traders. Many of the wealthiest did originate as energetic middlemen who risked their lives collecting the produce of inland tribes for export to Europe and distributing European produce likewise. A growing number after the seventeenth century were poor peasants prepared to work in mines and on plantations as 'coolies.'
The Chinese were the only ethnic group common to all countries of the Nanyang including Siam, the only independent state by the nineteenth century. Although speaking different dialects they maintained a common written language and culture. Illiterate migrants who 'made good' endeavoured to obtain instruction for their children in traditional language and literature. As

257

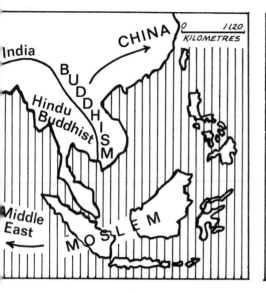

(Left) Major cultural division of Nanyang based on religion.
(Right) Major partition pattern by late nineteenth century showing
spheres of influence of Britain, Holland, France and Spain. (Thailand
remained independent.)

a result a vast intelligence network operated in the Nanyang via
the Chinese newspapers which few others could understand. This
was backed up by secret societies which acted to control and
police the behaviour of the communities.

Generally the Chinese were eager to evade political confrontation with the governments of South-East Asia. This encouraged
a general view that they were effete and cowardly. However, the
Chinese by maintaining a policy of non-confrontation, so con-
sistent with traditional philosophy, in particular Taoism, were to
become one of the strongest and most permanent elements of the
economy of the Nanyang.

Relations with the Countries of Settlement

The Portuguese and Spaniards feared the Chinese as rivals in
trade. They resented also their unwillingness to be converted to
Christianity. The Chinese community in the Philippines was
periodically wiped out and on each occasion the economy of the
islands collapsed. In 1603, 20 000 Chinese in Manila were killed.
The Portuguese sphere of influence declined after the loss of
Malacca to the Dutch in 1641. The Dutch were less evangelical,

258

being Protestants, but they attempted to restrict Chinese influence in trade in order to promote their own monopoly in Sumatra, Java, Borneo and the Malacca Straits. Some Chinese in the long established settlement at Palembang became wealthy through their appointment by the Dutch as tax collectors. By the nineteenth century the Chinese mining interests in Borneo had been severely restricted but at the same time the Dutch were encouraging migration into South Sumatra for work on the sugar and tobacco plantations.

The British considered a large Chinese community to be proof of the prosperity of a colony. They presented no apparent political danger and the Straits Settlements (including Penang founded 1785, Malacca in 1824 and Singapore in 1819) rapidly became major centres of Chinese occupation. The Moslem sultans of the western inland states of Malaya encouraged the Chinese to open up the rivers for trade and mining purposes and actually appointed Chinese 'River Lords' to control these developments. This system of indirect rule succeeded better than the British policy of direct intervention in Malaya, which failed to prevent outbreaks of fighting between rival secret societies, in which hundreds were killed. At a time when British administrators were mainly from the Indian civil service, speaking neither Malay nor Chinese, control of the Chinese community was only possible with the tacit consent of the leaders of the secret societies. Burma became a colony of Britain in 1886. Although sharing a border with China there was only a small settlement of emigrants and they were in Rangoon which represents the western limit of Chinese maritime migration in the Nanyang. There, they had to compete with Indians in trade and face the great hostility towards all foreigners from the Burmese.

Only in Malaya and Borneo were the Chinese of great numerical significance as a total proportion of the population. Elsewhere in the Nanyang they were relatively small minorities. In Siam they were assimilated to a much larger extent than in the colonial countries. Sanctions against migration had been in operation since the late Ming period and the zeal for ancestor worship is often considered as a stabilizing factor for the Chinese population, but economic factors were more important and acted to 'push' them as far away as San Francisco and Melbourne. (The latter two centres recruited Chinese labour for their respective gold rushes in the nineteenth century. Most of the miners were peasants from Si Yap which was a predominantly agricultural area in Canton.)

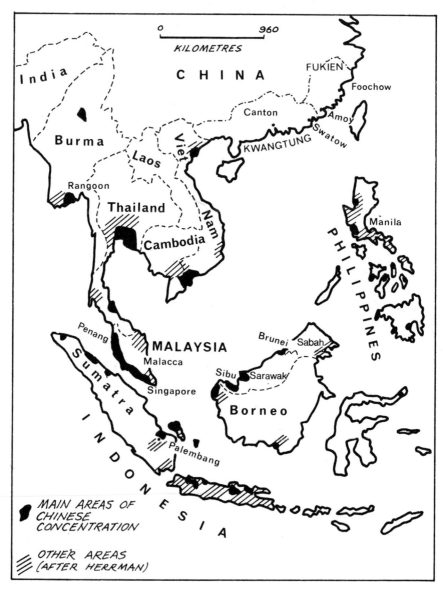

South-East Asia.

SOCIETY AND CULTURE

The Manchus were not destructive like the Mongols. They were semi-agriculturalists when general Wu San-kuei opened the gate at Shanhaikuan and invited them to enter the Great Wall. By the beginning of the eighteenth century the Ch'ing dynasty

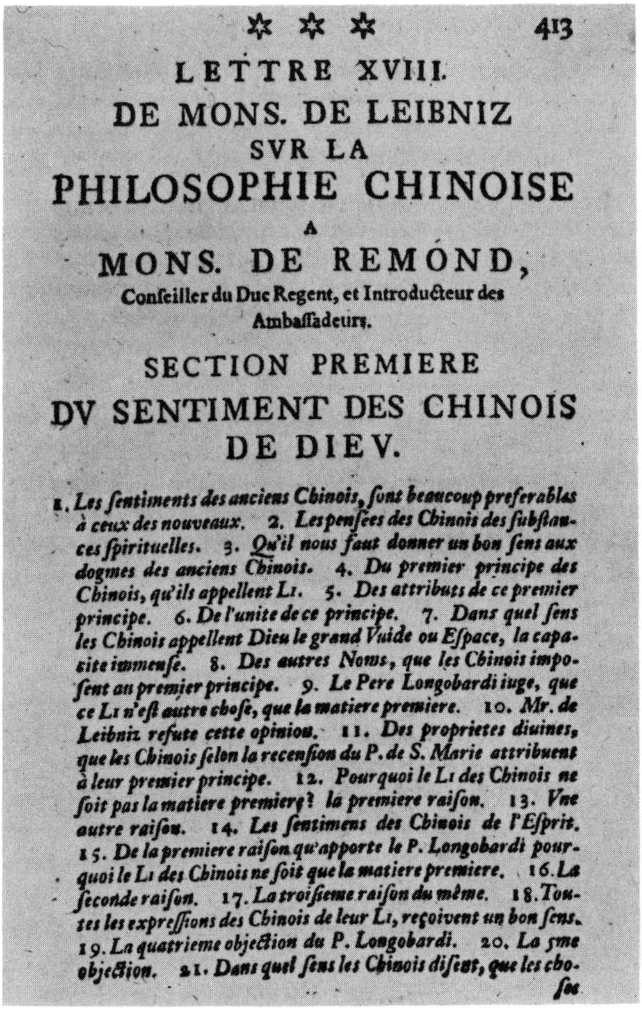

413

LETTRE XVIII.

DE MONS. DE LEIBNIZ

SVR LA

PHILOSOPHIE CHINOISE

A

MONS. DE REMOND,

Conseiller du Duc Regent, et Introducteur des Ambassadeurs.

SECTION PREMIERE

DV SENTIMENT DES CHINOIS DE DIEV.

1. Les sentiments des anciens Chinois, sont beaucoup preferables à ceux des nouveaux. 2. Les pensées des Chinois des substances spirituelles. 3. Qu'il nous faut donner un bon sens aux dogmes des anciens Chinois. 4. Du premier principe des Chinois, qu'ils appellent Li. 5. Des attributs de ce premier principe. 6. De l'unite de ce principe. 7. Dans quel sens les Chinois appellent Dieu le grand Vuide ou Espace, la capacite immense. 8. Des autres Noms, que les Chinois imposent au premier principe. 9. Le Pere Longobardi iuge, que ce Li n'est autre chose, que la matiere premiere. 10. Mr. de Leibniz refute cette opinion. 11. Des proprietes diuines, que les Chinois selon la recension du P. de S. Marie attribuent à leur premier principe. 12. Pourquoi le Li des Chinois ne soit pas la matiere premiere? la premiere raison. 13. Vne autre raison. 14. Les sentimens des Chinois de l'Esprit. 15. De la premiere raison qu'apporte le P. Longobardi pourquoi le Li des Chinois ne soit que la matiere premiere. 16. La seconde raison. 17. La troisieme raison du même. 18. Toutes les expressions des Chinois de leur Li, reçoivent un bon sens. 19. La quatrieme objection du P. Longobardi. 20. La 5me objection. 21. Dans quel sens les Chinois disent, que les choses

The title-page of the Letter on Chinese Philosophy *by Gottfried Wilhelm Leibniz (1646–1716).*

In 1598 Father Matteo Ricci arrived in Peking. The *shih* were opposed to his arrival, which had been largely arranged by the eunuch party; the Board of Rites respectfully reminded the throne of Han Yu's memorial on the religious excesses of Buddhism. Ricci did have some impact among the officials of the Court, but Christianity made little headway after his death (1610). Yet Chinese philosophy, the ideas of which were reported back in Europe by Jesuit missionaries from the East, had an important influence on Western thinkers, particularly Leibniz. While the Jesuits were making available to China Western science, Neo-Confucianism seems to have made a significant contribution to Western thought.

What stirred the philosophers in the West was the organic basis of Neo-Confucianism, which had derived from the ancient Chinese concept of the Yin-Yang. Leibniz wanted an explanation of the universe that was realist, but not mechanical. He rejected the con-

temporary view that the world was a vast machine, and proposed the alternative view of it as a vast living organism, every part of which was also an organism. He called these organisms 'monads.' They fitted into a pre-established harmony, like the *li* of Chu Hsi (A.D. 1130–1200). The organic view of the world, as first put forward by Leibniz, was to be most important in the nineteenth century, witness Hegel, Darwin, Pasteur and Marx. It has been suggested that Neo-Confucianism provided an initial stimulus. 'We may applaud the modern Chinese interpreters,' Leibniz wrote, 'when they reduce the government of Heaven to natural causes, and when they differ from popular ignorance, which looks on miracles and the supernatural as signs from God. And we shall be able to enlighten them further on these matters by informing them of the new discoveries of Europe, which have furnished almost mathematical reasons for many of the great marvels of Nature. . . .'

found that the process of cultural assimilation was becoming a serious threat to the survival of the Manchu tongue itself. Imperial insistence that all official documents should be written in both Manchu and Chinese, and the sponsorship of a huge programme of translation from Chinese, did ensure that Manchu lasted down till 1911, but long before that date it had changed into a 'dead language' which the Manchus themselves were forced to study in schools.

One of the chief reasons for the decline of Manchu was the intense admiration for Chinese culture that the conquerors felt. Emperor Ch'ien Lung (1735–95) was an enthusiastic patron of the arts and he gave a status to painters which they had not enjoyed since the days of the Sung Emperor Hui Tsung. The imperial collection acquired the greatest works of Chinese tradition, but, unfortunately, Ch'ien Lung could not resist the temptation to add his own poems to these paintings and stamp them with very large seals. Although such a practice was an old Chinese custom, Emperor Ch'ien Lung has embarrassed later admirers of Chinese painting by the sheer number of works he felt obliged to enhance. The Ch'ing Court was conservative in taste, so that architecture and painting tended to be rather pale imitations of previous dynasties, particularly the Ming. Not for nothing had the significant artists of the Ch'ing dynasty died before Ch'ien Lung mounted the throne. One of these painters, Wang Hui (1632–1720) was commissioned by Emperor K'ang Hsi to prepare illustrations for a book describing an imperial visit to the South, after the fall of Taiwan (1683). The great southern cities of Soochow and Hangchow produced all these painters, a monopoly of talent that clearly underlines the fact

A Chinese school in the nineteenth century. The teacher is listening to a pupil recite a classical text by heart. This test was called 'backing the book'; it had become the basis of the learning process during the Ch'ing dynasty, and reflected the uncritical and conservative attitudes prevailing among the shih.

that this early creative achievement was a legacy of the Ming Empire, not any fresh development. Indeed, the emphasis on tradition at the Ch'ing Court led to a vogue in making exact copies of old masters, which in turn took the painter and poet yet another step from the possibility of creative renewal, the right to experiment freely within a living tradition.

The narrowing of outlook in the Court at Peking, a rigorous censorship, and the reduction of places available for would-be officials in the Ch'ing civil service led to a growing disenchantment among the *shih* of the South. It seemed to many of them that the North was living off the wealth and toil of the South. Idle Bannermen were everywhere for people to see, and their military ineffectiveness became legend after the first Opium War. The *nung* were restive too. They bore the brunt of an agricultural economy annually proving itself more and more inadequate. Landless peasants formed the backbone of the T'ai P'ing armies, just as they had joined rebellions during the famine years preceding the fall of the Ming dynasty. Secret societies flourished everywhere.

K'ang Yu-wei (1858–1927)

To deal with the rising tide of confusion, reformers like K'ang Yu-wei tried to provide an intellectual basis for the changes in Chinese society that were necessary to save the Empire. The T'ai

263

P'ing rebellion had forced on the Ch'ing dynasty a moderate adoption of Western technology—arsenals, modern ships and improved communications—but peace took the urgency out of the need for reform. The Sino-Japanese War (1894–5) would have been the catalyst, but for the Empress Dowager Tz'u Hsi and the inherent conservatism of the *shih* themselves. K'ang's writings bear witness to the insoluble dilemma of the best of his class. The whole purpose of reform was to sustain the old order; thus, when innovation threatened that order, opposition was a natural response. K'ang had to work within a conception of reality that rested on a belief in the teachings of Confucius and Buddha.

In his book *Confucius as a Reformer* (1897), K'ang attempted to transform Confucianism into a viable system of thought that could hold its own in the modern world. The failure of Emperor Kuang Hsu's reform programme and his own exile forced K'ang to develop a radical line of argument that made Confucian tradition the framework for a single world civilization. *The Book of the Grand Unity* (1902) envisaged a world society of small democratically self-governing communities, each equally represented in a world parliament. Property and the family were to be abolished, because a false notion of Confucian righteousness had restricted affection to the enclosed circle of one's kin. K'ang was conscious of social injustice. He opposed the binding of women's feet and the restrictions placed on widows. The development of his thought reflects a profound discontent with existing conditions as well as a strong desire to change them. Moreover, the influence of Western ideas on K'ang pointed the way to the present intellectual renewal that has come through Communist theory. Unlike Confucianism, Taoism has proved to be most capable of modern political interpretation, possibly through its age-old subversive tendencies. Compare these two translations of a passage from the *Tao Teh Ching*:

> Thirty spokes together make one wheel
> And they fit into nothing at the centre;
> Herein lies the usefulness of a carriage.
> Clay is moulded to make a pot
> And the clay fits round nothing;
> Herein lies the usefulness of the pot.
> Doors and windows are pierced in the walls of a house
> And they fit round nothing;
> Herein lies the usefulness of a house.
> Thus whilst it must be taken as advantageous to have something
>   there,
> It must also be taken as useful to have nothing there.
>   *(Modern Western Version)*

264

Thirty spokes combine to make a wheel,
When there was no private property
Carts were made for use.
Clay is formed to make vessels,
When there was no private property
Pots were made for use.
Windows and doors go to make houses,
When there was no private property
Houses were made for use.
Thus having private property may lead to profit
But not having it leads to use.

(Modern Chinese Version)

The End of the Examination System
In 1905 the imperial examination system was abolished. At once the *shih* lost its privileged avenue of advancement to authority and influence, while the opening of modern schools caused a massive inflow of Western ideas. The Confucian Classics lost their eminence, which had been virtually undisputed since the Han Empire. Intelligent young men now looked outside China for an understanding of their lives and times. They realized that industrial products without the knowledge of the science and technology that lay behind them were valueless. They were prepared to take advantage of mission schools in order to acquire a Western language, which was a way into the modern world, not theology. China would be saved, not westernized, by their studies. However, the *nung*, who formed more than eighty per cent of the Chinese population, were hardly touched by this cultural change till the Communists came to power in 1949.

8 China in the Twentieth Century

From the foundation of the Republic in 1911 to the present day

HISTORICAL OUTLINE

From the moment that Emperor Kuang Hsu's programme of reforms failed and it became obvious that the Empress Dowager Tz'u Hsi would resist any fundamental change in Chinese society, serious revolutionary activity concentrated on the overthrow of both the Ch'ing dynasty and the Empire. Revolutionaries were convinced that the republican model of government would be the saving of China. Accordingly, Dr Sun Yat-sen, the leader of the revolutionary movement, the T'ung-meng hui, or Alliance Society, spent many years raising funds and support from the overseas Chinese. There were ten abortive revolts in the South before, on 9th October 1911, a bomb exploded accidentally in the office of the main revolutionary organization in Hankow, one of the three cities that comprise Wuhan, the great industrial and communications centre of the middle Yangtze valley, and precipitated an anti-Manchu revolution that captured fifteen of the eighteen provinces in the Empire by the end of November. In February 1912 the six-year-old Emperor Hsuan T'ung formally abdicated.

Sun Yat-sen and the Warlords
Sun Yat-sen (1866–1925) was the culmination of a tendency that had begun when the T'ai P'ings first looked outside China to Protestant Christianity for a solution of the problems that were besetting the Empire. For Dr Sun was an 'overseas Chinese'; though born in Kwantung, he had lived in Hawaii, receiving his education in Western schools there and at the Medical College in Hong Kong. In outlook Dr Sun was scientific and modern— his own answer to China's plight was the establishment of a democratic republic. He and his followers worked hard for this liberal goal, but it was too immense a change to introduce at

266

once. The revolutionaries had been able to form cells among the officers of the modernized regiments from 1905. This move proved decisive in the struggle against the Ch'ing dynasty, but it left military governors at the apex of the provincial administrations of the Republic. Many of these officers were warlords, men determined to exploit the uncertainty of the times and the power of their troops for the sake of personal ambition. The *shih* were in disarray with the end of the imperial examination system and the rise of modern schools. So the civil arm of government lost prestige as different generals asserted provincial independence.

Yuan Shih-k'ai.

Yuan Shih-k'ai, recalled by the Ch'ing dynasty as a last resort, was the best placed to take advantage of the confused situation. His military reputation was sound and he controlled the strong northern army. Disposing of the Manchus and intimidating the rebel forces, Yuan obliged Dr Sun, the provisional president, to retire in his favour. By 1914 President Yuan felt secure enough to dismiss not only the National Assembly but all the provincial assemblies as well. Supported by Western powers—they preferred a ruler who would keep the peace in China and protect trade—he made a bid to found a new dynasty, hoping to demonstrate clearly that he had received the Mandate of Heaven. But there

267

were two factors he had overlooked, namely the historical sense of the Chinese people and the empire-building intentions of the Japanese.

Japan was alarmed at the rise of Yuan Shih-k'ai, since another dynasty might lead to the recovery of the Chinese Empire, so reducing its own ability to expand on the Asian continent. Joining the Allies in 1914, Japan had seized the German-leased territories in Shantung, claiming that this was done 'with a view to its eventual restoration to China.' In January 1915 the Japanese government presented Yuan Shih-k'ai with the Twenty-One Demands, whose purpose was the reduction of China to a virtual protectorate of Japan. With no more than moral support from the Western powers, now locked together in total war, Yuan was forced to accept the least offensive Demands. The news led to a nation-wide protest by the Chinese. It seemed that the would-be Emperor was about to betray the country, as he had the Emperor Kuang Hsu (1898), the boy Emperor P'u-yi (1911–12), and the Republic (1914). The Confucian virtues of loyalty and righteousness were singularly lacking in Yuan: he commanded neither respect nor confidence. His downfall came as one military governor after another declared for the Republic. Japanese agents and money found these warlords easy prey for the simple reason that Yuan himself had shown them the way to power. In 1916 Yuan was dead, after a nervous illness caused by disappointment.

The removal of Yuan Shih-k'ai from the political scene left a power vacuum, particularly in the North, where competing generals sought to control Peking. Yuan's personal eminence had permitted the almost peaceful transition from Empire to Republic in 1911–12; political revolution was contained within the continuity of the military establishment. The Warlord Period (1916–26) showed the real extent to which the Empire had disintegrated. In the South Dr Sun resumed as President of the Republic, but there was a complete breakdown of government at a national level. Since all foreign countries persisted in seeing the various régimes in Peking, not the South, as the legal government of China, the country remained divided till after the launching of the Northern Expedition in 1926. Financial motives were behind this diplomatic *impasse*, for foreign loans were financed by custom duties collected from Peking. It appeared that the 'barbarians' were only concerned to keep China weak, when, suddenly, the Russian Revolution (1917) provided the struggling Republic with a new friend, the USSR.

The Kuomintang and the Chinese Communist Party

In order to maintain its political base in the South the Republic had to depend on the protection of local warlords. So precarious was the position that Dr Sun barely escaped with his life in 1922, when the Kwantung warlord, supported by the British, moved against him. Against this background of continued imperialism in alliance with the warlords three events should be placed. They are:

● *The May Fourth Movement*, which marked the continued influence of *shih* in Chinese society. The scholars had gained control of the modern universities, colleges and schools; a new generation had appeared by the Treaty of Versailles (1919), when the Allies awarded the former German-leased territory to Japan. In Peking 3 000 students protested in T'ien An Men square and then burnt down the houses of the puppet ministers. Soon the country had followed the lead of the new young *shih*; cities and towns joined the protest; even *nung* in the remote countryside were stirred by the patriotic appeal. Pro-Japanese ministers fell, the Chinese delegation at Versailles was instructed not to sign the peace treaty, and modern Chinese nationalism emerged.

● *The Chinese Communist Party* had its First Congress in Shanghai (1921). Among the delegates was Mao Tse-tung, one of the leaders of the May Fourth Movement. Although the CCP joined Comintern (the Communist International), the Russians found Dr Sun's nationalist movement more promising at first.

● *The Kuomintang*, the Nationalist Party of Dr Sun, accepted Russian advice and aid. What prompted this alliance was the attitude of the new Communist government in Moscow. 'The Unequal Treaties' obtained by the Tsars were declared void and normal relations established. The *shih* were deeply impressed by this change in policy. It was so unlike the behaviour of other foreign powers, despite their talk about the defence of freedom and democracy. Throughout his life Dr Sun's government was never recognized by any other Western country—on the grounds that his was not the legal one. The Kuomintang, therefore, opened its membership to communist and non-communist members alike, though the differences between Left and Right rent the party asunder after Dr Sun's death (1925).

Chiang Kai-shek (born 1887) became Dr Sun's military adviser in 1917. He was the son of a well-to-do landowning family from Chekiang; his revolutionary beliefs were confirmed in Japan, when he was training as a military officer at the Tokyo Military Academy. But, unlike Mao Tse-tung (born 1893) and

269

Dr Sun Yat-sen and his wife photographed with officers trained at Whampoa Academy. In 1923 Chiang Kai-shek had been sent to Russia to study the organization of the Red Army. A year later Whampoa was opened with Russian aid; Chiang Kai-shek became its military commandant and developed his influence in the Kuomintang through his appointment.

other left-wing followers of Dr Sun, Chiang was less concerned with a thorough transformation of Chinese society than the creation of a strong national state. He had little sympathy with Mao's trust in the *nung*, for by both birth and training he felt called to command those below him in rank. His associates tended to be the military and the new Chinese business class in Shanghai and other commercial centres. Soon after Dr Sun died a struggle developed inside the Kuomintang between the leftist-political officials and the rightist-military group: Chiang emerged as the new leader, though his power within the party was still limited by the ever active Left. As Mao Tse-tung said: 'Political power grows out of the barrel of a gun.' What Dr Sun had striven to avoid most of all had happened—the Kuomintang military, like another set of the warlords, had become the dominant force in the Republic. The Northern Expedition gave the Kuomintang control of all the South: Nanking and Shanghai fell in 1927. But the victory brought Chiang and the Communists into open conflict, since the extent and violence of the agrarian revolt encouraged by Mao Tse-tung frightened many of Chiang's officers, themselves members of southern landlord families. Chiang ordered Kuomintang troops and underworld toughs to

270

Dr Sun Yat-sen and
Chiang K'ai-shek.

attack the rebellious workers in Shanghai. Chou En-lai, an important organizer of the Communist movement there, just escaped the massacre. From this moment the CCP and the Kuomintang were bitter enemies, despite the Japanese invasion of China, which produced a temporary united front.

Mao Tse-tung and the Long March
By 1927 Chiang had driven all the Communists out of the Kuomintang. From Nanking, the Nationalist capital, he gradually extended his influence northwards till few independent warlords were left. But over the *nung*, particularly where Communist guerillas were operating, Chiang had no effective control, for in 1928 Mao established a separate peasant state in the wilds of Hunan, his native province. On the advice of Moscow, the CCP had tried armed risings in cities, such as Canton, but they were quickly crushed. Limited to a Western historical perspective, Karl Marx, the German-Jewish revolutionary on whose writings

271

communism is based, had argued that the peasantry could never be a truly revolutionary force. Only the proletariat, the urban wage-earners, could be expected to seize power—as in 1917 the Russian experience seemed to confirm. Mao disagreed with this view of revolutionary change. For him the proper order of Chinese society was:

- *nung,* the peasant farmers;
- *kung*, the artisans;
- *shih*, the gentry and scholars;
- *shang,* the merchants.

Though the Comintern disavowed Mao, and Chiang's armies were thrown against him, the peasant movement spread. The National-ists were allied to the Shanghai business world, representing

'The ruthless economic exploitation and political oppression of the peasants by the landlord class forced them into numerous uprisings against its rule. . . . It was the class struggles of the peasants, the peasant uprisings and peasant wars that constituted the real motive force of historical development in Chinese feudal society.'

Mao Tse-tung in 1939

international finance as well as the *shang*, while the Communists drew on the historical rebelliousness of the *nung*. Between these two opposing forces the *shih* found themselves with little choice but to wait and see.

'While we recognize that in the general development of history the material determines the mental, and social being determines social consciousness, we also—and indeed must—recognize the reaction of mental on material things, of social consciousness on social being and of the superstructure on the economic base. This does not go against materialism; on the contrary, it avoids mechanical materialism and firmly upholds dialectical materialism.'

Mao Tse-tung in 1937

'In many ways dialectical materialism is familiar to the Chinese mind. Neo-Confucianism subsumed a long tradition of organic thinking that stretched back through early Taoists to the ancient Yin-Yang theory.

So serious had the peasant movement become by 1934 that Chiang made an all-out attempt to crush Mao. The Communist base areas were encircled with blockhouses and other military barriers in order to deny them supplies. To escape and continue the revolution the Communists were forced to break out of the closing Nationalist vice; the trek to safety, the famous 'Long

Mao during the Long March. It was at this time that he wrote 'On Protracted War'.

'Weapons are an important factor in war, but not the decisive factor; it is people, not things, that are decisive. The contest of strength is not only a context of military and economic power, but also a contest of human power and morale. Military and economic power is necessarily wielded by people.'

Mao Tse-tung in 1934–5

March,' took them a distance of 9 600 kilometres, through eleven provinces and 200 million *nung*, before reaching the safety of Shensi. Only about a quarter survived the ordeals of the journey—the rugged terrain and the numerous battles—but Chairman Mao emerged as the respected leader of the CCP.

Japanese Aggression
Since the Sino-Japanese War of 1894–5, the military faction allied with the new business and industrial class had come to dominate the political life of Japan. The spectacular victories of the Russo-Japanese War of 1904–5—the majority of the Tsarist navy was sunk and an entire army surrendered in Port Arthur—gave the Japanese Empire immense confidence: this conflict was the first one in which an Asian power, albeit modernized through Western technology, had inflicted total defeat on any European nation for several hundred years.

As a result Japan extended her influence from Korea into Manchuria, which the Russians had been developing. At first Dr Sun had looked upon modern Japan as a friend of the Chinese Republic, but the Twenty-One Demands (1915) and the continued

273

Troops on the Long March. Of the 80 000 men that set out only 20 000 arrived in Yenan.

occupation of the German-leased territories permanently soured relations. Japanese infiltration of the North became open aggression in 1931, when an incident was faked at Mukden by Japanese officers in order to serve as an excuse for occupying all Manchuria. Despite opposition from the Japanese government itself, the military took over control of the province and installed the deposed Ch'ing Emperor P'u-yi as a puppet ruler of a new state, called Manchukuo.

The Kuomintang wavered. Nation-wide demonstrations, strikes, boycotts, and protests failed to induce Chiang to declare war on Japan. Chang Hsueh-liang, the Manchurian warlord, was in China with half his troops, and Chiang advised him to stay there. In the minds of Chinese patriots Nanking became associated with a policy of appeasement, for Chiang used his forces against the Communists, not the steadily encroaching Japanese. The assassination of the Japanese Prime Minister by a group of young officers freed the military establishment from all restrictions in its Chinese campaigns (1932). Atrocity and widespread destruction marked the Japanese advance.

But at Sian, near the ancient site of Chang-an, Chiang was obliged to reverse his policies by a mutiny (1936). The army there was supposed to be pressing a final attack on Mao's Yenan base area, but Chang Hsueh-liang and his men had come to the conclusion that a united front of Kuomintang and Communists was needed against the Japanese. 'Chinese should not fight

274

Chinese' propaganda by Communist agents had sapped the will of Chang's army, though for these troops a guerrilla war in Shensi made little sense when the Japanese armies were looting and raping their native provinces. Taken prisoner by the mutinous soldiers, Chiang was persuaded to end his harassment of the Communists. Chou En-lai came and agreement was reached.

In 1937 Japan captured Peking and hostilities became general. The North was soon overrun and, using the International Settlement at Shanghai as a base without regard to international law, the Japanese launched an offensive along the Yangtze valley. Nanking suffered dreadfully; there were several weeks of massacre, rape, looting and arson. Although the Japanese armies had complete technological superiority, they had not the measure of Chinese resistance, particularly in those areas where the *nung* had come under Communist influence. While they sought to destroy the Chinese field armies, those of the Kuomintang, they failed to check guerilla activities, even behind their own lines. In effect, the Japanese armies held only the major cities and towns besides the main lines of communications. Chiang retreated to Chungking, where from 1938 to 1944 he remained inactive, much to the embarrassment of his American advisers. Accumulating equipment and military supplies via the Burma Road and later airlifts from India, Chiang claimed he was awaiting the right moment to strike. But it soon became obvious that he still regarded Mao as his main opponent and was saving his strength for an anti-Communist campaign after the withdrawal of Japan, now involved in a global conflict in alliance with the Fascist powers and overstretched in South-East Asia and the Pacific.

What the Japanese invasion meant for Chinese history was the triumph of Communism. While Chiang's troops deteriorated in idleness at Chungking, Mao raised a militia force of two million *nung*, whose bravery and determination ensured that they were liberated not only from the Imperial Army of Japan but also the military domination of the Kuomintang landlord and business faction.

The People's Republic of China
When in 1945 the dropping of atomic bombs on Hiroshima and Nagasaki caused the surrender of Japan, the Kuomintang held the West and the CCP controlled the North, apart from cities with Japanese garrisons. To whom these Japanese should surrender proved an immediate point of dispute. As the legal government of China and an ally, the Kuomintang demanded

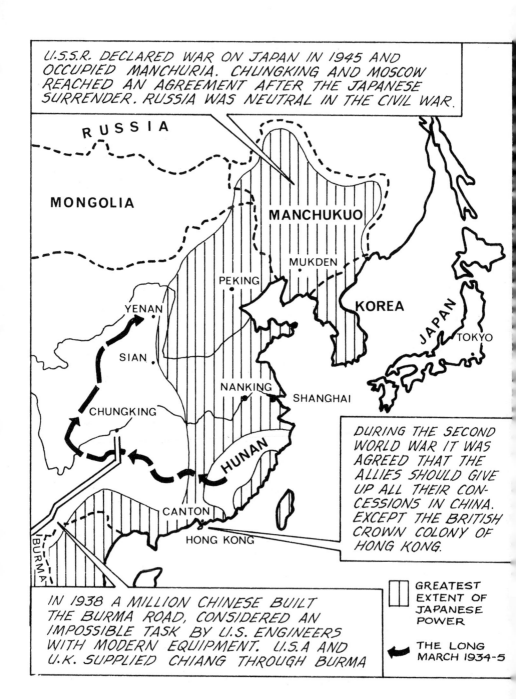

U.S.S.R. DECLARED WAR ON JAPAN IN 1945 AND OCCUPIED MANCHURIA. CHUNGKING AND MOSCOW REACHED AN AGREEMENT AFTER THE JAPANESE SURRENDER. RUSSIA WAS NEUTRAL IN THE CIVIL WAR.

RUSSIA

MONGOLIA

MANCHUKUO

MUKDEN

PEKING

YENAN

KOREA

JAPAN

TOKYO

SIAN

NANKING

SHANGHAI

CHUNGKING

HUNAN

DURING THE SECOND WORLD WAR IT WAS AGREED THAT THE ALLIES SHOULD GIVE UP ALL THEIR CONCESSIONS IN CHINA. EXCEPT THE BRITISH CROWN COLONY OF HONG KONG.

CANTON

HONG KONG

BURMA

IN 1938 A MILLION CHINESE BUILT THE BURMA ROAD, CONSIDERED AN IMPOSSIBLE TASK BY U.S. ENGINEERS WITH MODERN EQUIPMENT. U.S.A AND U.K. SUPPLIED CHIANG THROUGH BURMA

GREATEST EXTENT OF JAPANESE POWER

THE LONG MARCH 1934-5

The Sino-Japanese War.

276

air support from the United States and its troops were flown into occupied cities. Peace efforts by the Americans failed and in 1947 the CCP and Kuomintang were fighting earnestly. The low morale of Chiang's forces and their dismal wartime record inspired no one. The CCP seemed to offer a viable alternative to the corruption and weakness of the Kuomintang. Isolated and disliked the Nationalists lost ground before the poorly equipped but disciplined People's Liberation Army. On the surrender of Peking to the CCP in 1949, a massive victory parade in T'ien An Men Square included *nung, kung* and *shih.* This combination of classes signalized the defeat of the Kuomintang. During the Yenan years Chairman Mao had transformed the ideology of the CCP into something distinctly Chinese, a system of thought attractive to many of the *shih.* Mao, the Hunanese school teacher and peasant leader who had never been abroad nor learnt a foreign language, had achieved the successful combination of *nung* and *shih,* but, unlike the first Ming Emperor, he was not prepared to give the scholars a privileged position. From the outset he made it clear that their skills should be used for 'serving the People.' Meanwhile, Chiang, like the last Ming partisan, retired to Taiwan with 300 000 troops. More fortunate than his historical predecessor, the Kuomintang leader had a foreign ally whose navy could defend his refuge.

American opposition to the People's Republic of China (formally established on 1st October 1949) compelled the Chinese Communist leaders to seek aid exclusively from Russia. Technical assistance and loans were made—by 1965 China had repaid its debts through exports to the Soviet Union—but differences in ideology have caused friction between Peking and Moscow. It should not be forgotten that Mao, like Hung Hsiu-ch'uan, has translated foreign doctrines into a Chinese form. The Thought of Chairman Mao offers a radical interpretation of socialism, an unnecessary disturbance of communist theory from the point of view of the Russians, who abolished the Comintern in 1943.

Land reform and the nationalization of businesses prepared the way for a large-scale industrial revolution, which began in 1952. Membership of the CCP increased as more urban workers have joined and the initial violence of the civil war has altered to an emphasis on re-education for dissidents. 'Remoulding through labour' and political study has been the lot of reluctant *shih* and *shang.* The 'Hundred Flowers' episode in 1957, when Chairman Mao relaxed censorship and encouraged the educated classes to voice their views, was followed by a programme of

Troops of the People's Liberation Army on their arrival in Nanking in 1949. 'Without a people's army', Mao Tse-tung had written in 1945, 'the people have nothing'. In contrast with the Nationalist forces, these soldiers did not live by pillaging the land. They were expected to follow three commandments, 'Do not even take a needle or a thread. Consider the people as your family. All that you have borrowed you must return'.

re-education for those 'rightists' who did criticize the régime from mistaken viewpoints. The revolutionary *nung* and *kung* were their teachers.

The Great Proletarian Cultural Revolution (1966–68)

The Cultural Revolution was nothing less than an attack on the CCP by its leader, Chairman Mao. He is one of those rare individuals who seem to reverse the usual effects of growing old—that is, he has become more radical as the years have passed. Since the Great Leap Forward in 1958, when an ambitious drive to increase both agricultural and industrial production met with mixed success, Mao had less influence on the direction of policy than Liu Shao-ch'i, whose outlook was 'revisionist.' Two main issues between Mao and Liu were the education system and the People's Liberation Army. Under Liu's 'rightist'

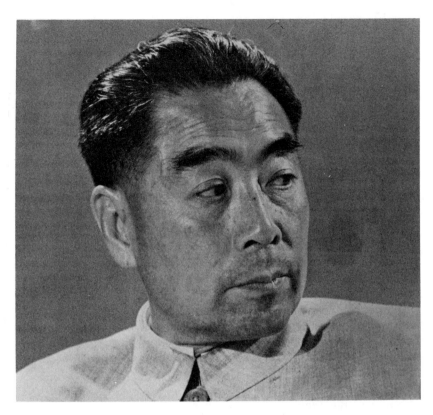

Chou En-lai a year after the Bandung Conference (1955). He was born in a family long-established as shih. *His encounter with communist theory occurred when he was a student in Paris (1921).*

philosophy both of these institutions were divisive, encouraging the re-emergence of the old class divisions of Chinese society. This was Mao's view. Liu claimed that China needed technicians and a strong army, so that Mao's insistence on truly proletarian organization was a mere day-dream inspired by nostalgia for Yenan. In 1962 Mao succeeded in introducing a programme of 'social education,' and in 1965 military ranks were abolished in the PLA. However, this proved to be the limits of his power in spite of the support of Lin Piao, then Minister of Defence.

On 5th August 1965 Mao wrote a wall poster entitled *Bombard the Headquarters!* It represented a call to the young to rout out the 'revisionists' and purify the revolution. Within months 13 000 000 Red Guards had travelled to Peking as the revolutionary fervour spread from universities and colleges into schools. The movement split the CCP and the country. Chiang Ch'ing,

279

Mao's wife, directed the activities of the Red Guards, who had denounced Liu Shao-ch'i as the 'top person in authority taking the capitalist road.' Conditions in China were chaotic but Mao removed his opponents.

Lin Piao used the PLA to good purpose and Chou En-lai, a consummate politician in any crisis, managed to arrange compromise governments in the provinces and save officials from unjust attack. 'The working class,' Mao said, 'must exercise leadership in everything.' Whether this will be the result of the Great Proletarian Cultural Revolution remains to be seen. The CCP has been weakened at the very time that the leadership had to rely on the PLA. Perhaps the disappearance of Lin Piao was Mao's reassertion of control over the military arm of government (1971), just as the more recent campaign against the philosophy of Confucius represents continued pressure on those who would 'take the capitalist road' (1974). Whatever is concluded about the Cultural Revolution in one respect it remains unique. For it was a movement of the young, a continuing revolution in a revolution. Sensing the frustrations of young people, Mao guided their revolt into an attack on the complacency of their parents. Grandfather and grandchildren opposed the 'rightist' tendencies of the middle-aged.

China and the World
Today, China is a world power again. Here are the events that have led to the international acceptance of the People's Republic:

● Recognition of the Communist government by Britain, but Peking resented the consulate which London maintained on Taiwan (1949). The United States continued to support Chiang Kai-shek.

● Mao went to Moscow and Sino-Soviet alliance was signed (February 1950). This was the first contact between Chinese Communists and Russian Communists since the Shanghai massacre of 1927. Mao had proved that peasants could be a truly revolutionary force.

● Korean War (1950–53). North Korea, a Russian ally, invaded South Korea, an American ally. Chinese 'volunteers' went to the aid of the North when United Nations forces under the command of General MacArthur approached their own borders. The PLA acquitted itself well and a ceasefire left Korea divided into two separate countries. This was the first time that Chinese arms had matched those of the West.

● Liberation movements, 'People's Wars,' were aided by

China in South-East Asia. Ho Chi-minh was helped to expel the French in Indo-China, where a decisive victory was gained at Dien Bien Phu (1954). The region had been a Chinese protectorate under the Ch'ing dynasty.

● At the Bandung Conference, Chou En-lai told Afro-Asian neutralist nations that China had no intention of interfering in their affairs (1955). However, the United States, France, Australia and Britain had set up the South-East Asian Treaty Organization in 1954 to contain China's growing power. In the event, only Pakistan, Thailand and the Philippines joined.

● Vietnam War (officially over in 1973) was a continuation of the struggle between the North and the Western powers, through their client rulers in the South. In the 1960s the United States became embroiled and fighting spread into Laos and Cambodia. The Vietcong, Communist guerrillas, had the edge in the war, despite the advanced technology of the Americans.

● Tibet (1959). The People's Republic had drawn Tibet back into the Chinese sphere of influence in 1950, though the Dalai Lama at first remained head of state. A revolt against Communist influence caused the intervention of the PLA in 1959.

● India (1962). The PLA invaded and occupied territories in the Himalayas claimed by India. Peking disclaimed the Simla Agreement and the MacMahon Line; these had been forced on a weakened Ch'ing dynasty by the British Empire in the nineteenth century. The Indian army was soundly beaten by the PLA, though after the fighting the Chinese only retained the Aksai Chin plateau, which lies between Sinkiang and Tibet.

● Differences arose between China and Russia, whose advisers were soon withdrawn (1960). Khruschev had offered arms to India and was attempting to improve relations with the United States, the antithesis of Communism in Mao's eyes. In 1963 Russia, Britain and France signed a treaty banning further nuclear tests. But there were border disputes too. Tsarist aggression had taken large areas of Sinkiang and Manchuria from the Ch'ing Empire. Armed clashes occurred in the late 1960s.

● China exploded its first atomic bomb (1964); three years later an H-bomb was set off. Hence, the People's Republic is the only non-Western country possessing nuclear weapons.

● The People's Republic replaced the Nationalists (Taiwan) as the representative for China at the United Nations (1971).

● President Nixon visited Peking (1971). The U.S.A. and China set up liaison offices in each other's capitals in 1972.

281

LITERATURE AND PAINTING

The outstanding modern writer of twentieth-century China was Lu Hsun (the pen name of Chou Shu-jen, 1881–1936). An opponent of the Empire, Lu Hsun's writings have a very strong element of social criticism in them. His short story, *A Madman's Diary*, was the first modern work of fiction; it appeared in 1918 and was written in the vernacular. But *The True Story of Ah Q* (1921) is justly regarded as his masterpiece. By choosing as his main character an illiterate, landless labourer, Lu Hsun struck on a brilliant device for ridiculing those who still believed in Confucian values. The 'polite' classes are shown up as hypocrites, using a system that depends on the misery of countless *nung*. Like a true fool, Ah Q always succeeds in winning a 'moral victory' over his tormentors. Here is an episode from the story:

THE TRAGEDY OF BEING IN LOVE
Ah Q felt so buoyant, it seemed as though he would fly away. His sense of elation came from pinching the cheek of the young novice who had passed him in the street. . . . So he floated for most of the day, till in the evening he found himself in the barn, where his sleeping quarters were situated. Normally, he would have turned in and gone to sleep, but tonight he was restless. He felt something smooth between his index finger and thumb. He wondered: was it something soft and smooth from the face of the novice, or had his fingers become smooth and soft through touching her face?

'May all the generations of Ah Q perish,' (rather strong language from such a young nun) the novice had cried out. Her curse still rang in his ears. He thought she had spoken correctly. But again, there certainly was a need for a woman. 'Perish.' . . . There was no-one to cook him a meal, he pondered; he did need a woman. Had not Mencius said: 'Among the three great sins of the unfilial, the greatest of all is the discontinuation of the family line.' His thoughts were perfectly attuned to the teaching of the sage. It is indeed a pity that later he should have run amok. 'Woman, woman!' he said to himself, 'the monk could touch . . . woman, woman, woman!'

It is not certain when Ah Q actually fell asleep that night. His fingers seemed very smooth, more so each day. 'Woman!' he used to think all the time. (Clearly, from this example, we can tell that women are harmful. Indeed, Chinese men, the vast majority of them that is, are the material from which saints are made, but, they are ruined by women. It's a shame! Shang kingdom was ruined by Ta Chi, Chou kingdom by Pao Ssu, Ch'in . . . though not clearly recorded, it could hardly have fallen otherwise. It must have been because of a woman. Tung Chok was definitely ruined by Chou Shan.)

Ah Q himself is a gentleman. We cannot be sure which illustrious teacher he followed, but he was precise in his behaviour towards men and women. Normally, he was very careful, particularly with novices and imitation 'ocean devils.' He had come to a number of philosophical conclusions, like all nuns have affairs with monks, a lone woman walking through the town is trying to catch a man, and a conversation between any man or woman must be underhand. Accordingly, Ah Q often glared, mumbled rude comments, and even threw stones.

Now, Ah Q, who would have thought that a novice should have so affected you? The feelings which oppressed him were outlawed by religion and society. (How disgusting is a woman! If only the novice had worn a veil. A little piece of cloth would have made so much difference. No sensation would be troubling Ah Q's fingers.) Once Ah Q did pinch the bottom of a woman in a crowd of people watching a street opera. However, there had been a layer of trousers between the woman's flesh and Ah Q's fingers, so nothing had happened. With the novice, the situation was entirely different.

'Woman!' Ah Q thought. He had guarded himself against women. They tried to entice him, though they did not smile. Indeed, he paid special attention to those women who spoke to him, though he had never encountered a hint at anything clandestine. 'Oh dear!' Ah Q reflected, 'how detestful are women, ever pretending to be respectable!'

One day Ah Q was pounding rice for his master, Chou. After dinner, he sat in the kitchen, smoking a pipe. . . . The Chou household had an early evening meal and went to bed. No light was allowed, unless young master Chou was preparing for his degree examination or, more likely, Ah Q had been given the job of pounding rice. . . .

Wu Ma, the only maidservant in the Chou household, came and sat in the kitchen, when the washing up was done.

'Our mistress,' she told Ah Q, 'has not eaten for two days, not since our master bought a young lady. . . .'

'Lady . . . woman . . . Wu Ma,' Ah Q thought.

'Our mistress,' the maidservant continued, 'is having a baby in August. . . .'

'Woman,' Ah Q thought, putting down his pipe. He stood up.

'Our mistress . . .' rattled on Wu Ma.

'Sleep with me,' Ah Q suddenly said, kneeling at Wu Ma's feet. Complete silence followed, then, with a scream, the maidservant fled, trembling, from the kitchen. Trembling himself, Ah Q got up and leant on the bench. He felt uncertain as he tucked his pipe in his belt. 'Better get back to work,' he thought, when 'pong'—a big bamboo descended on his head.

'You rebel, you!' shouted young master Chou, a first class *shih*, as he struck Ah Q on the skull again. Ah Q used his hands to shield himself but the bamboo stung his finger joints so badly that he was forced to quit the kitchen in haste.

'Turtle's egg!' shouted young master Chou, using an oath favoured by high officials.

Ah Q rushed to the shed for pounding rice. Despite the pains in his finger joints, he could not help recalling the oath. 'Turtle's egg!' was not a phrase belonging to the speech of rustic folk. No *nung*

283

used it. Only the rich and noble classes, Ah Q was sure, understood what was meant. So impressed and frightened was he that the idea of women left his mind without trace. (In fact, a beating and a scolding usually seemed to solve his problems.)

He began pounding. Hard and hot work it was. Soon he had shed his shirt. Pounding away, Ah Q heard a commotion in the Chou house. Attracted by the noise—he loved to watch a scene—Ah Q made his way towards his master's rooms. In the dusk, he was able to discern many people, including the entire Chou household and their next door neighbour. . . .

Mistress Chou was dragging Wu Ma out of her room. She told the maidservant: 'Come out of your room and stop brooding over what has happened. Who doesn't know you are an honest girl? . : . Suicide is silly!'

While Wu Ma, crying and weeping, was being dealt with by the Chou family, Ah Q approached, full of curiosity. 'I wonder what it all means,' he thought, 'perhaps I had better find out.' Unexpectedly he saw young master Chou rush in his direction, brandishing a bamboo.

In a flash it all came back to him. Another beating seemed inevitable. . . . But he succeeded in making an exit through a side door and ran off to his sleeping quarters in the barn. There he sat for a time, shivering in the chilly evening air. Although he knew that he had left his shirt in the pounding shed, the bamboo deterred him from going back to collect it. . . .

As a punishment it was agreed that Ah Q should:

1. give the Chou household expensive candles and joss-sticks as well as apologize in person;
2. pay for a priest to drive the evil spirit of suicide from the Chou house;
3. no longer enter buildings belonging to the Chou family;
4. be blamed if Wu Ma died;
5. not ask Master Chou for any wages or the return of his shirt.

Fortunately for Ah Q, Spring had arrived. He was able to sell his cotton quilt in order to raise enough cash to carry out the conditions forced on him. What little money he had left afterwards, he spent on drink. . . .

Lu Hsun was no advocate of wholesale change. China, he maintained, had to adopt from the rest of the world only those things that suited its essential nature. By 1930 he had decided that the CCP offered the best hope for national renewal.

Two great artists have continued the tradition of painting this century. They are Ch'i Pai-shih (1863–1957) and Huang Pin-hung (1864–1955). The humble origins of Ch'i have impressed the officials of the People's Republic as much as his marvellous paintings. A man of the people, he has done much to revive and reinterpret the role of the painter.

Ch'i Pai-shih (1863–1957):
Mountains, pinetrees and sailing
boats; painted at the age of 89.
Hanging scroll; ink and slight
colour on paper.

Huang Pin-hung (1864–1955): Landscape; painted at the age of 89.
Hanging scroll; ink and slight colour on paper.

Shanghai in 1973. A cyclist delivering yarn casts a glance at an enormous revolutionary street poster, which exhorts him 'To be vigilant and protect China'. The people represented in it are all holding 'Quotations from Chairman Mao', the little red book. Such public art is a feature of the contemporary scene in China.

MODERN CHINA—THE ECONOMIC MIRACLE

In the past twenty-five years China has undergone a revolution which is still continuing. This revolution contains three inseparable elements:

- a change in the social system typified by public ownership of the means of production;
- a change in technology reflected by increased productivity and output which results from the substitution of small-scale handicrafts by large-scale mechanization;
- a revolution in philosophy by which China maintains its cultural identity but which inevitably forces it to participate in world affairs as a model for other underdeveloped countries.

286

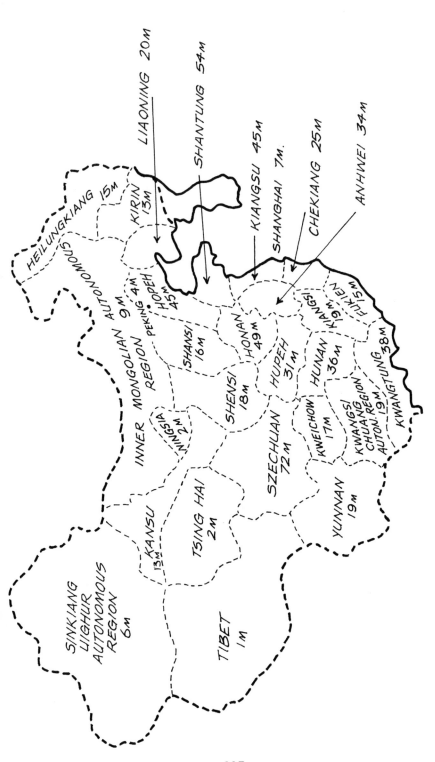

Provinces and autonomous regions of China with size of population to nearest million in 1957.

HEILUNGKIANG 15M

SINKIANG UIGHUR AUTONOMOUS REGION 6M

INNER MONGOLIAN AUTONOMOUS REGION 9M

KIRIN 13M

LIAONING 20M

SHANTUNG 54M

PEKING 4M

HOPEH 45M

SHANSI 16M

SHENSI 18M

NINGSIA 2M

KANSU 13M

TSING HAI 2M

TIBET 1M

SZECHUAN 72M

HONAN 49M

HUPEH 31M

KIANGSU 45M

SHANGHAI 7M

ANHWEI 34M

CHEKIANG 25M

KIANGSI 19M

FUKIEN 15M

HUNAN 36M

KWEICHOW 17M

YUNNAN 19M

KWANGSI CHUANG AUTON. REGION 19M

KWANGTUNG 38M

Land Reform, or the Transformation of Agriculture

An English economist in 1932 considered much of the unrest reported in China was less a product of theoretical Marxism than one of irregularity of land holding and unemployment. The peasants were successively exploited by Manchus, Europeans, warlords, landlords, bandits, government troops and Japanese invaders; they were subject to the age-old irregularities of climate; they were increasingly forced to sell their land to pay taxes or buy grain in times of famine. It is not surprising that they were likened 'to a man standing permanently up to the neck in water, so that even a ripple is sufficient to drown him.' When the Communists not only proposed, but implemented land reform in their areas of influence, it was understandable that they received the support of the masses.

The *nung* are essentially conservative. The peasant's ambition would be to own land. While Communist doctrine implied state ownership of land, the leaders were generally pragmatic enough to recognize the need for gentle and informed change. The first reform known as *'land to the tiller'* involved total redistribution of land on the basis of family need. Since this broke up the estates it increased fragmentation of holdings, already an acute problem with the rapid population growth, and initially decreased productivity. This did not automatically lead to worsening conditions of life since, before this, great food surpluses had often been achieved. The main reasons for starvation had been the inability or unwillingness of those with reserves to transfer them to areas of need.

Between 1949 and 1952 *mutual aid teams* of 3–6 families were encouraged to form permanent production groups. Individual ownership of land was maintained but any reclaimed land became common property and was jointly cultivated. Thus socialism was gradually introduced. The next stage was the establishment of *independent producers co-operatives* with voluntary membership and the right of withdrawal. Land was amalgamated and decisions were formulated by a democratically elected management committee. In practice leadership increasingly fell into the hands of CCP members. By 1956 ninety per cent of the rural population was involved. Labour was organized to build roads, dams and ditches in the winter and increasingly the government was able to control and direct agricultural output.

Advanced co-operatives or *collective farms* comprised of up to 200 family units were introduced in 1956. Land under individual ownership, draught animals and implements were forfeited and

288

Legend:
- 500000 +
- ○ 1000000 +
- ■ 2000000 +

U. S. S. R.

Tsitsihar

Harbin ○

Changchun
Kirin
○ Fushun
■ Shenyang
Anshan

Peking ■

Tientsin ■

Talin

Lanchow

○ Taiyuan

Tzepo
Tsinan
Chengchow

Tsingtao

Sian ■

Suchow

CHINA

Nanking ○

Chengtu ○

Chungking ■

Wuhan ■
Wuhsi
Soochow
■ Shanghai
Hangchow

Kweiyang

Changsha

K'unming

Foochow

Canton ■

Major Cities.

289

some compensation paid. The increasing bureaucracy of these large units and the decrease in personal motivation led to discontent and a decline in productivity. They gave way in 1958 to the *commune*, which was an even larger unit but which in fact took over the administrative functions of the *hsiang* while remaining in the traditional *hsien* framework. A State Planning Organization passed targets to the Commune Management Committee, who in turn fed the information to brigade leaders. Each brigade was made up of several production teams and they alone made the decisions as to how to achieve the targets.

The reform of agricultural organization was consistently adopted more rapidly in the North than the South, where the numerous minority groups resented the seemingly perpetual intervention of Chinese governments into their affairs.

To increase the output of food during the gradual process of socialization, the Communist government opened its own large, modern and efficient farms. Because of the shortage of suitable land for expansion within the eighteen provinces, they have been

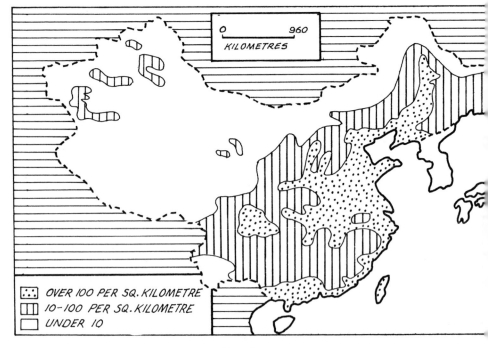

0   960
KILOMETRES

[.:.] OVER 100 PER SQ. KILOMETRE
[Ⅲ] 10-100 PER SQ. KILOMETRE
[ ] UNDER 10

Population.

290

increasingly concerned with reclamation of wastelands, particularly in frontier and coastal areas, and these schemes have served to stimulate migration to such areas. Some of the state farms in the South are used to train and resettle Chinese returning from overseas.

To back up agricultural improvements the State initiated three five-year plans from 1953–7, 1958–62 and 1966–70. Under these Mao Tse-tung hoped to completely transform production through mechanization and settlement of virgin lands in order to meet the escalating demands for foodstuffs and industrial raw materials. Industrial development was seen to be completely dependent on an efficient agricultural base. The success of agricultural policy was revealed from 1959–62 when China survived one of the worst droughts in history without the mass starvation typical of former times. This was partly due to increased production but also to better distribution of reserves and strict rationing.

'The Great Leap Forward,' or the Socialization of Industry

The 'Hundred Days Reform' of 1898 failed in its objectives of modernization of industry because of Tz'u Hsi's opposition and the conservative nature of most Chinese administrators. Even so, by 1913 there were nearly 700 firms involved in mining, smelting, textiles, food processing and public utilities.

	Foreign owned	Chinese owned
Number of firms	136	549
% of total	45%	55%
Capital		
(total £30 m)	(Main investors Britain 50% Japan 25%)	

From this point on industry increased to satisfy the demands of Japan and the West. The Chinese resented the role of foreign imperialists and many activities were taken over as the Kuomintang and CCP took control of the Yangtze valley, by 1930. This coincided with the annexation of Manchuria by Japan which the Chinese Nationalists were helpless to prevent. The Japanese played an important role in developing the industrial regions of the north-east for their own benefit, and maintained control over them until 1945. When the Chinese regained control, the Russians had already stripped Manchuria of much industrial equipment. The civil war between the CCP and Kuomintang created industrial stagnation and commercial chaos; the result was rapid inflation. The Communists, on taking power,

- took over entire wholesale trade;
- took control of banks;
- established a price index related to the basic commodities of rice, flour, oil, coal and cotton and successfully held down prices;
- began a take-over of industry which was completed by 1956.

Initially industrial development was made a priority receiving nearly sixty per cent of total capital investment, most of which went on new plant and modernization of heavy industry. Consumer industries were a low priority. Aid was given by the USSR in the building of 156 key productive units including integrated steel works at Anshan and Wuhan, electric power stations, tractor and lorry factories, cotton mills and coal mines. The increase in bureaucracy resulting from the first five-year plan (1952–7) led to Mao Tse-tung's 'Hundred Flowers' policy under which constructive criticism could be freely voiced. Some economists criticized the economic policy for being inefficient and over-centralized. The government had directed much new industry away from the coast and into the interior, but this in itself was restricting the efficiency and raising their costs. They also suggested more material incentives to production. For their pains they were demoted and criticism ended.

Mao, however, was too astute not to heed the rumblings from below and under the second five-year plan, starting in 1958, he allocated a greater proportion of capital to agriculture and set no detailed production targets. He rejected the Russian pattern of planned urban industrialization and put the onus on the people to expand production with the 'Great Leap Forward.' The commune movement which accompanied this 'spontaneous' and 'unplanned' surge facilitated the development of hundreds of small units of production such as 'back-yard iron-smelters.' While production increased rapidly, the main result was chaos.

In 1960 the Russians withdrew their experts and cancelled their policy of co-operation. A new policy of 'readjustment, consolidation, filling out and raising standards' was introduced with increased emphasis on agriculture and light industry, both of which suffered during the 'Great Leap.' The resulting successes in creating a more balanced and better integrated system still did not satisfy Mao Tse-tung who feared that stability would bring complacency. Thus one aspect of the Cultural Revolution of 1966 was to shake up the bureaucrats and intelligentsia to maintain their awareness of the grass root problems of industrial production.

Transport, Trade and Urbanization
Industrialization inevitably increased urbanization, and created landscapes similar to any other industrial society. The juxtaposition of allotments and fields with factories, warehouses and new housing projects stresses the overall shortage of land and interdependence of the two types of economy. At the 1953 Census, 163 settlements had over 100 000 people, with nine over a million strong. Today the number of 'million' cities is nearer twenty. The proportion of people living in urban settlements (i.e., over 2 000 inhabitants) has risen slowly from thirteen per cent in 1953 to a figure probably not exceeding twenty per cent.

To facilitate industrialization, transport and communications have been improved. Before 1949 the densest railway coverage was found in Manchuria where it had been financed by Russia, then Japan. The Civil War and Sino-Japanese war reduced the

One of the most important factors contributing to the vast material development is the rapidity with which the Chinese have acquired the skills and techniques of modern industry. This shows the State Northwest Printing and Dyeing Mill.

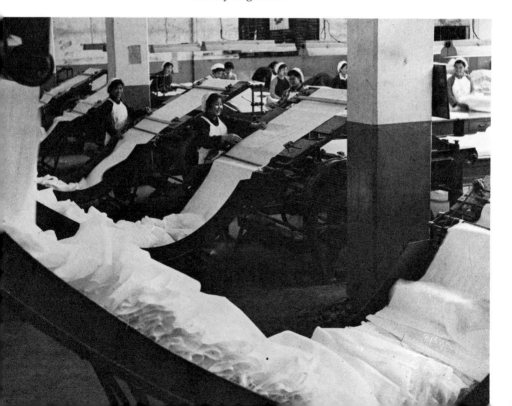

total distance covered by about 1 920 kilometres to 3 200 kilometres. Most of this has now been restored and most of current capital investment seems to go on improvement and maintenance of these predominantly industrial networks. New developments on both economic and military grounds have extended the network 1 120 kilometres to the oil fields of Sinkiang; they have linked the upper Yellow River valley with Szechuan, joining Paoki, Chengtu, and Chungking, going both through and over the Chin-Ling Shan: and Liuchow in Kwangsi was linked to Hanoi in 1951. The river is still a major means of transporting both goods and people, witness the lack of railways in the lower Yangtze valley. The road network was long limited by topography and until 1950 most was unfit for motor vehicles. Now, great arterial highways are being built by the government, leaving local road maintenance and extension in the hands of the communes.

China's ports have continued to develop. Greater Shanghai now has twelve million inhabitants. The Communist victory in 1949 heralded the end of semi-colonial trade bases (with the exception of Macao, Hong Kong and Taiwan). Initially the necessity for obtaining urgent credit facilities and supplies of capital equipment from sympathizers led to the reopening of the 'Jade Gate' as the main trade route. The embargo imposed by the UN during the Korean War, the continued cessation of trade

Between 1955 and 1960 the annual road construction leaped from 20 160 kilometres to 64 000. This picture shows the Changan Boulevard in Peking.

with the USA after this, and growing anti-imperialism in China, further restricted contact with the non-communist countries. In 1951 seventy-eight per cent of exports went to Russia and seventy per cent of imports came from there. With the withdrawal of Russian technicians and increasing hostility between the two countries in 1960, this figure has declined to be replaced by trade with Cuba and countries outside the Communist bloc. Since 1956 China has maintained a favourable balance of trade allowing it to repay its Russian loans in full by the mid 60s. The continual import of grain does not necessarily reflect constant shortage as China finds it profitable to sell rice abroad and buy cheaper wheat. Trade forms a very small percentage of GNP (about four per cent) and China's increasing self-sufficiency even in the most advanced goods, coupled with her increasing willingness to give no-interest aid to other developing countries such as Tanzania, may become an increasing embarrassment to those trying to foster Western-type 'democratic' solutions to their problems.

SOCIETY TODAY

The People are the sea: the government is the fish
—*Mao Tse-tung*

Social Change since 1949
The social revolution in China has largely been one revolving round the relationship between the masses and the leadership. Since Mao Tse-tung knew his Chinese history, he realized the importance of *nung* support in the maintenance of power. For him the 'Revolution' was neither theoretical nor geared to an urban proletariat, but practical and based on the countryside. To convert and maintain the confidence of a traditionally conservative peasantry he recognized the need for involvement and decision-making by them. This would give them proof of their role in changing the destiny of China and give them confidence to carry it through without falling prey to the 'revisionists' or 'progressives,' whether *shang* or *shih*.

Mao's doctrines on contradiction state that life is a struggle, but that this is a good thing. For any given situation with conflicting viewpoints there is always a right way which can be achieved, given discussion and experiment. So Mao accommo-

The Yangtze River bridge (1810 yards long) carries a lower double railway track and an upper six-stream vehicle and pedestrian highway. It is an engineering feat of which the Chinese are justly proud.

dates genuine mistakes as well as providing workers and peasants with the confidence required to take initiatives and make suggestions. In this manner the continuing revolution is carried through by the workers who are credited with seventy per cent of the contribution by Mao. Needless to say this has created problems with the communist intelligentsia and theoreticians who have frequently criticized the failure to follow the orthodox pattern of communist development.

THE FOOLISH OLD MAN WHO REMOVED THE MOUNTAINS
The Foolish Old Man's house faced south and beyond his doorway stood the two great peaks, Taihang and Wangwu, obstructing the way. He called his sons, and hoe in hand they began to dig up these mountains with great determination. Another greybeard, known as the Wise Old Man, saw them and said derisively, 'How silly of you to do this! It is quite impossible for you four to dig up these two

296

huge mountains.' The Foolish Old Man replied, 'When I die, my sons will carry on; when they die, there will be my grandsons, and then their sons and grandsons, and so on to infinity. High as they are, the mountains cannot grow any higher and every bit we dig they will be that much lower. Why can't we clear them away!' Having refuted the Wise Old Man's wrong view, he went on digging every day, unshaken in his conviction. God was moved by this, and he sent down two angels, who carried the mountains away on their backs.

The Role of the Commune

The total frenzy of the early commune days with their complete insistence on public ownership of virtually all private possessions has given way to a better balanced and more viable set-up. Initially, the commune was a combat unit with a high degree of infused motivation to get China out of its immediate problems. Collective living under the 'five-together' system (working, eating, living, studying, and drilling) has been replaced by a return to the normal family pattern. The commune's success lies in the width of its responsibilities—agriculture, rural industry, water conservancy, afforestation, communications, education, civil defence, health and public hygiene, and cultural and recreational activities. Some members of the commune management committee are paid officials but most are rewarded by a system of work points according to the jobs they do in the production teams.

The income of a production team of a commune is generally divided so that about half distributed goes to members and one-quarter to production expenses. But these figures vary according to region and year. All-out attempts are being made to increase the earnings of backward communes.

Here is the distribution of expenditure in 2nd Team of Paching Brigade 1964 Yangtan People's Commune—South Shansi (covering 11 000 people and 61 production teams):

	% of expenditure	
Production expenses	38·6	heavy rain necessitated replanting
Agricultural Tax	6·5	
Reserve Fund	5·0	used for capital expenditure
Welfare Fund	1·0	
Reserve Grain	4·4	
Members	44·5	

297

The large state farms and collectives of the northern plains lend themselves to the use of machinery. This shows harvesting on the Eastern plains.

The Welfare fund caters for accidents, sickness and old age, as well as for those with no relatives. Senior citizens are entitled to the Five Guarantees—enough to eat, adequate housing, clothing, day-to-day needs, and a decent burial. The standard of living is undoubtedly rising; taxation is stable; there is no extortionate rent to meet; employment is constant. Furthermore, the relaxed rules allow cultivation of one's own allotment. Thus more can buy consumer goods such as bicycles, sewing machines and radios.

Population Growth
The first census of individuals as opposed to number of households was carried out in 1953. It revealed a population of nearly 600 million, over 100 million higher than a Post Office census of 1926. The distribution of the population was uneven. On the Chengtu Plain of Szechuan densities of up to 1 200 people per square kilometre were found. Kiangsu, overall, had a density of 154 per square kilometre, while the Tibetan Plateau and the Taklamakan desert averaged less than 1 per square kilometre. Over 85 per cent of the population were under 50, giving a great percentage of productive labour. The reasons for the rapid growth in population since 1949 are obviously the comparative

A production team planting rice in the small terraced paddy-fields. Here mechanization is much more difficult.

Anshan Integrated Steel Works. Over 4 million tonnes of steel a year are produced by the Anshan Steel Works, which is the greatest integrated centre in the country. Other big centres are now at Paotow and Hankow.

peace and secure food supply, coupled with a vast improvement in public hygiene and personal cleanliness. Communism has brought a 'puritanism' which imposed much responsibility for street cleanliness and sewage disposal on the public; it also removed prostitutes and beggars from the streets overnight. Striking advances in preventative medicine have halved the infant mortality rate in the cities; Shanghai 1952 had an IMR of 8·12 per cent; by 1956 this was 3·11 per cent.

The Chinese thought themselves well able to feed any number of mouths, and actually encouraged an increase in the number of hands available to work for the revolution. However, since population growth began to exceed food output, this had to be revised so that in 1957 a birth control campaign was introduced. Mao's critics of the 'Hundred Flowers' period stressed the need for greater mechanization and automation, if living standards were to be raised, and pointed to a large population as a major impediment to development. The birth-control programme was lost in the confusion of the 'Great Leap Forward' until the three hungry years of 1959–61 re-emphasized the need. Today, the birth-rate has been reduced by the recommendation of late marriages and planned childbirth by the state. Not surprisingly this policy has achieved more success in the cities than in the country.

Since Communism aimed to abolish feudal exploitation, it was not unexpected that the Confucian family system came under heavy criticism in the early days. A law of 1950 banned bigamy, concubinage, child betrothal and arranged marriages. It gave opportunity for divorce proceedings by either party and encouraged, sometimes by coercion, self-criticism and public confession, which led to the break-up of many families. Now that women are fully emancipated and can live completely independent lives—thanks to crèches and nurseries—the family unit is more secure from party interference.

Chinese by Blood and Chinese by Birth
Chinese communities in the Nanyang. With the exception of Malaya and Singapore, the Chinese in South-East Asia were worse off after the Second World War than before. Because:

● during the Japanese occupation much of their property was expropriated by collaborators;
● the growth of anti-imperialist nationalism was directed at all who had become prosperous under the system;

300

● the Communist success in 1949 persuaded some of the indigenous peoples that the Chinese communities must be fifth-columnists working for a world communist movement;

● even Socialist governments have feared the sheer size and power of China.

Wherever the Chinese took the lead, the rest of the people have been reluctant to follow. Hence, they failed to win any ground in the 'Emergency,' in post-war Malaya. Before the war the Kuomintang had a conscious policy of encouraging strong nationalism in the Nanyang. It had traditionally supplied revolutionary leaders and funds for resistance to the Japanese and the CCP. The nationalism and wealth of the overseas community led to increasing migration control in the 1930s, so that they were not reinforced by new members and increasingly they were Chinese in blood, not by birth.

Enforced educational integration and sometimes restriction on their language has not in any way submerged the communities, which have remained the target for suspicion and sometimes violence. The Chinese government has consistently shown a lack of interest in using the communities overseas as staging posts for communist expansion. In the 1950s they were recommended to adopt the language and customs of the countries they were in, in a policy of 'survival.' Chinese communist parties in the Nanyang were seen as counter-productive. The Communist Party of Indonesia positively reacted against Chinese membership. The official Chinese attitude was attacked as being 'revisionist' by the Red Guards in 1966. As yet little change of policy has occurred. The reason for fifteen years of official 'revisionism' is basically the insecurity of the new Chinese State, which needed breathing space from foreign entanglements to develop economically. The major exception to the general political indolence of the Nanyang Chinese was Singapore, completely independent from Malaysia after 1965. Its population is eighty-five per cent Chinese and again, though its government leans to the left, the Communist Party is severely suppressed. Malaysia itself may prove to be an enduring democratic country in which people of Chinese origin can play their full part; the constituent states of Sarawak and Sabah, in Borneo, could well act as a balance to any conflict between Malays and Chinese in West Malaysia. These two states of East Malaysia possess more diverse populations and have long traditions of multi-cultural harmony.

Minority Communities within China. In 1953 the 'national minorities' within China numbered over thirty-five million, or

A contemporary painting of Bako, a village on the coast of Sarawak, by an overseas Chinese artist, Chin Khee. The work is in the Lin Nam style, which seeks to combine Western perspective with traditional Chinese brushstrokes. The painter is also a teacher in a Chinese language school, an institution concerned with the preservation of Chinese culture. It is customary among Chinese families living outside China to ensure that at least one boy in every generation receives a full Chinese education.

six per cent of the total population. These comprise over fifty different groups, ten of which have over one million each. In areas where they are concentrated they have been allowed some measure of autonomy and self government—in Kwangsi Chuang Autonomous Region, in Sinkiang Uighur Autonomous Region, in Ningsia Hui Autonomous Region and in Inner Mongolian Autonomous Region. The majority of smaller tribes are found in the highlands of the south-west provinces of Szechuan, Kweichow and Yunnan. The policy towards such groups who have frequently come into conflict with the Chinese in the past, is now one of preserving their unique cultures and languages, while gradually introducing the facilities for education and economic improvement which will bring these people more fully into the communist system. These tribal peoples will become Chinese by birth, if not by blood.

A Hokkien temple in Kuching. The photograph presents some interesting contrasts. The British roadsign is a survival from colonial days, whilst the Chinese villa on the hill behind has become a boarding house for local girls attending the Anglican Mission School. Meanwhile the daily life of the street continues around the temple entrance, as younger children buy tit-bits to eat in the late afternoon. Opposite the front entrance, on the other side of the road, stands a covered stage, which is used for dramatic performances, particularly opera, during religious festivals.

Education, Science and Technology

China exploded its first nuclear bomb in 1964; it leads the world in the development of advanced steam dynamos; it has a satellite—'the man-made earth guiding star'—circling the earth; it has developed a high speed teleprinter capable of coding, decoding and printing out 1 500 Chinese characters per minute. It might be easy to dismiss these as prestigious copies of Western technology designed to impress the world. In actual fact, they merely pick up the threads of medieval and earlier Chinese technology, which we have shown to be the forerunners of many nineteenth-century Western developments. If these advances were produced while China starved and stagnated, we might be justified in our early dismissal, but on looking closely we can see that they are just one part of a whole range of developments stretching back to the grass roots. Southern communes have pioneered the extraction of creosote from coconut refuse. To transport it they have constructed their own narrow gauge railways *and* diesel locomotives.

The people who bring about such changes are not necessarily well educated specialists. The *nung* may work from childhood and receive only part-time education, but increasingly they are

303

The Fengman Hydroelectric Power Station in North-East China. It has an estimated generating capacity of 56 700 kilowatts.

being taught techniques of problem-solving stemming from Mao's view that all is possible, and that every problem has a solution. Another aspect of this is solving one's own personal contradictions, such as the desire for wealth and power which can conflict with the desire to see a classless society where each receives according to his need rather than according to his job. Whether this doctrine will be fostered long enough for it to succeed is uncertain. Because so many of the people in power were not educated under its principles, it may not survive Chairman Mao, though the future of China will be socialist. His recruitment of the Red Guards was to mobilize the young in order that they might be aware of the conservatism which comes with relative prosperity and middle age.

To help China develop, three distinct methods are now equally applied. *Yang Fa,* 'the foreign way of doing things,' recognizes that most modern science and much technology has been developed in the West and that there are no satisfactory alternatives to explain things such as nuclear fission or electricity. *Thu Fa,* 'earth methods,' are those long employed by local people who have subjected them to the test of time. Some of these have declined in the past and are now being revitalized. Even Western societies are acknowledging that there is more to folklore and tradition than was ever previously imagined. *Hsin Fa,* 'entirely new methods,' are those being pioneered by the Chinese 'three

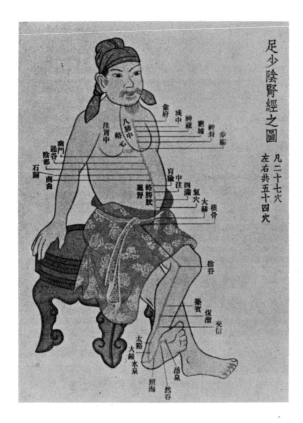

足少陰腎經之圖

凡二十七穴 左右共五十四穴

A Ming
acupuncture chart.

in one' groups of 'revolutionary workers, progressive administrators, and sympathetic scientific and technical personnel.' These three can be illustrated well in the development of modern medicine in China.

Chinese medicine evolved from alchemy, with an emphasis placed on healing drugs of plant and mineral origin. Ancestor worship restricted surgery and autopsies so that scientific knowledge of the body remained relatively primitive. The development of acupuncture and moxibustion 2000 years ago are recorded earlier. In the nineteenth century Chinese medicine began to be neglected in higher circles and a great effort was made to modernize the training of doctors. This trend continued throughout the twentieth century until in the 1940s when the number of Western-trained doctors was in the ratio of around 1 to 25000 of population. By 1957 the growth of medical schools reduced this ratio to 1 to 6000, but at the same time traditional medicine regained its respectability and half a million of its practitioners swelled the ranks of the medical profession. Now not only are the two branches well established with mutual co-operation between them, but the Chinese are making the traditional methods more scientific and virtually creating '*Hsin Fa*,' or new methods. Complicated surgical parts such as artificial kidneys, cardiac pumps, artificial hands are produced and the Chinese have a reputation in the restoration of severed limbs and fingers and bone grafts. In acupuncture, which relies on subjective diagnosis, greater attempts are being made to understand and capitalize on a treatment that obviously works in specific cases in conjunction with other treatments. Electric currents can be passed through needles, and hollow needles can contain minute anaesthetic or biological solutions. Radio isotopes have been added to needles and the paths of the radioactive elements in the body have been traced with a geiger counter. In 1956–7 a group of Soviet doctors completed a course of traditional medicine at the Institute of Experimental Acupuncture and returned to practice in the USSR. Elsewhere in the West the use of traditional Chinese methods is generally limited, though one London hospital is investigating acupuncture techniques.

THE FUTURE

> The unification of our country, the unity of our people and the unity of our various nationalities—these are the basic guarantees of the sure triumph of our cause.
>
> *Chairman Mao in 1957*

Few Chinese would disagree about the need for unity. National cohesion, as we have seen, is a very old idea in China. When a petty king begged for independence in A.D. 960, the first Sung Emperor asked: 'What wrong have your people done to be excluded from the Empire?' Nor would many Chinese doubt that the Mandate of Heaven did pass to the CCP in 1949. But 'the sure triumph of our cause' might give reason for pause. For the two chief pillars of Chinese society, the *shih* and the *nung*, the experience of communism has been somewhat different. While the peasant has enjoyed a measure of freedom and peace unknown in human memory, the scholar has suffered from the loss of both these prized possessions. In the aftermath of the 'Hundred Flowers' episode constructive criticism was difficult to sustain. The Cultural Revolution, however, may represent an attempt to reopen discussion on important aspects of the revolution. How far the *shih* will be allowed to interpret and to criticize, remains a mystery. As a class the educated are indispensable for the smooth running of government. The old saying: 'Confucianism is the doctrine of the *shih* when in office, and Taoism is the attitude of the *shih* out of office,' could well apply to Maoism. Patient opposition has been a constant Taoist virtue, for:

> As the soft yield of water cleaves obstinate stone,
> So to yield with life solves the insoluble:
> To yield, I have learned, is to come back again.

A humorous tale which has recently done the rounds in Kwantung makes the point exactly. Uncle Chang, tiring of nightly sessions of political study, asked to address his study group before the meeting one evening. Since he insisted that he had something of the greatest importance to say, the group leader was forced to agree. 'What I should like you to know,' Uncle Chang announced, 'is that I agree one hundred per cent with whatever you are going to explain to us about Chairman Mao, even before you say it.' With a shrug of despair, the group leader told Uncle Chang to go home.

A painting of Mao addressing a revolutionary meeting. Meetings were also called by the workers themselves, at which they criticized Liu Shao-ch'i's revisionist line.

But the Thought of Chairman Mao does relate powerfully to the conditions in China at present, as contemporary eye-witness reports testify; revolutionary excitement is not waning, though such dogma could prove stifling in time. While the success of the mass literacy campaigns among the *nung* will do much to help de-centralize the administration, the nerve centre of the country needs must stay alive in order to ensure national survival. What happened to Confucianism in the Manchu Court is a nightmare that probably haunts Mao. Could not Maoism become just as inflexible after his own death?

The young people of China are the future of China. Population growth ensures that they will remain the majority for many years to come. Between 1970 and 2000 the population is expected to rise from nearly 800 million to over 1000 million. To them Chairman Mao has given the task of continuing the revolution. Their experiments may, or may not, advance Chinese civilization, but they will have an effect on the course of events in China and the world. For China today has become as fascinating a country as Cathay was to Marco Polo. It is a place to look on and be amazed. An ancient culture and a quarter of mankind are striving to meet the challenges and complexities of life in the twentieth century. Perhaps China will regain its early pre-eminence and have things to teach the world again, particularly the developing countries.

Specific predictions about the future are always difficult to make. However, a study of China does illustrate how history repeats itself, if nothing else. The CCP will survive as long as it retains the Mandate of Heaven. Although Chairman Mao has emerged as a new Emperor figure following the Cultural Revolution, everything has not been perfect since 1949. The PLA remains an unknown quantity, while the rising standard of living enjoyed by the mass of the Chinese people may bring the country eventually into the World Economy itself. China, which maintains an annual trade surplus, would be a huge market. Yet the Chinese could decide to isolate themselves, as they have chosen to do on previous occasions. What is certain is the survival of Chinese civilization as a powerful cultural and political force in the world. Because China is an ecosystem it has come through the enormous stresses and strains of the past hundred and fifty years intact. Modern China is a reality, which even the United States, reversing its entire post-war foreign policy, had to recognize in 1972.

OUTLINE CHRONOLOGY OF CHINESE HISTORY, WITH MAIN DYNASTIES

PREHISTORIC	Old Stone Age	500 000–7 000 B.C.
PERIOD	New Stone Age	7000–1500 B.C.
	(Hsia Kingdom?)	(2000–1500 B.C.?)
HISTORICAL	Shang Kingdom	1500–1027 B.C.
PERIOD	Chou Dynasty	1027–256 B.C.
BEGINS	Warring States period	481–221 B.C.
IMPERIAL	Ch'in Dynasty	221–207 B.C.
UNIFICATION	Han Dynasty	202 B.C.–A.D.220
	Usurpation of	
	Wang Mang	A.D.9–23
DARK AGES	Three Kingdoms	A.D. 221–265
	T'sin Dynasty	A.D. 265–316
	Northern and	
	Southern Dynasties	A.D. 316–589
REUNIFICATION	Sui Dynasty	A.D. 589–618
OF CHINA	T'ang Dynasty	A.D. 618–907
DIVISION AGAIN	Five Dynasties period	A.D. 907–960
SECOND	Northern Sung	A.D. 960–1126
REUNIFICATION	Dynasty	
	Southern Sung	A.D. 1127–1279
	Dynasty	
MONGOL	Yuan Dynasty	A.D. 1279–1368
INVASION		
CHINESE	Ming Dynasty	A.D. 1368–1644
RECOVERY		
MANCHU	Ch'ing Dynasty	A.D. 1644–1912
INVASION		
END OF	Chinese	A.D. 1912–1949
IMPERIAL ERA	Republic	
COMMUNISM	People's	A.D. 1949 onwards
TRIUMPHS	Republic	

Chinese Index

An Lu-shan, the T'ang rebel 安祿山

Annam 安南

Anyang, the ancient capital of Shang 安陽

Book of Odes 詩經

Canton 廣東

Chan, School of Buddhism 禪

Chang-an, ancient capital 長安

Chang Hsueh-liang, the Manchurian warlord 張學良

Chao, the ancient state of 趙

Chao Kuang-yin, northern general and the first Sung Emperor 趙匡胤

Cheng Ho, the Ming admiral 鄭和

Chengtu, the town of 成都

Ch'i Pai-shih, the modern painter 齊白石

Chia Ching, the Ming Emperor 嘉靖

Chiang Kai-shek 蔣介石

Chieh, the last Hsia king 桀癸

Ch'ien Lung, the Ch'ing Emperor 乾隆

Ch'in, the ancient state of 秦

Ch'in Dynasty 秦朝

Chin Ling Highlands 秦嶺山

Ch'ing Dynasty 清朝

Chou Dynasty 周朝

Chou En-lai 周恩來

Chou Hsin, the last Shang king 紂辛

Chou Kung 周公

Ch'u, the ancient state of 楚

Chu Hsi, the Sung philosopher 朱熹

Chu Yuan-chang, the First Ming Emperor 朱元璋

Chu Ssu-Pen, the Sung geographer 朱思本

Chuan Chou, the port of 泉州

Chuang-tzu, the Taoist philosopher 莊子

Chungking, the city of 重慶

Confucious 孔夫子

Foochow, the port of 福州

Feng-shui, 'Wind and Water' 風水

Grand Canal 運河

Han Dynasty 漢朝

Han, the ancient state of 韓

Han-shan, the T'ang poet and recluse 寒山

Han Yu, the T'ang minister 韓愈

Hangchow, the city of 杭州

Honan, the province of 河南

Hopeh, the province of 河北

Hsia Dynasty 夏朝

Hsia Kuei, the Sung painter 夏桂

Hsiung Nu, the Huns 匈奴

Chinese index

Red Basin (Yunnan)	紅河	Tsin dynasty	晉朝
San Kuo, the Three Kingdoms	三國	Tu Fu, the T'ang poet	杜甫
Sian, the city of	西安	Tun-huang, the great Buddhist cave temple complex	敦煌
Sinkiang, the province of	新疆		
Shang Dynasty	商朝	Tung-meng hui, the Alliance Society	同盟會
Shanghai, the city of	上海	Tz'u Hsi, the Ch'ing Empress Dowager	慈禧
Shen Tsung, the Sung Emperor	神宗	Wang An-shih, the Sung reformer	王安石
Shantung, the province of	山東	Wang Mang, the usurper	王莽
Shansi, the province of	山西		
Shang, the merchants	商	Wang Shu Ho, author of the 'Pulse Classic'	王叔和
Shih, the scholars and gentry	士	Wang Wei, the T'ang poet and painter	王維
Shih Huang Ti, the Ch'in Emperor	始皇帝	Warring States	戰國
Shu, one of the Three Kingdoms	蜀	Wei, one of the Three Kingdoms	魏
Shun, legendary ruler	舜	Wei, the ancient state of	衞
Su Sung, the Sung scientist	蘇頌	Wei River	渭河
Sui Dynasty	隋朝	Wei-hai-wei, British leased territory	威海衞
Sun Yat-sen, the revolutionary	孫中山	Wen Ong, Han governor of Szechuan and educationalist	文翁
Ssu-ma Ch'ien, the Han historian	司馬遷		
Sung, the ancient state of	宋	Wu Ti, the Han Emperor	武帝
Szechuan, the province of	四川	Wu, one of the Three Kingdoms	吳
T'ai P'ing rebels	太平	Wu San-kuei, the Ming general	吳三桂
T'ai Tsung, the T'ang Emperor	太宗	Wuhan, the industrial centre	武漢
Taiwan	臺灣	Yang Chien, founder of the Sui Dynasty	楊堅
Tali, the Kingdom of	大理		
Tao Teh Ching	道德經	Yang Kuei Fei, the favourite of Ming Huang	楊貴妃
Tarim	塔里木盆地	Yang Shao (culture)	仰韶
T'ang dynasty	唐朝	Yang Ti, the Sui Emperor	煬帝
Tibet	西藏	Yangtse River	揚子江
Tientsin, the city of	天津	Yao, the legendary king	堯

312

Further Reading

Historical and General

JEROME CH'EN, *Mao and the Chinese Revolution*, Oxford University Press, 1965.

C. P. FITZGERALD, *The Birth of Communist China*, Penguin, 1964: 3rd ed. Praeger, 1966.

C. P. FITZGERALD, *China: A Short Cultural History*, Cresset, Praeger, 1961 edition.

C. P. FITZGERALD, *The Empress Wu*, Cresset, 1956.

C. P. FITZGERALD, *The Southern Expansion of the Chinese People*, Barrie and Jenkins, Praeger, 1972.

J. K. GALBRAITH, *A China Passage*, Houghton Mifflin, André Deutsch, 1973.

J. GERNET, *Daily Life in China on the Eve of the Mongol Invasion 1250– 1276* (translated by H. M. Wright), George Allen and Unwin, 1962, Stanford University Press, 1970.

E. R. HUGHES, *The Invasion of China by the Western World*, 2nd ed., A. and C. Black, Barnes and Noble, 1968.

KEESING'S Publications, Ltd., *The Cultural Revolution in China: Its Origins and Course Up to August 1967*, Keesing, 1967, Charles Scribner's Sons, 1968.

M. LOEWE, *Everyday Life in Early Imperial China*, G. P. Putnam's Sons, Batsford, 1968.

JOSEPH NEEDHAM, *Within the Four Seas*, George Allen and Unwin, 1969.

JOAN ROBINSON, *The Cultural Revolution in China*, Penguin, 1969.

EDGAR SNOW, *Red Star over China*, rev. ed., Grove Press, 1968, Gollancz, 1969.

RICHARD WILHELM, *A Short History of Chinese Civilization* (translated by J. Joshua), Harrap, Kennikat Press, 1929.

Literature

CYRIL BIRCH, *Anthology of Chinese Literature*, Grove Press, 1965, Penguin, 1967.

WITTER BYNNER, *The Jade Mountain*, Random House, 1957.

CLARA CANDLIN, *The Herald Wind*, John Murray, 1955.

GARY SNYDER, *A Range of Poems* (includes his translations of Han Shan), Fulcrum, 1966.

ARTHUR WALEY, *The Life and Times of Po Chü-I*, George Allen and Unwin, 1949, Hillary House, 1951.

ARTHUR WALEY, *Monkey*, George Allen and Unwin, 1959.

ARTHUR WALEY, *One-Hundred-and-Seventy Chinese Poems*, Jonathan Cape, 1969.

ARTHUR WALEY, *The Poetry and Career of Li Po*, George Allen and Unwin, 1950.

314

Philosophy and Religion
C. F. BAYNES, *I Ching* or *Book of Changes* (translated by Richard Wilhelm), 3rd ed., Princeton University Press, 1967, Routledge and Kegan Paul, 1968.
WITTER BYNNER, *The Way of Life According to Laotzu*, G. P. Putnam's Sons, 1962.
H. A. GILES, *Chuang Tzu: Taost Philosopher and Chinese Mystic*, George Allen and Unwin, 1926, Hillary House, 1961.
L. GILES, *Taoist Teachings*, John Murray, 1947.
D. H. SMITH, *Confucius*, Temple Smith, 1973.
ARTHUR WALEY, *The Analects of Confucius*, George Allen and Unwin, 1938, Hillary House, 1964.
A. W. WATTS, *The Way of Zen*, Pantheon Books, 1957, Penguin, 1962.
A. F. WRIGHT and D. TWITCHETT, *Confucian Personalities*, Stanford University Press, 1962.

Science
JOSEPH NEEDHAM, *Clerks and Craftsmen in China and the West: Lectures and Addresses on the History of Science and Technology*, Cambridge University Press, 1970.
JOSEPH NEEDHAM, *The Grand Titration*, George Allen and Unwin, 1969.
JOSEPH NEEDHAM, *Science and Civilization in China*, Cambridge University Press, from 1954. The first volume is essential background reading, but all of this remarkable series should be looked at.

Art and Architecture
CHIANG YEE, *The Chinese Eye: An Interpretation of Chinese Painting*, Faber, 1935, Indiana University Press, 1964.
LIN YUTANG, *The Chinese Theory of Art*, Heinemann, 1967.
L. SICKMAN and A. SOPER, *The Art and Architecture of China*, Penguin, 1956.
ANIL DE SILVA, *Chinese Landscape Painting in the Caves of Tun-Huang*, Methuen, 1967.
MICHAEL SULLIVAN, *A Short History of Chinese Art*, rev. ed., University of California Press, 1970.

Geography and Economics
M. ELVIN, *The Pattern of the Chinese Past*, Eyre Methuen, Stanford University Press, 1973.
A. HERRMANN, *An Historical Atlas of China*, Aldine, Edinburgh, 1966.
THEODORE SHABAD, *China's Changing Map: National and Regional Developments, 1949-71*, rev. ed., Methuen, Praeger, 1972.
R. H. TAWNEY, *Land and Labour in China*, George Allen and Unwin, 1932, Octagon Books, 1964.
T. R. TREGEAR, *An Economic Geography of China*, Butterworth, American Elsevier, 1970.
T. R. TREGEAR, *A Geography of China*, Aldine, 1965, Butterworth, 1967.
YI FU TUAN, *The World's Landscapes: China*, Longmans, 1970.

Index

Index

Index

201–8; Manchu dynasty, 260–5; today, 295–306
Soil erosion, 13
Soochow, 262
Southern settlements, 87–9
Stirrups, appearance in China, 75
Stone Age settlements, 16
Sui dynasty, 90–1, 99
Sun Yat-sen, Dr, 266–70, 273
Sung dynasties: northern, 123–4; southern, 125–7
Sung Empire, 120, 122
Szechuan and the Red Basin, 251, 252, 253, 299

T'AI P'ING REBELLION, 240–1, 249, 264, 266
T'ai Tsung, Emperor (Supreme Ancestor), 94–5, 96, 111, 112, 228
Taiwan, 233, 242, 244, 247, 262
Talas River battle, 99
Tali Kingdom, 204
T'ang dynasty and the restoration of unity, 94–119, 120, 227
Taoism, 34–6, 38, 71, 102–3, 113, 114, 187, 240, 258, 264, 307
Tartar partition, 90, 95, 103, 182
Technology: in classical times, 40–6; in First Empire, 72–8; education in, 76–7; and tenure, 80–2; in T'ang and Sung empires, 136–45; today, 303–4
Tenure and technology, 80–2
Three Kingdoms, 56, 90
Thu Fa, 304
Tibet and Tibetans, 63–4, 99, 100, 123, 234, 244, 252, 281
Togan Timur, Emperor, 187
Town Planning, 153–7
Trade growth during Sung Empire, 147–8; in the twentieth century, 293–5
Treaty Ports, 153, 245, 251, 255, 256
Tsang Kung, 77
Tsin dynasty, 90
Tu Fu, 112, 113, 115–16
T'ung-meng hui revolutionary movement, 266
Tungus of Manchuria and Hopeh, 64
Turks, 64, 99
Twentieth-century China, 266–306
Tz'u Hsi, Empress Dowager, 242, 253–4, 264, 266, 291

UNIFICATION and foundation of Chinese Empire, 28, 47–89
United Nations and China, 9, 281
United States and China, 247, 256, 277, 308
Urbanization, 293

VIETNAM, 99, 206, 244; war, 281
Vladivostock, 245, 247, 253
Voyages by Chinese, 209–13

WALLED SETTLEMENT DEVELOPMENTS, 150–3
Wan Li, Emperor, 200
Wang An-shih (leader of the Innovators), 124, 146–7
Wang Chin, general, 199, 200
Wang Hui (painter), 262
Wang Mang (revolutionary reformer), 61–2, 66, 76, 147
Wang Wei (painter and poet), 166
Warlord Period, 268
Warring States period, 28–32
Weapons: iron, 30, 46; early advanced types, 126–7; lack of modern, 241; nuclear, 281
Weddell, John, 214
Western: idea of Cathay, 188–91; debts to China, 192–3; travellers to the Orient, 193–6; imperialism, 233–66
Wheelbarrow, invention of, 75
William of Rubruck, Friar, 195–6
World reaction to Communist China, 279–81
Wu, the Warlike Emperor, 55, 56, 58, 60, 61, 64, 65, 66, 79, 90
Wu Ch'êng-ên, 228
Wu, Empress, 96–7, 111, 113
Wu San-kuei, general, 200, 233, 260
Wu Tsung, Emperor, 111
Wu Yueh (last independent state), 123

YANG CHIEN, GENERAL, 90
Yang Fa, 304
Yang Kuei Fei (concubine), 97, 98, 117, 119
Yang Shao cultural group, 16, 18
Yang Ti, Emperor, 91
Yangchow, 192
Yangtze valley, 88, 89, 147–8, 206, 207, 235–6, 251, 255
Yao, Emperor, 22
Yellow Emperor, 22
Yellow River (Hwang-Ho), 10–11, 14, 42, 43, 45, 202, 249
Yelu Ch'u-ts'ai (scholar-statesman), 127, 181–2, 185, 189
Yin Lu-ch'in, 105–6
Yin-Yang philosophy, 14–15
Yo Fei, general, 125
Yü the Great Engineer, King, 21, 22–3, 45
Yuan Empire, 179–96, 199, 225
Yuan Shih-k'ai, President, 242, 267–8
Yung Lo, Emperor, 198–9, 205, 206, 209
Yunnan annexed, 197, 206